ENCOURAGING PRIMARY SCIENCE

Encouraging Primary Science

An Introduction to the Development of Science in Primary Schools

GEORGE RAPER

and

JOHN STRINGER

CASSELL

Cassell Publishers Limited
Artillery House
Artillery Row
London SW1P 1RT

Distributed in North America by
Taylor and Francis Inc
242 Cherry Street
Philadelphia, PA 19106–1906

British Library Cataloguing in Publication Data

Raper, George
    Encouraging primary science.
    1. Science — Study and teaching
    (Elementary)
    I. Title   II. Stringer, John
    372.3'5   LB1585

ISBN 0-304-31372-6

Photosetting by Oxford Print Associates Ltd
Printed and bound in Great Britain by Mackays of Chatham Ltd

Last digit is print no: 9 8 7 6 5 4 3 2

Contents

The experiments in this book have been used with safety and success in a great many primary schools. Teachers using the activities should take note of the safety guidelines in the text, and take account of factors such as class size, degree of supervision, and the age and experience of the children. Teachers are strongly advised to rehearse activities before introducing them to children.

Acknowledgements

Our thanks are due to the many people who have helped directly or indirectly in the preparation of this book.

The Leverhulme Trust financed the secondment of one of us (John Stringer) to a one-term Schoolteacher Fellowship in 1983 when some of the original work was initiated. The University of Warwick and Coventry LEA have also supported our work. Views expressed in this book, however, are our own.

We are particularly grateful to the many LEAs who provided copies of their primary science guidelines, and in particular to the following for permission to quote from certain of their works:

Cheshire   – the investigation of a rook's nest.
Fife   – walks around the Eden estuary.
Oxfordshire   – investigations into vegetable dyes and sticky tape.
Tameside   – an acceptable structure for primary science.
Warwickshire   – seizing an opportunity in the primary classroom.
West Cumbria   – concern for the management and selection of investigations.

We have drawn on original material from a variety of sources and so we also thank the following individuals and publishers for permission to quote their copyright material and reproduce photographs:

The Association for Science Education.
Councils and Education Press (Education), Longman Group.
W. H. Freeman & Co.
Wynne Harlen.
Macdonald and Co.
John Murray (Publishers) Ltd.
Osmiroid International Ltd.
Janine Wiedel (photographer).

Many students and teachers have tried and criticised our ideas and we thank them as well as the children whose enthusiasm for science activities has persuaded us that there is a central place for science in every school and classroom.

The whole has been drawn together with skill and patience by Eleanor Howard, Anne Daffern, Gwen Payne, Elizabeth Robbins and Vivienne Stringer during the typing of the manuscript.

Preface

Science is becoming established in primary classrooms and it is our intention in writing this book to encourage and inform those wishing to develop this aspect of teaching.

We begin with a review of what the science education of primary school children might involve as perceived by a number of agencies including the DES; and we then go on to discuss the attitudes, concepts and skills which can realistically be developed through a range of science-based experiences.

When children talk about science and the work of scientists, their notions have implications for our teaching. Personal experiences of children's 'Why?' questions, and the observations of others looking at concept development in young children, demonstrate the importance of encouraging situations conducive to problem solving and also the importance of intuition. Such studies also highlight the need to match classroom activities to children's own scientific understandings and to their attitudes to science.

The apprehension of many, when first called upon to develop science in the classroom, is a concern both understandable and widespread, and we attempt to put it into perspective by analysing some of the reasons for it. Many teachers have overcome their initial concern through a variety of approaches in school. Crucial to the implementation of science is the role of the head, and also the role of the post-holder or teacher with responsibility for the science curriculum. These roles are mutually supportive, and some of the strategies by which head and post-holder can begin to develop school policy with the active involvement of the rest of the staff are outlined.

Recent policy statements from the DES stress the need for schools to construct individual schemes of work in science. Case studies introduce ways in which science can develop from a variety of opportunities and from a range of approaches, including practical problem solving and technology in the classroom. For those with little previous science experience, several tried and tested areas of investigation are suggested, each of which has excellent potential for success. Further and more ambitious developments can follow.

There are several ways in which teachers might organise their classroom for science activities, each of which has individual strengths and weaknesses. Criteria for classroom management decision making are listed and strategies explored from small group involvement at a 'science table' to more ambitious and organisationally complex techniques. We conclude with a chapter headed 'Practicalities' in which we try to answer some of the everyday questions associated with science in school – safety aspects; keeping animals and plants; equipment and resources – as well as ways of assessing progress.

Our aim is to encourage science for younger children. We hope that having read our book you will help us to achieve it.

All photographs reproduced with the permission of Janine Wiedel.

Chapter 1

The Nature and Context of Primary Science

OPPORTUNITIES

Children's questions, their notions of science and of the work of 'scientists' highlight their interest in, and their need for, information about the environment. They are very keen to be involved in practical discovery of information of the sort which will help to provide some of the answers to their questions. A major aim of primary science must be to encourage and stimulate this curiosity; to require them to explore, observe and question their environment and so to develop their experience.

Integration across the curriculum is a strength of primary practice and any area of work must be capable of free and constructive integration. Even though they are not always recognised as such, by teachers or pupils, many primary classroom activities can be called 'science' and many of the attributes of science and ways of working in science are common to other areas of the curriculum. Science can evolve from these areas – possibly by altering the emphasis of the work, increasing the breadth of a topic or by looking at particular aspects in greater depth.

Science in the primary school is not merely teaching children a mass of scientific knowledge or content for its own sake, but it is concerned with stimulating the development of a curious and questioning attitude so that children can begin to understand more fully their natural and man-made environments; to begin to appreciate a variety of problems; and to develop a framework for their solution. This is best begun during the infant and junior years.

Thus, opportunities for science-based investigations can arise from a variety of starting points: An easily identifiable science area such as 'electricity in the home' might be chosen, and a range of pupil activities provided to familiarise children with some of the more important aspects can be undertaken. This might lead on to safety in the home – the cost of cooking, lighting, keeping warm, etc. and a range of classroom activities which can 'grow out' of the science. Another class might be working on a more general topic such as 'colour' and eventually some of them might look at certain of the science aspects which 'grow out' of this area: paint and light mixing, road safety and clothing colours, and the dyes in felt-tip pens. Yet other classes might be involved in some less obvious science areas: work in a local church might lead to a consideration of structures and materials; a music lesson might develop into new ways to produce and propagate sounds.

Space is a topic with a wealth of potential for work across the curriculum.

Likewise, science activities will enhance and consolidate other curriculum areas. Communication skills and mathematical skills are, of necessity, important aspects of science activities, and craft and design work is closely linked to problem solving, especially of a technological nature.

INFLUENCES

During the past 20 years a vast amount of curriculum materials for primary science have been produced commercially and influenced by a variety of groups such as the Department of Education and Science, the Association for Science Education, the Assessment of Performance Unit and the School Natural Science Society.

National initiatives such as the 'Schools Council Science 5–13 project' have been well publicised and are relatively well known by teachers. Commercially produced materials are legion, from relatively simple guidelines to highly structured courses (see Appendix III). Small working groups of teachers and their Local Education Authorities are responsible for a wealth of curriculum documents, newsletters and local directories, all of direct relevance to primary practice.

And yet, concern has been expressed in many quarters over the lack of impact of these ideas and materials in schools.

The Department of Education and Science

The Department of Education and Science (DES) report in 1978, *Primary Education in England: a Survey by HM Inspectors of Schools*, introduced its science comments thus:

Few primary schools visited in the course of this survey had effective programmes for the teaching of science. There was a lack of appropriate equipment; insufficient attention was given to ensuring proper coverage of key scientific notions; the teaching of processes and skills such as observing, the formulating of hypotheses, experimenting and recording was often superficial. The work in observational and experimental science was less well matched to children's capabilities than work in any other area of the curriculum.

Concern was expressed that, although children were introduced to plants, animals and objects able to stimulate scientific enquiry, very few opportunities were taken to encourage children to make careful, detailed observations or to plan science investigations – especially those initiated from their own questions and experiences. Although about half the classes surveyed had undertaken work on topics which contributed to children's understanding of the characteristics of living things, few studied, in depth, reproduction, growth and development in plants and animals. Physical science activities were less well pronounced, sources of energy being considered in about half the eleven-year-old classes but rarely with younger children. Much of the work done in the primary school that is of a scientific nature can be undertaken and developed without the aid of specialist equipment and materials. Thus children can look closely at, and identify patterns in, the arrangement of leaves on a twig, the ways in which materials react to various stimuli such as heat and light, and in the behaviour of light when reflected by mirrors or refracted by water or split into its component colours by raindrops.

Of course, the survey found examples of good practice too – although much was biological in nature, no doubt reflecting the interests, past experiences and training of the teachers. The neglect of the physical sciences continues to cause great concern. However, biological topics can afford valuable insights into the science of materials, structures and forces, and energy. For example, in one nine-year-old class:

> the teacher had arranged a visit to a bird sanctuary. The preparatory work involved drawing children's attention to the characteristics of different species of birds which would assist in their identification, examining the construction of birds' nests and relating the materials used and the method of construction to the size of the bird and the shape of its beak. At a later stage the children constructed a bird table and went on to collect bird droppings; they placed them in sterilised seed compost and witnessed the germination of seeds which had been carried by the birds.

More recently (1983) the HMI Science Committee introduced a discussion paper *Science in Primary Schools* offering comments 'on the variety of ways in which children of primary school age can be taught to think scientifically and some suggestions for the consideration of Local Education Authorities and Heads'. In order that a framework for the development of science skills, concepts and ways of thinking can be constructed, broad areas of content which should be inclined in the primary curriculum are mentioned:

- the study of living things and their interaction with the environment
- materials and their characteristics
- energy and its interaction with materials
- forces and their effects.

Of course this is in no way restrictive – most science activities will fall into one or more of these categories!

The importance of 'systematic enquiry' is stressed. For example,

> the building of a model bridge is not in itself either scientific or technological. But scientific and technological development is taking place when a sustained investigation is being made of forces and structures; when pupils are asking questions and seeking answers through experiment or in books; and when what they have learned brings to influence their design of the model bridge.

This, of course, has implications for the teacher, in that an understanding of the importance of experimental investigation is essential. Most teachers will have had little experience of such approaches either at school or at their training establishments. However, experience shows that from small, self-contained beginnings, such approaches can be achieved.

The discussion paper attaches importance to the notion of continuity. Sequencing within the areas already mentioned (Living Things, Materials, Energy and Forces) is important, and the need for teachers within a school to have a policy and general scheme of work for science is emphasised. Examples are given of how scientific ideas might develop in, for example, 'Living Things', and how a range of concepts might be approached over several years.

Science in Primary Schools is one of a range of publications which exercises an encouraging influence on primary science practice, and which has given substance to *Science 5–16: A Statement of Policy* (1985). In this most recent science statement from the DES, priorities are clearly stated and the processes to which all children should be progressively introduced are listed.

In order to achieve its broad aims, the policy statement includes ten principles on which science education in schools should be based:

Breadth	For all pupils science should introduce them to the main concepts of the whole range of science, to a range of scientific skills and processes and to the technological applications and social consequences of science.
Balance	Elements from each of the main areas of science should be studied, and courses should balance the acquisition of scientific knowledge and the practice of scientific method.
Relevance	Courses should draw on the everyday experience of the pupils and aim at preparing them as effectively as possible for adult and working life.
Differentiation	Courses should be sufficiently demanding to test the most able pupils to the full, and to encourage those of average ability and below to new levels of achievement.
Equal opportunities	Ways should be found to excite the interest of girls in aspects of science which some of them at present find 'unappealing or intimidating'. Girls and boys alike should receive a broad science education.
Continuity	Links should be created between phases of education so that pupils can build on work already done.
Progression	Courses should be designed to give progressively deeper understanding and greater competence.

Links across the curriculum	The contribution which science can make to the teaching of other subjects, and vice versa, should be fully exploited.
Teaching methods and approaches	Science should be taught at all stages in a way which emphasises practical, investigative and problem-solving activities.
Assessment	Progress in science should be assessed in ways which recognise the importance of the skills and processes of science as well as rewarding the ability to reproduce and apply scientific knowledge.

LEAs and schools are urged to develop and publish their own policies for science education in the primary schools, as well as plans for implementing such policies. The policy statement recognises features that are crucial if such plans are to succeed:

(a) each school concerned should include the teaching of science among the curricular aims which it formally adopts, should develop programmes of work and should monitor its own progress in putting its aims into effect;

(b) the head teacher should be committed to the principle of science education for primary pupils and should be accountable to the governors and to the LEA for the rate at which progress is made;

(c) the school needs to have at its disposal at least one teacher with the capacity, knowledge and insight to make science education for primary pupils a reality; in the case of small schools such consultant teachers may need to offer advice to more than one school;

(d) the objective should be that all class teachers, without exception, should include at least some science in their teaching, making use of their colleagues' specialist knowledge and experience as necessary;

(e) teachers need continuing access to permanent points of support outside the school, such as advisers or advisory teachers, a teacher training institution, teachers' centre or SATRO.

The policy statement also emphasises the need for schools to produce their own individual schemes of work which should:

emphasise progression in content, concept and intellectual demand, and in scientific skills and processes, appropriate to the children's ages and abilities;

avoid risks of sex stereotyping;

identify the fundamental aspects of science to which every pupil should be introduced;

secure appropriate differentiation for children of differing abilities;

contain not only a list of topics but also advice on suitable approaches, on practical work that has been found successful and on resources that are available within the school and outside it;

be drawn up as a result of discussion between the head teacher and all of the staff, in the light of discussion of LEA documents where appropriate and with support from staff from outside the school;

reflect discussion with other primary schools and with the schools to which pupils will transfer, so that receiving schools are clear about the range and depth of the science education provided in the primary school.

These documents invite discussion on the rich variety of scientific experiences open to primary school children and we shall attempt, in this and subsequent chapters, to explain and extend them.

The Association for Science Education

In 1981 the Association for Science Education (ASE) published a policy statement, *Education Through Science*, a comprehensive document of relevance to all involved with the teaching of science at every level. Few would argue with the conclusions reached on the place of science in the school curriculum. The Association urges that 'schools . . . accept the need to develop an approach to science studies which is based on the notion of science across the curriculum and sees science as essential in the development of a common core curriculum at the primary and secondary levels'. Moreover, the Association re-emphasises the findings of the HMI survey (and similar conclusions in Scotland outlined in a Scottish Education Department report published in 1980) and stresses that the 'failure to make science an integral part of the primary curriculum is almost totally due to the shortage of suitably trained teachers (due in part to weaknesses in the current organisation of science teaching in secondary schools) and the lack of adequate support facilities and continuing in-service opportunities.'

Many Local Education Authorities have, however, within their resources, made distinct efforts to support science in the primary schools through the appointment of advisory teachers and through in-service programmes. The Association itself, in partnership with teaching institutions and LEAs, has established guidelines for nationally recognised in-service courses in science for primary teachers, including a professional diploma validated by the Association. In the longer term the need is stressed for initial training courses for those intending to teach at primary school level to contain a compulsory course component in the teaching of science.

In order that the primary teacher can incorporate scientific work in the normal schedule of teaching and learning activities, the provision of adequate resources is essential:

the provision of a wide range of simple equipment and materials that is likely to be of use in support of scientific activities and enquiries

the provision of suitable storage facilities that enable resources to be found easily and used by teachers and children.

Thus space is needed for children to keep and observe living things such as plants, fish, tadpoles, worms, insects and small mammals in safety; and for stimulus materials, including books, pamphlets, pictures, charts, diagrams and extracts from newspapers, magazines and comics.

Finally, the Association suggests that primary schools should seek to establish working relationships with the science departments of local secondary schools in order that more specialist resources can be made available as and when required.

The Assessment of Performance Unit

The Assessment of Performance Unit (APU), set up within the Department of Education and Science in 1975 to provide information about national levels of performance in a number of curricular areas, began its first survey of the science performance of 11-year-olds in 1980. Since then other surveys have been undertaken and the findings published in a series of substantial reports. More recently a number of booklets for teachers have been made available, covering a range of issues relevant to those involved in the teaching of 'science' to primary school children.

The view of primary science which the surveys attempt to reflect is that it:

is a rational way of finding out about the world, involving the development of a willingness and ability to seek and use evidence;

involves the gradual building of a framework of concepts which help to make sense of experience; and

fosters the skills and attitudes necessary for investigation and experimentation.

Practical tests were used to give information about the children's:

ability to perform investigations
skill in observing
ability to use simple measuring instruments and equipment
reactions to science-based activities.

Written tests were used to assess the children's ability to:

plan investigations
interpret and explain information given in the question, by making use of patterns in the data or suggesting hypotheses
use graphs, tables, charts.

The process skills, attitudes and concepts which are implied by the Unit's view of primary science were identified, and tests were devised to assess them.

The categories and sub-categories assessed are shown on the next page.

These categories are only a framework for assessment. The teaching and development of skills should gradually and progressively be extended during the pupils' school experience, and examples throughout this book indicate how this might be achieved.

The surveys provide information about children's performance in the tests, about their reactions to science activities and about provision for science in schools. The main findings are summarised thus:

Most 11-year-olds

- set about practical investigations in a relevant manner
- observed broad similarities and differences between objects
- read the scale of simple measuring instruments correctly
- classified objects on the basis of observed properties
- read information from flow charts, tables, pie charts and isolated points from line graphs

About half of 11-year-olds

- reported results consistent with the evidence from investigations
- were more fluent at observing differences than similarities between objects
- made predictions based on observations
- suggested controls in planning parts of investigations
- used given information to make reasonable predictions

- applied science concepts to solve problems
- proposed alternative hypotheses to explain a given phenomenon
- added information to a partially completed graph or chart

Category	Sub-Categories	Form of test
Use of symbolic representation	Reading information from graphs, tables and charts. Representing information as graphs, tables and charts.	Written
Using apparatus and measuring instruments		Individual practical
Observation	Making and interpreting observations.	Group practical
Interpretation and application	Interpreting presented information. Distinguishing degrees of influence. Applying science concepts to make sense of new information. Generating alternative hypotheses.	Written
Planning investigations	Planning parts of investigations. Planning entire investigations. Identifying or proposing testable statements.	Written
Performance of investigations		Individual practical

Few 11-year-olds

- repeated measurements or observations to check results
- controlled variables necessary to obtain good quantitative results
- recorded the observation of fine details of objects
- observed the correct sequence of events
- produced an adequate plan for a simple investigation
- gave good explanations of how they arrived at predictions
- described patterns in observations or data in terms of general relationships

Not surprisingly, the surveys found that children liked, and were interested in, science activities. They were willing to be involved in all types of investigations, using both living and non-living things. They appeared willing to tackle written tests but there was little evidence of critical and reflective consideration of their own work. Performance between girls and boys was not markedly different, although girls were slightly ahead in using graphs, tables and charts, in making observations of similarities and differences and were better able to plan investigations and record data. Boys were ahead in using measuring instruments, in applying physical science concepts to problems and in recording quantitative results.

The APU outlines the implications for classroom practice indicated by their surveys. The overall picture, as it emerges, seems to suggest that children are much more confident in their use of general skills important across the curriculum – skills such as observing, measuring and keeping written records; but less competent in skills more specifically related to science such as defining patterns in observations, explaining, predicting, hypothesising, controlling variables and planning investigations. This is possibly due to reduced opportunities to develop these skills. Specifically, the APU suggests that schools might:

* encourage children to design their own approaches to solving problems and allow them to try out their ideas;

* discuss with the children the progress of their investigations and encourage them to discuss with each other;

* discuss the children's results and challenge them to show how they were worked out from the evidence;

* listen to children's ideas and probe their 'wrong' responses; encourage them to explain their reasons for their ideas; use this knowledge in planning further activities for their children;

* help children to review critically their practical procedures and to consider alternative strategies for solving problems or investigation.

It might also be worth bearing in mind that:

* girls may need more encouragement to take an active part in science activities, especially in using equipment and making measurements;

* boys may need guidance in recording their procedures systematically and in describing their experiments so that others can follow what they have done.

The School Natural Science Society

Primary School Science Skills, published in 1984 by the School Natural Science Society, discusses in detail those science skills and attitudes that can be fostered in the primary school. The SNSS stresses that the booklet is intended to be directly relevant to general school discussions about ways of working and classroom organisation in the context of the Society's perceived nature of primary science. In particular, the sort of science recommended is:

(a) learnt mainly through genuine practical experiences
(b) discussion of that experience
(c) not merely understood but also used for problems that the children meet and perceive at home and school
(d) drawn from a wide range of topics from the man-made as well as the natural world. Because it applies the knowledge gained, it includes making things as well as scientific exploration. We can call this technology: producing things using some science ideas, as well as others not from science.

The authors go on to discuss, in some depth, what they consider to be implicit in certain well-defined skills. It is hoped that their skills list will aid teachers in the selection of material for the development of their skills, to see the inter-relationships between these various skills, and to assess and analyse the work done in the classroom. Ultimately the planning of school schemes of work should benefit, as should the recording of progression in science by the pupils.

The Society envisages this document to be more relevant to those teaching the seven to eleven age range. However, they hope to produce material more appropriate to five- to seven-year-olds and possibly list topics useful in developing certain skills. They also intend to propose core concepts to be grasped by the end of the primary stage and provide help with teaching methods and organisation allied to progression through the school.

Secondary school

Transfer procedures between primary and secondary schools vary between, and even within, Local Education Authorities. Primary schools can 'feed' several secondary schools, who in turn have intakes from many primaries. In the past, contact between the schools, in a meaningful sense for science, has been poor. The main mechanisms for such contacts can be summarised in four points.

1. A report form, with some provision for science comments, sent from the primary to secondary school when the pupil transfers.
2. Informal contacts between schools and/or individuals.
3. Meetings of a more formal nature, probably involving several schools and possibly set up by LEA Inspectors.
4. Some form of teacher exchange or attachment.

What little research there has been in this area seems to suggest that informal contacts are the most common form of liaison and potentially the most beneficial. Report forms mentioning science have been exchanged, but there is little evidence of their having any impact on secondary provision. Formal contact and staff exchange are less frequent occurrences. Secondary schools can rarely rely on a common science experience amongst their intakes and, in many cases, tend to start from scratch. This can be very discouraging to those pupils with a well-established science background, and to their teachers; and it would appear that a detailed assessment of the type and form of science experienced by pupils should enable the secondary school to build on good primary practice. In order to achieve this, liaison is essential and much more likely if LEA's can initiate and develop links formally in order to agree procedures, and then for individuals to develop such links to their mutual advantage. In particular, secondary school science staff should be invited to visit the primary schools in order to appreciate the work in science being accomplished there.

DEVELOPING SKILLS, ATTITUDES AND CONCEPTS

Science is an ideal vehicle for acquiring skills, fostering attitudes and developing an understanding of a range of concepts relevant to everyday experience.

Usually there is no need to isolate these interrelated areas. Some of the science-based activities of the children will enable them to develop certain techniques or meet

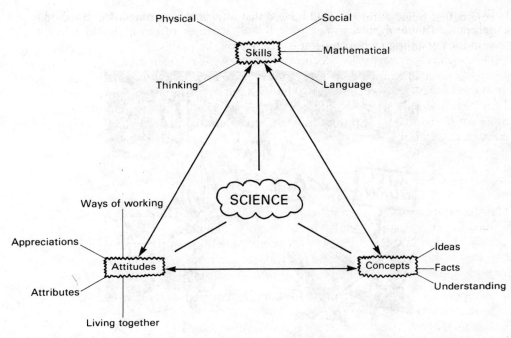

Figure 1.1   Attitudes, concepts and skills are interrelated and developed by science activities

new ideas, and other areas will be enhanced by a different range of activities. Over several years of a balanced science experience, the child will have used most of the skills, met a range of ideas and facts, and will have become used to ways of working which can be applied to everyday life.

Fable of a lost child keeping warm

Once upon a time a small child became lost. Because the weather was cold, he decided to gather materials for a fire – *he asked questions*. As he brought objects back to his campfire he discovered that some of them burned and some of them didn't burn – *he made observations*. To avoid collecting useless substances, the child began to keep track of those objects that burned and those that did not – *he collected data*. After a few trips his lists contained the following information – *his classification*:

Will burn	*Will not burn*
Tree limbs	Rocks
Broom handles	Blackberries
Pencils	Marbles
Chair legs	Paperweights
Flagpoles	

This organisation of the information was quite an aid in his quest for warmth. However, as tree limbs and broom handles became scarce, the child tried to find a regularity that would guide him to new flammable materials.

Looking at the pile of objects that failed to burn, and comparing it with the pile of objects that would burn, the child noticed that a regularity appeared. He proposed a generalisation – *he hypothesised*.

'Perhaps Cylindrical Objects Burn'

Figure 1.2   'Cylindrical objects burn.'

The next day the child went looking for materials to burn, but he forgot to bring along his list. However, he remembered his generalisation. So, he returned to his fireside hauling a tree limb, an old walking stick and three rounders bats – *successful predictions*. What's more, he reflected with pleasure, he hadn't bothered to carry back some other objects: a car radiator, a piece of chain, and a large door. Since these objects weren't cylindrical there was no reason to expect them to burn – *he interpreted data*.

Because of his successful predictions, the child became confident of his generalisation. The next day he deliberately left the list at his campsite. This time, with the aid of his rule, he came back heavily laden with three pieces of pipe, two lemonade bottles, and the axle from an old car, while spurning a huge cardboard box of old newspapers.

During the long cold night that followed *he drew these conclusions*:
The cylindrical shape of a burnable object may not be ultimately associated with its flammability after all.
Even though the cylindrical rule is no longer useful, tree limbs, broom handles, pencils and other burnables in the table still burn.
I'd better bring the list along tomorrow.
But, thinking over the long list, he saw a new regularity that fitted the table and the newly acquired information as well.

'Perhaps Wooden Objects Burn'

(From Pimentel, 1963.)

And so we begin to see what science is all about. Our observations and data collection add to our personal store of knowledge, which in turn will help us answer our questions. We hypothesise and make predictions which are held to be true until we find a situation that doesn't fit our theory. We modify our views until, eventually, we can successfully answer our questions.

The child has made his first steps; he will eventually realise that newspapers burn!

Skills

Once children embark on a science activity or investigation, there are well-defined skills or processes (not necessarily unique to science) which will help them in their approach to their work and to its successful completion.

Even very young children naturally use their skills of *observation* and *communication* in their everyday pursuits, and their *questioning* can often provide starting points for further development of these basic skills. As they get older and more experienced their work might possibly require them to make *estimations* and eventually *measurements*; and to *classify* and *look for patterns* in their data. As they mentally and physically develop, they will increasingly use more complex *manipulative* skills and the need for *testing* and *experimenting* will become apparent. Later still, they can be gradually introduced to higher-level processes – although they will, in all probability, have used them in a rudimentary or less structured way earlier: *predicting* on the basis of their accumulated data, and *inferring*, *hypothesising* and *applying* their findings to new situations. For many children, however, these latter will be more profitably developed in their secondary schools. It is very unlikely that these processes can be developed linearly; in practice mutual interaction will be inevitable – they are linked in so many ways.

In the early stages these skills can be introduced gradually. From small and simple beginnings they will be developed through a variety of activities, some spontaneous, some contrived, but all contributing to the science experiences of the children.

Observation

Careful, accurate observation is fundamental to science studies. We sometimes forget that we have five senses and, when we are asked to describe something, often merely report our visual impressions, and then only in a superficial way.

If they are involved in a study of trees, for example, children should be encouraged not only to *look* at the tree as a whole, but also to study carefully its various parts. When making a detailed examination of leaves, they can spot variation in shape and size of leaves from different parts of the tree; they can carefully talk about the colour of leaves – is it uniform over the leaf, on both sides, over several leaves? Individual differences in a collection of specimens can be recorded and the beginnings of explanations made. Eventually, they will have observed as much as possible using the sense of *sight* and so the need to involve the other senses becomes apparent.

Touch is particularly attractive for young children. They like to feel and discuss the various textures; the crinkle of paper, the smoothness of silk, the warmth of the fur on small animals. Thus they can extend their observations. Is the leaf rough or smooth or warm or brittle?

Sound can be informative. When does our leaf make sounds? Is it an autumn leaf? Does it crackle? Does it break? What about the rustle of leaves on the tree? What causes these sounds? Do they vary? Most of us are very sensitive to *smell*. It is now becoming more difficult to describe our observations. We tend to say that something has a smell which is pleasant or otherwise. We tend to compare odours. We might, for instances, describe our leaf as smelling of perfume – *judgement* is being used. (*N.B. Teachers must warn children that smelling some substances, even household ones, can be irritating or dangerous.*)

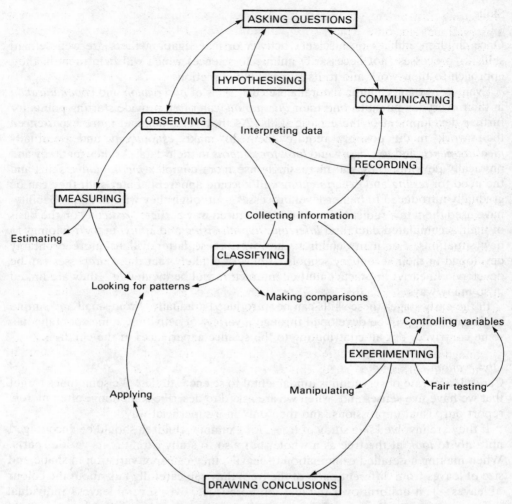

Figure 1.3   A range of skills will be used during investigative work

Finally, the sense of *taste*. Now we must take much more care. *Indiscriminate tasting of unfamiliar substances is not to be encouraged, especially with young children*. If taste is to be used, very small quantities should be tentatively introduced to the tip of the tongue (different areas of the tongue are sensitive to various categories of taste – but that is another area of investigation!). The judgement of the teacher is important here. *If in doubt, don't taste*.

Children enjoy competition. Give them a leaf, or an insect or a burning birthday candle. Let them see how many observations they can make, using as many senses as appropriate.

There are many aids to observation. A good supply of hand lenses will enable children to extend their observations. They can be used anywhere; in the classroom and in the field. A simple microscope will give extra clarity to fine detail while leaving hands free to record and make detailed drawings. Apart from the fundamental measuring instruments found in the typical classroom, there are many robust observational aids on the market. Osmiroid have the tripod magnifier allowing three powers of magnification and useful for looking at leaves, insects, fibres, etc. The Magnispector and Midispector are four-inch and three-inch diameter magnifying boxes with a base grid in centimetre and millimetre divisions. The lid is a lens and so specimens can be contained and magnified.

One final word on observation. It is very easy and widespread to confuse *observation* and *interpretation*. We describe someone as wearing a woollen cardigan because of its visual appearance. However, it might easily be a man-made fibre manufactured to give the appearance of wool. We made an interpretation or judgement not really justified by our limited observations.

Measurement

Observational skills using the senses only begin to describe our environment. Eventually the need for a quantitative or *measurement* description becomes apparent. Initially children describe objects in an elementary way without formal measurement. They use *relativities* – a long stick, a short twig; they make comparisons through handling – a heavy stone, a light bucket. Later, they begin to *rank* objects they can order by size, such as a pea, a marble, a tennis ball, a football. Gradually the use of a scale develops, such as a hand span, a stride, a measuring stick, a ruler; the levels of graduation increase as the child progresses through school.

Estimating is a skill with relevance to a variety of situations – to maths work; for deciding how to hit a ball on the sports field; or how much dinner to put on a plate! In science, estimation often needs confirmation by accurate measurement.

Encourage children to construct their own measuring instruments.

There are many measuring instruments available – for length, for weight, papers which change colour to measure acidity, meters to register or detect electric currents. For particular investigations the children can make their own measuring instruments – a yoghourt pot anemometer for wind speed, a 'current balance' for testing batteries, or a chart for testing eyesight. Links with mathematics are strong, both areas needing to develop and use higher level concepts. Thus, children might look statistically at the size of a sack of potatoes they have grown or the percentage germination of seeds grown under different conditions. They encounter the need for accurate scale models when looking at the strengths of bridges or the construction of canal locks.

Classifying

Every day we make subconscious use of *classification*. We classify Greece as a Mediterranean country, and so, when deciding on a holiday destination, we immediately assume various attributes of the country – its climate, its food, its people. We are using classification in order to make *predictions* about what our holiday will be like.

In the classroom a teacher might ask a child to get some drawing paper. It is classified as stationery so he knows roughly where to look – the stationery cupboard. Classification is being used to help find something. Mention has already been made about the elementary classification skill of arranging marbles and balls in a rank order according to size. *Grouping* is also extensively used in science. Initially children will group items into two sets, using some easily observed property, colour or shape. Of course the groups can change – the paper might not be in the stationery cupboard, it could be grouped with art materials in the art cupboard! Thus from a box of green and yellow circles and triangles a child might group the items thus:

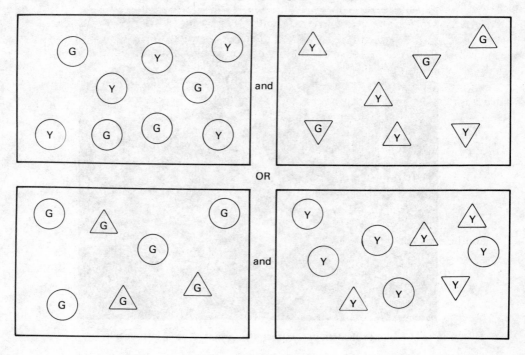

When confronted with a larger 'population' older children, especially, can group or classify in many ways:

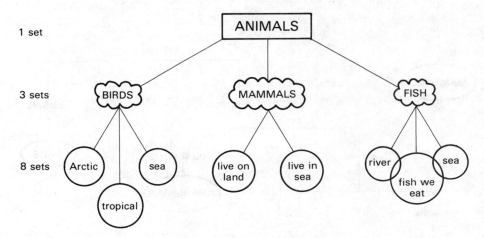

The actual activity will usually determine how the classification might be made, and as children get older they will be able to use more sophisticated reasons for forming the sets. They might decide to rank, not by considering the size as the younger child does with marbles and balls, but by considering other properties they come across in their science. Work on eating utensils might lead to a consideration of spoons and their suitability for use in a variety of situations – eating cold sweets or hot soup, etc. Thus they might be ranked in order of heat conductivity for a particular use, or size for another use, or attractiveness in a particular setting.

Ranking and setting can be combined. The set of objects which conduct electricity can be ranked in order of ease of conduction – possibly by reference to how brightly a bulb in a common circuit glows.

The use of simple *keys* can help a child's science, especially in identification work. Grouping of vertebrates can be done using a common key (see next page). There are exceptions, of course, which children find very interesting.

Alternatively, a numbered key can be used:

1. Hair present   *Mammals*
   Hair absent   go to 2

2. Feathers present   *Birds*
   Feathers absent   go to 3

3. Scales present   go to 4
   Scales absent   *Amphibians*

4. Nostrils present   *Reptiles*
   Gills present   *Fish*

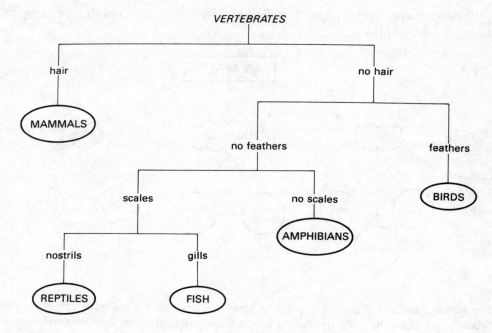

Experimenting

I kept six honest serving men
They taught me all I knew
Their names where WHAT and WHY and WHEN
And HOW and WHERE and WHO   (Kipling)

'What happens if . . .?' At some stage the young science investigator needs to *experiment*. Children find out about, and begin to understand, their environment. One of the ways they do this is to do something to this environment, to change the surroundings or alter conditions slightly – to begin to experiment.

During their practical activities children will practice and develop most of the skills already mentioned. Even the very young can begin to experiment in a formal way – they have been doing so since birth. However, in science, experimenting is not usually a random process, even though some important discoveries have apparently resulted from chance or even accident.

Asking questions, the right questions, leads to practical work. Even an unstructured 'What happens if . . .?' is a valid reason for doing experimental work to find out. Eventually, much later, *hypothesising* occurs; generalisations are made and supported by experimental evidence.

If we ask a question of an experiment we must ask it fairly. *Fair testing* or *control of variables* is essential if correct deductions are to be made from our work. Children themselves are usually very conscious of this – the referee of a hockey match ensures fair play, the competitors on sports day all start from a common line.

Supposing a group of children decide to find out which washing-up liquid gives the best value for money. After some discussion they agree on what they mean by value for money, and plan their testing accordingly. They intend to wash some greasy plates. For a fair comparison several factors must be considered, *variables to control*: the water temperature, the amount of water, the amount of washing-up liquid added, the amount of grease on each plate, the number of 'scrubs' – all must be kept the same – what about the various prices and volumes of washing-up liquid in the bottles? These variables must be identified before testing – are there others? – and ways of keeping them constant must be agreed.

Younger children, of course, will be less likely to spot all the variables, but they will find some and appreciate the need for 'fairness'.

As older children, or those with some science experience, begin to hypothesise and make generalisations, the need to control variables becomes increasingly important. They might decide to find out about the optimum conditions for growing beans in the classroom. As many variables as possible should be isolated:

growing medium	soil
	compost
	sawdust and blotting paper
	gravel, etc.

position	constantly kept in sunlight
	on a north facing window sill
	near a radiator
	in the dark, etc.

watering	a measured amount once a day
	a measured amount once a week
	standing in water
	cold water
	hot water, etc.

There are many other variables to consider – feeding, staking, keeping under glass, for instance.

It soon becomes evident that a seemingly simple problem can be quite complex to solve. Variables must be altered one at a time, the hypotheses of the class tested and optimum (and reasonably practical) conditions found.

Communicating
Obviously an efficient recording and communication system is necessary to deal with the increasing amount of data deriving from investigative work. Depending on the activities undertaken, there are many ways of recording, and hence communicating, as the variety of techniques suggested by the practical activities described in later chapters will show, and as the following example can, in part, illustrate:

The children were investigating the dyes in inks. They put an ink blot on blotting paper and watched it spread out. They added a drop of water – the spreading continued. Eventually they saw a separation of colours. The blotting paper itself, when dry, makes an excellent record of their findings. It communicates much better than words; little additional information is needed, except the technique; and even this can be pictorally represented.

Other activities will lend themselves to other methods of communication: drawing, writing, charts, histograms, plaster casts, model-making and oral communication (further discussed in chapter 2) – what we require is the most efficient, effective way.

As the descriptive powers of children develop they need encouragement to be more accurate or definite in their reporting. They will describe a tree as being tall. What is the reference point – as tall as the tallest pine tree, tall compared with a person, a child or a flower? Likewise, hot and cold, fast and slow, light and heavy, and many more. A reference point eliminates doubt or uncertainty and sharpens the observation: heavier than an equivalent sized block of wood, but lighter than an equivalent sized block of iron. There are obvious links with classification skills and the need for measurement.

Physical skills
Science affords further opportunities for children to develop and extend their physical skills. They will, in the course of their practical work, use many different pieces of equipment; some delicate, some robust; some requiring fine control such as the adjustments to a microscope, others delicate manipulations such as the preparation of a specimen microscope slide. Yet other activities will require them to acquire techniques such as marking out a sample plot of ground to enable them to look at earthworm populations. They will develop organised, safe and careful methods of working; learn to handle common tools, and look after them; become confident in handling living things with care and concern – plants and small animals. Science will help them develop ways of working which will serve them in many other fields.

Attitudes

Teachers will decide for themselves which attitudes they wish to encourage through science activities. We have already seen how skills and processes relevant to the whole curriculum can be reinforced by science studies. Likewise, positive attitudes can be developed through activities which are themselves interesting and thought-provoking, and which can harness the child's natural curiosity and questioning.

Assessment of Performance Unit surveys indicate that a *questioning* attitude towards the surroundings and enjoyment of science-based work is closely linked to the basic skill of observation as primary goals for science-based activities with 11-year-olds. Indeed, throughout the school these must be areas of major importance and concern.

Science studies are particularly appropriate for fostering attitudes of *curiosity*, *working co-operatively* and *persevering*. We have already seen that, as scientists, we must have an *open mind*, be willing to *test our theories* before accepting or rejecting them, and *question myth and superstition* as explanations of natural phenomena. Children will become willing to assume responsibility for the *care and maintenance* of plants and animals and develop a *respect*, not only for living things, but also for their physical surroundings. They will appreciate not only the functional properties of materials, but develop an *aesthetic* awareness too. During practical work, fair testing will develop values of *honesty* and they will be *objective* in seeing that a 'failed experiment' is important – it, also, can provide valuable information.

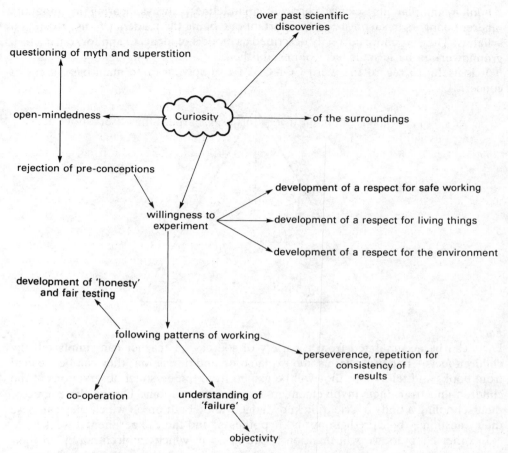

Figure 1.4   Initial curiosity can be used to encourage the development of a range of attitudes

Concepts

Several authors have produced lists of concepts in science of particular relevance to primary school children.

Wynne Harlen (1978), in a notable *School Science Review* article, 'Does Content Matter in Primary Science?'* concludes with a comprehensive list of content and concept guidelines relative to children in their primary schools (see Appendix I). Likewise, the Assessment of Performance Unit reports *Science in Schools: Age 11* contains a list of science concepts and knowledge which may be required for some of their assessment categories (see Appendix II).

Such lists can, of course, be daunting, and are always open to arguments of omission or inappropriate inclusion. However, they are useful frameworks on which a

---

* The discussion begun in the SSR article is further developed by Professor Harlen (1985) in *Teaching and Learning Primary Science* (Chapter 4) London: Harper and Row.

school might plan its science curriculum guidelines, always bearing in mind the inherent dangers in such lists – an important one being the tendency to use them as a syllabus. They are more correctly described as models of ideals to aim for, once a firm groundwork in basic skills has been established.

It is useful to regard the word CONCEPT as implying three main basic areas of concern:

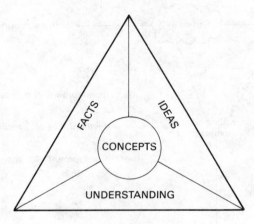

Facts

Facts can be accumulated from a variety of sources. A teacher can simply tell the children facts – hopefully with some explanation and discussion; they can be gleaned from books and television; they will be gained from the personal observations of the children and from their involvement in a range of situations. During the course of their schooling a body of scientific knowledge will be built up on which they can base their questions, their predictions and hypotheses, and their experimental work.

In other chapters we will mention broad areas in which children may plan their investigations – the study of living things, materials, energy and forces. We will look at the facts associated with these areas that children will become familiar with: different types of food assist growth, provide us with energy, help in our fight against disease; different materials have their own unique properties and characteristics which make them suitable for building bridges, providing insulation or clothing us; useful work can be done when a spring uncoils.

Ideas

Ideas are usually of a more abstract nature, and concept lists contain many of them: everything is attracted to the centre of the earth, this causes things to feel heavy; if we change the shape of a piece of plasticine from a ball to a sausage, the amount of material stays the same.

A recent discussion paper, *Science in Primary Schools*, produced by the HMI Science Committee (1983), mentioned (p. 2) that 'there are certain fundamental facts and ideas that pupils must meet and grasp if they are to make any significant progress in their studies'. Sequencing is very important if children are to have this 'grasp'. It is often difficult to dissect a theme and isolate a hierarchical list of components, but it is essential if ideas are to be fully appreciated.

One way which has been found useful is to list statements about a particular theme which may or may not be relevant to the children concerned. If these statements are written on card which can be cut into individual statements, some order can be achieved. Some statements will be rejected, the need for additional ones seen. Before work on magnets we might list the following:

- magnets only attract certain things
- stroking iron or steel with a magnet makes it magnetic
- a compass needle is a magnet
- there are many different metals
- most metals are shiny
- like poles of two magnets repel
- most metals are hard
- magnets attract some metals
- magnets produce a field around them
- magnets are made of iron or steel
- heating destroys magnets
- the poles are labelled N and S
- banging destroys magnets
- some metals ring when struck
- many metals feel cold
- unlike poles of two magnets attract
- the poles of a suspended magnet are attracted by the poles of the earth
- iron and steel becomes a temporary magnet in an electric coil
- magnets have two poles

A first attempt at ordering might produce a result like that shown overleaf (Fig. 1.5).

On reflection we can rearrange, decide that other ideas should be fed in at various stages, and leave other less appropriate ideas out to be considered again when the children are older and have experienced other concepts.

Once such an exercise has been done, the types of activity related to the acquisition of these ideas can be considered, bearing in mind the skills and attitudes already mentioned.

Understanding
Understanding must be one of the most important aims at any level:

I hear and I forget
I see and I remember
I do and I understand

Without understanding at the various levels there is little point in progressing further. Some concepts must be gradually developed over many years, using many experiences, before complete understanding is achieved. The ideas are constantly being reinforced and gradually built upon in an ever-upward pyramid towards particular goals (see Fig. 1.6, page 25).

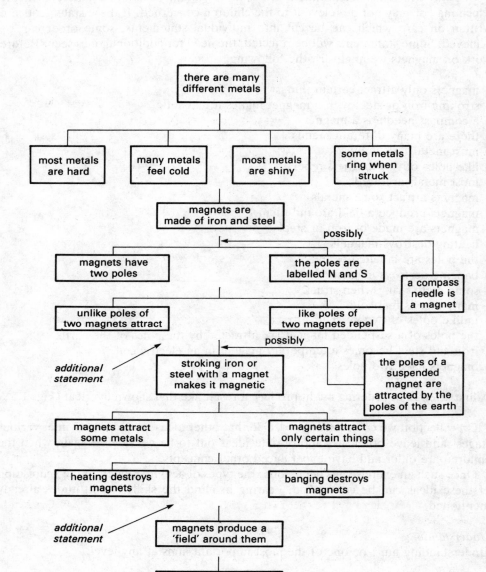

Figure 1.5   A first attempt at ordering information

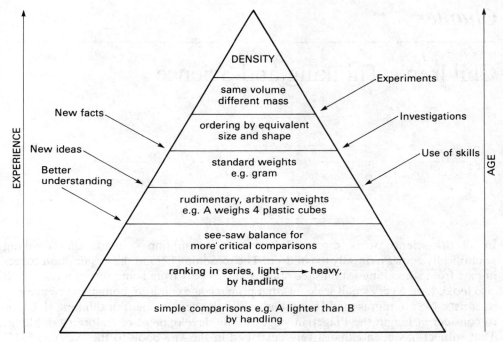

Figure 1.6 Pyramid of ideas

REFERENCES

Association for Science Education (ASE) (1981) *Education Through Science: Policy Statement*. Hatfield. ASE.

Department of Education and Science (1978) *Primary Education in England: A Survey by H.M. Inspectors of Schools*. London: HMSO.

Department of Education and Science (1983) *Science in Primary Schools: A Discussion Paper produced by the HMI Science Committee*. London: HMSO.

Department of Education and Science (1985) *Science 5–16: A Statement of Policy*. London: HMSO.

Department of Education and Science (1981) *APU Science in Schools age 11, Report No. 1*. London: HMSO.

Department of Education and Science (1983) *APU Science in Schools age 11, Report No. 2*. London: DES.

Department of Education and Science (1984) *APU Science in Schools age 11, Report No. 3*. London: DES.

Department of Education and Science (1983) *APU Science Report for Teachers: 1. Science at age 11*. Hatfield. ASE.

Harlen, W. (June 1978) Does Content Matter in Primary Science? *The School Science Review*, **59**, 209 pp. 614–625.

Harlen, W. (1985) *Teaching and Learning Primary Science*. London: Harper & Row.

Pimentel, G. C. (ed). (1963) *Chemistry – An Experimental Science*, Fable – A lost child keeping warm. pp. 3–4. New York: W. H. Freeman.

School Natural Science Society (1984) *Primary School Science Skills*. Gillingham: SNSS.

Schools Council, (1972) *Science 5–13 Project: Units for Teachers*. London: Macdonald.

Scottish Education Department (1980) *Learning and Teaching in Primary 4 and Primary 7: A Report by H.M. Inspectors of Schools in Scotland*. Edinburgh: HMSO.

Chapter 2

Children's Thinking and Science

In all the science work discussed here, the assumption is made that thinking scientifically comes naturally to children. The reasoning behind this assumption comes in part from some long-established studies and in part from some recent work which also looked, on a very small scale, at what primary-age children thought of science and scientists. No attempt is made here to consider the development of thinking skills, or to consider at length the Piagetian stages in the development of children's thinking. That subject has been exhaustively described in the key book to the 'Science 5–13' series, *With Objectives in Mind*. This recognises three main stages in the development of the ability to learn. At 'Stage One', two substages are identified – the transition period from intuition to concrete operations and the early stage of concrete operations. The former, pre-seven, 'infant' stage, described as 'Intuitive' by Piaget, is concerned with immediate observation and physical activity. Children cannot be expected to reach logical conclusions from their experiences and so, understandably, cannot be expected to predict the consequences of an action. In the later, 'early concrete operations' stage, children begin to handle things mentally as they handle objects physically.

In the second major stage called 'concrete operations – later stage' by the Science 5–13 team, this mental manipulation is growing in power and variety. As a result, problems can be solved in a more organised manner. In the third stage, children are in the transition from concrete to abstract thinking. Only then can they confidently handle hypotheses.

Each level demands a different approach, not just in the teaching of science. Stage one is best met by opportunities to explore the immediate environment and to make some sense of it by discussion and communication with others. At this stage then, as the concrete operations stage is entered, practical examples should be used to introduce new ideas. With the later concrete operations stages these examples can become more specific. At the abstract stage, hypotheses can be understood, and a number of variables systematically handled.

This outline grossly over-simplifies Piaget and a reading of *With Objectives in Mind* is to be recommended. If time does not allow that, each of the 'Science 5–13' books has an appendix briefly describing stages as the team interpret them, and linking these with developing skills.

CHILDREN'S 'WHY?' QUESTIONS

Piaget is only one of a number of authors to look at children's scientific thinking, much of which can also be directly applied to classroom teaching. Take, for example, a light-hearted article by Professor Ted Wragg that appeared in the *Times Educational Supplement* in 1981.

Ted Wragg, challenged by practitioners to 'spend some more time in the classroom', arranged to work with a group of infants. What should he teach them? What would they *like* him to teach them? What did they want to know about? The response to this request was a wealth of questions, many of them prefaced with the familiar 'Why?' What, he wondered, deadened this curiosity as children grew older?

He was not the first to ponder children's 'Why?' questions. Nathan Isaacs had first explored their curiosity back in 1930, and later (in 1958) returned to the subject. Gwen Allen, in 1966, also explored 'Questions Children Ask'. They both found that children's natural curiosity, as shown by their interest in reasons and explanations, led on to investigation. This interest is similar to that demonstrated by any scientist, in that it leads to a cohesive body of knowledge. In other words, children think as scientists do – or scientists' thinking is much like that of young children – since both are interested in 'why?'

Four groups of 'why?' questions can be identified, although they overlap so much that it would seem difficult to discriminate. First are the demands for *explanation*; the ones familiar to Ted Wragg – 'Why do people have hair?' for example. Then there are the 'why?' questions for a *purpose* – usually greater understanding – 'Why aren't we shopping today?' Scientific in nature are the quests for *causes* – 'Why does soap bubble?' Most irritating of all are the demands for *grounds or reasons* – 'Why should I?' Isaacs and others recognised that the trigger to many important questions is anomaly. Children encounter anomalies when they meet with experiences which they are unable to relate to previous learning.

'You've got two eyes; why can't you see two of everything?' Isaacs gives the example of playing with a child and lying on the ground for a protracted length of time. 'You aren't dead', said the child, 'Why not get up?' These questions are a child's response to puzzlement and disorientation. Put another way, children want to fit apparent anomalies into the pattern they have of their world. Like scientists, they want to reconcile new with previous experiences. Again, like scientists, they are open to ideas challenging previous thought. 'Why?' questions are often an expression of open-minded puzzlement, a demand for any help which will put them right. 'Why is my Daddy bigger than you?' asked one child, 'He is younger than you are.' 'Why?' is response to apparent anomaly.

A study of the development of science concepts comes in the work of Albert (1978). She examined the way in which the concept of 'heat' developed in young children; she found that it developed early, and in logical stages of understanding. Children, understandably, recognise what is meant by 'hot' from a very young age – 16 months, on average. First comes an understanding about the effect of heat upon themselves; and then heat as an entity. The concept of energy as a source of heat takes us further into the abstract. Then comes an understanding of temperature and levels of heat; compare the old, but valid, teaching chestnut 'Which would you rather have thrown at you, a bucket of boiling water or a red-hot pin?' (The difference being, of course, that the pin is at a higher temperature, but the water contains more heat.)

What is important about all this is not so much that it is academically interesting, as that it confirms the importance of matching activities to children's scientific understanding. In the same way that many younger children are slow to grasp the (more easily demonstrated) difference between the volume and pitch of sound, so many will find it hard to understand the difference between degree and amount of heat. Added to this, are children's own attitudes to science as a school subject, which may alienate and then disaffect them altogether.

Selmes (1969) found, along with others, that secondary-age pupils frequently described science as 'boring', 'uninteresting', or 'monotonous' and, in 1969, had little understanding of science as a method of investigation.

'DO FISHES GO TO SLEEP?'

Faced with this kind of evidence, one of the present authors worked with groups of junior-age children (Stringer, 1984) to explore their attitudes to science and scientists. In taped interviews young children were invited to ask the questions they might ask of a scientist. Then they were given the instruction 'draw me a scientist, please', and drew, individually, and without help or collaboration. Lastly, they examined four fairly anomalous little demonstrations, and tried various strategies to resolve *why* their experiments turned out as they did.

The eight-, nine- and ten-year-olds in schools in county and city were requested to ask the kind of questions they might ask a scientist. The hundreds of replies were transcribed and classified according to their content. Few of their questions were of a 'practical' kind and fewer still would lead on to realistic classroom investigation, although several would be appropriate starting points for work with reference books – 'is there water underground?' or 'how does a baby grow?' The majority were deep and demanding, and many were unanswerable – certainly in simple terms, possibly in any way at all. They expressed children's interest in the imponderable, and their natural curiosity. 'How did God become God?' 'When did people start getting cancer?' 'How do we get the names of things?' – were all questions of *origin*. Similar were the questions that were, so to speak, *moral* in nature – 'Is the day fixed when we die?' 'Do people have to die to give someone else the chance to live?' Then there were *astronomical* questions – 'Why isn't the moon round all the time?' 'When they [scientists] look up in space with those things, what do they get out of that?' Closely related, and unanswerable by study in some cases, were questions concerned with first-hand *environmental observation* – 'Why is the sky so blue?' 'Why don't clouds float down onto the earth?' 'Do birds have a fixed number of feathers?' or 'Do fishes go to sleep?'

But, by far, the largest category and classification, often arbitrary, when questions covered several fields, was that of the 'record breakers'. Scientists were expected to have encyclopaedic knowledge of firsts and extremes. 'How fast can light travel?' 'How long can man stay in space?' 'How many things have scientists found out?' 'Who was the first animal/ man/ woman/ in space?' 'Who discovered glass/ the weather/ computers?'

Few of the questions, then, were directly related to practical problem solving. Teachers, in these circumstances, might need to consider engineering circumstances that lead to the asking of problem-solving questions. It would be interesting to examine the questions of children who have had considerable experience of the problem-solving method of working. Do they ask more questions that are answerable by experiment? Does experience show young children the limitations of the scientific method?

An interesting sidelight on children's opinions of scientists arose from a request to draw a scientist. All the children, given this general brief, drew scientists with enthusiasm. Asked to include in their picture one or two things a scientist might work with, the children elaborated their pictures accordingly. A Sikh boy named his scientist 'George'; other children chose 'Fred', 'Jason' and exotic names like 'Professor Zed' and 'Sir Rolf'. All men? Yes, boys and girls, whatever their background, drew men without hesitation, although the brief was carefully defined without mention of gender.

Most of the scientists wore spectacles; but they weren't universally bald. Television has glamorised younger, more hirsute scientists ('Professor Nigel, Age 22'). But all toiled single-mindedly ('he's working too hard; his eyes are sore') at the two great problems facing mankind – a cure for cancer or a more efficient way of blowing people up. The crackpot scientist, meddling with the world, is far from dead.

Few of the girls involved in this study, and few of the boys from minority groups, had considered that science was a career for anyone other than white males. And this attitude, if it is general, needs countering. The role of women and men all over the world and from every kind of background can be presented in story and by the careful use of audio-visual aids. Books like the 'Wide Range' Science Stories introduce us to the stories of great scientists, and to explorers at the boundaries of knowledge, both men and women. They also broaden our understanding of what constitutes science and emphasise the human characteristics of scientists.

Children have a great interest in how things work, and also in how things were discovered. First-hand discoveries of their own can be tempered with stories of how others made progress, by accident, by inspiration, or by sheer sustained effort.

Some small insight into children's thinking about science resulted from inviting them to predict, experience, and explain four little 'experiments' of a semi-magical nature. Remembering that 'why' questions often arose from anomaly, these demonstrations were chosen to be apparently anomalous. One was Newton's Disc, which mixes the familiar 'rainbow' colours as it spins, to produce an effect very close to whiteness. Another was the 'blue bottle' – shaking a colourless transparent liquid in a stoppered bottle turns it deep inky-blue. Third was a solar-powered oscillator, producing a whining noise when turned to face a light source. The last was Crook's Radiometer, a tiny merry-go-round seated in the vacuum in a glass globe that spins when brought close to a source of light.

All were tested, explored and tentatively explained by the children. Their predictions and explanations were elaborate and often well-reasoned. Three distinct responses could be recognised. Some children related the demonstrations to *previous experience*; often to related learning in school. Thus a group with experience of studies in light were unsurprised by Newton's Disc; if raindrops could 'split' the light into constituent colours, of course the disc could mix them once again.

A second response was one of *curiosity and testing*, so that the experiment could be related to previous experience and an acquired body of knowledge. The 'solar buzzer' was turned through different angles by one child, with a resultant change in the pitch of the noise it made. This was linked by the child to the change in the quality of sound when you turn a transistor radio to get better reception.

Yet another response was purely *intuitive* – jumping, rightly or wrongly, to a conclusion. Thus Newton's Disc was 'only colours stuck on the cardboard; when you spin the disc the cardboard colour comes through'.

A lot can be learnt from uninterrupted time with small groups like these that can be adapted to the far more demanding task of working with a class. Firstly, the tremendous gains that children can make from experiencing the fresh, the new, and the unknown. It challenges previous thought, introduces anomalies, and makes demands on children.

Next, the need to give credit for the intuitive, the inexplicable, or even the apparently wrong, answer. A junior boy, asked by a perceptive teacher to suggest ways in which he might convince his classmates that he had seen a flying saucer, answered 'I'd ask it to come back next Thursday.' The class collapsed in laughter, and the flustered teacher was led to comment, 'that wasn't a very good idea.' And yet it *was* a good idea. The essence of good science includes the concept of repeatability. If the 'experiment' could be repeated – if the saucer came back – its existence would be proved beyond doubt. We need to be open to the unexpected answer – a point we return to in considering science and language.

The freedom to contribute ideas in unthreatening circumstances can lead children to discuss, in the broadest sense of the term. If we can compare, contrast, accept or reject ideas on rational grounds, without personal hurt, then we are a long way towards co-operation and progress.

Finally, children (and adults) can gain enormously by talking through their experiences. Only by talking, it seems, can we see the patterns in what happens to us, rationalise, and internalise. Teachers experience this when they 'learn by teaching'. Many of us gain far more by putting our experience into words – the audience in a play or concert interval, for example. Sometimes we need to talk to come to terms; thus a colleague who had had a car accident bringing him close to death rationalised it by bringing it into almost every possible conversation.

This little study served to demonstrate the importance of encouraging situations that are conducive to problem solving, and showed the importance of intuition. It would be wrong to expect children to follow the scientific method uncritically in every case; like scientists, children can make inspired leaps in understanding, and should not necessarily be expected to account for every answer. But by giving them first-hand experience of problem solving, we can help them to develop thinking skills that they can apply more widely than in science alone.

PRIMARY SCIENCE AND LANGUAGE

Science has its own special contributions to make to language development; if this aspect especially interests the reader, the ASE book on the subject edited by Brenda Prestt (1980) is recommended. Its contributors use transcriptions to consider the role of 'Language in Science' – chiefly secondary science.

Interested or not, it is important to primary science practitioners to recognise the relationship between language and learning, and especially between language and learning in science. In teaching and learning situations there is transmission of knowledge and a common language is generally necessary for this to take place. It must be recognised that verbal language is both writing and talking, and that both are important.

John Holt asks 'Who needs the practice in talking? Who gets it?' In his estimation, two-thirds of education is talk, and two-thirds of that is teacher talk. Science is a fine medium for encouraging constructive discussion; what constitutes 'a good discussion' will be considered later. First, let's look at teacher talk.

We can recognise a familiar chain in any teacher-led lesson, especially if it is a class lesson. Indeed, teachers might recognise it as good practice, and praise it from a student or probationer teacher. Questions are asked and answers received, often with commendation. From the satisfactory answer, the teacher frames a further question, and so progress is made. But what sort of progress? If you observe such a lesson, you will notice that teacher talk far outweighs pupil talk. Indeed, this kind of didactic teaching often encourages single-word answers; since the questions are 'closed', the teacher already has in mind (with some precision) the 'right' answer, and there is little room for the unusual answer, however contributory it might be to the lesson. Indeed, the unexpected answer – and many of the expected ones! – are re-formed to the plan already in the teacher's mind. Most important of all, there is no evidence even from one pupil's right answer, that the *whole* group is following the teaching. Take this conversation over a snail crawling on a glass plate.

Teacher	What do you think those are, on the snail's head?
First Pupil	Eyes?
Teacher	No, I mean the long things.
Second Pupil	Tentacles?
Teacher	No, not quite. No, that's not the word I was after.
Third Pupil	Feelers?
Teacher	Feelers, that's right, feelers. Now how many feelers can you see?
Fourth Pupil	Four?
Teacher	That's right. Two pairs. Do you see that? One long and one short pair. And what do you think those are, at the end of the long pair?
Third Pupil	Eyes?
Teacher	Yes, that's right. Not very good eyes. Snails have poor eyesight. What do you think they can see?
Second Pupil	The ceiling?
Teacher	No, I mean, how well can they see?
Fifth Pupil	Not very well.
Teacher	Yes, but how well?
Second Pupil	They can't see us.
Teacher	They've got very simple eyes. They can just distinguish light and dark. You see?
Third Pupil	Ah, yes.

Now this is not a straight transcription, but a compilation collected from an enjoyable science lesson given by a student teacher moving from group to group of Middle Juniors and trying, generally successfully, to focus their observations on animals that they found both fascinating and a little repulsive. As an experience, and in the resulting art work produced, it was an excellent lesson. And the dialogue above will not be unfamiliar to many teachers. But consider it again.

Notice, first of all, that the teacher does nearly all the talking. The longest pupil-answer is four words. And many of the pupil-answers are in question form, as they grope for the answer the teacher is expecting. One or two of the answers are 'right' but unrecognised ('eyes' from pupil one – and 'tentacles' from pupil two – not expected). All the answers are modified – sometimes into other forms – 'four' becomes 'two pairs'. A loosely framed question 'What do you think they can see?' gets the answer 'the ceiling', which a teacher might then take to be unthinking, or even deliberately silly. Finally, the teacher supplies the answer, that snails can 'just about distinguish light and dark' – but what do the pupils make of that? Indeed, what do any of these answers prove, except that on each occasion *one* pupil was able to make a stab at what was in the teacher's mind. There is no evidence that the whole group is being carried along by the dialogue, especially the sixth pupil, who made no contribution at all.

We all teach like this, of course. It is fundamental to any group-teaching and some class-teaching. But it is important to guard against certain implicit assumptions, the most common of which is that if the teacher says it, the pupils automatically know it. Of course, the teacher directs the dialogue, but it is unwise to assume that we can put across difficult ideas by sheer weight of words.

Children can experience a good deal more spoken language, both as transmitters and receivers, if they discuss things together. The days of silent classrooms have generally gone, but pupil-talk is still connected in most teachers' minds with lack of class control. Teacher-controlled talk is secure talk. Much of pupil-talk – especially if you record and transcribe it – may seem incoherent and irrelevant. We need to recognise that pupil-talk is as important to their understanding as the pseudo-communication inherent in pupils' essay-writing for teachers, and has the same function – fitting new pieces of experience into an existing framework. By talking experiences out, we make sense of them. This is the conversation during an interval – at a stimulating play or film – which is as much for the speaker as the listener. In extreme cases, we can make the intolerable more acceptable and people who internalise their problems may find it harder to come to terms with them.

To talk is to learn; all teachers should recognise that. And, like science, which is concerned with forming order out of chaos, talk helps to shape our ideas, to determine for us what we think. One of the authors experienced this vividly when joined in a train compartment by two orthodox rabbis. They discoursed vigorously for over an hour on a small point of scripture. Learning is rarely linear, as it is in a lecture or article. Talk helps to reshape and resolve a rag-bag of experiences.

Transcriptions of pupil discussion about science activities show that the known presence of a microphone orders talk. A structure of planning, with the organisation of materials and the digestion of the task instructions, may be followed by deviation from the set task and independent discovery before the work is completed and recorded. Teachers, understandably, fear this deviation; but it may have a unique value to the pupil. Certainly, as in mathematics, we need to recognise that experience will be needed for real understanding, and that co-operation is a learned skill – and how many discoveries today are made by lone scientists? Teamwork is fundamental.

Lastly, as stated elsewhere, we must understand the importance of intuition – the kind of thinking that made a nine-year-old girl suggest that a postage stamp would fall as fast as a book if it were put *on top* of the book – the book pushes the air out of the way. Greater sensitivity to children's ideas – to their use of language – might encourage more of them to make that sort of inspired contribution. Many science lessons end with a 'discussion' – but how accurate is it to describe this activity as true discussion. If we are insensitive, we can undermine, or even destroy, pupil contributions. Teacher scorn at pupil ideas should be a thing of the past, but incredulity is nearly as bad. And incredulity can stem from ignorance. A little Asian boy joining a reception class was asked to 'make tea' in the Wendy house as a practical test of his understanding of English. When, with a large spoon in a saucepan, he mimed stirring, his teacher quite reasonably suspected that his understanding of the request was limited. But she did not know that it is not uncommon, in many Asian homes, to make tea by boiling all the ingredients in a saucepan. Similarly, an example quoted by Torbe (1980) describes how one child suggested washing-up liquid to soften bath-water. The teacher dismissed the idea, unaware that bath salts were commonly replaced by cheap detergents in some homes.

If children are to pool their ideas, they must be accustomed to a non-threatening atmosphere, but that doesn't mean that it should not be critical. A lot can be learnt from frank, objective discussion of children's ideas on why one activity worked, and another didn't. Real discussion will arise from this sort of common experience, and the objective rejection or selection of suggestions. A true discussion will explore information in some depth. It is a vital part of learning, but we so often discount it because it is ephemeral, and leaves no lasting record. If they do not write, have they really learnt? And if they have discussed at their level have they understood without the imposition of our own more complex explanations on theirs? It takes considerable confidence for teachers to answer 'yes' to both these questions.

So far, we have considered spoken language, but written language can be so much more than the pseudo-communication of a report to the teacher.

It is relatively easy to structure a situation where some form of recording is actually necessary for the successful completion of the science. Experience suggests that it may mean the 'sacrifice' of an initial piece of science. Take the popular little activity of separating the dye colours from a tube of Smartie chocolate beans. This is successful and absorbing – almost foolproof – but when the point is reached where the blotting paper used for separation is covered in multi-coloured smears which, then, was the red Smartie? And which the dark brown? They may look very much alike, and children seldom label the paper before starting. They *need* to write, to make sense of their records. Similarly, an experiment carried out over a long period of time – plant growth, for example – is useless unless careful records are kept. In technology, the need to plan carefully and record instruction techniques actually arises from the activity, and pupils not keeping design records are at a serious disadvantage when it comes to practice. In the same way that writing to a real person, rather than completing a letter-writing exercise, gives reality to the task, so experimental recording adds relevance to paperwork.

This is further enhanced when the records are for the use of others. It is valuable, for example, to record how you went about an experiment for other groups to avoid your pitfalls. This can be elaborated into actual direction of others, either verbally or in writing. A lot of fun can be had from children instructing other children in unfamiliar activities; greater precision is demanded from the preparation of written directions. A step on from this is informing others of your experience, and the outcome of your activity. This can be by oral or written means, possibly with illustrations. It need not be in the stilted 'method, observation, result' style so many of us remember from secondary school. But it should be clear enough for others to follow, and appreciate something of the original experience. Younger children, especially, are unlikely to see any difference between factual objective reporting, and aesthetic, subjective description, and while this may be a desirable distinction for older children, the contribution of science to creative writing and to other artistic expressions should never be underestimated. Alan Ward, co-author of *Sciencewise*, (see Appendix III) has collected children's responses – both scientific *and* aesthetic – to his work with 'giant bubbles'.

What is of critical importance in any writing arising from science experience is that it has immediate relevance to the child – i.e. that the experience was so stimulating that it demanded recording. It would be foolish to suggest that work-shy children will suddenly be seized with the desire to write, but there is certainly more instigation from a practical activity than from a book of exercises.

Science also provides an opportunitity to develop – and study – listening skills. From the traditional listening walk, through studies of the sensitivity of the ear, to the identification of tape-recorded sounds, science encourages children not only to listen carefully – a skill transferable to instructions, advice, a broadcast or an animal's activity – but also to understand what listening and hearing are all about.

Beyond reading for understanding – work cards, instructions, charts and diagrams – science can encourage children to read more deeply and widely. Many publishers are developing science readers to meet the need for vicarious experience and knowledge of the history of science. Identification books and background books support a variety of classroom activities. 'How it works' books are very popular, and can satisfy a natural curiosity that cannot be met by practical experience. And as publishers produce more elaborate books and children are asked to do more than read passively, lively texts are illustrated by the moving parts of a car engine, or follow the development and metamorphosis of a 'Very Hungry Caterpillar'. Books like those by Eric Carle encourage children to think about the future of the world. Whatever the science topic, there will always be related fiction – on sailing and fishing to accompany a project on water, for example.

Science can enrich language, and the use of language can extend the range of science. The interrelationship is rewarding to both.

REFERENCES

Albert, E. (1978) Development of the Concept of Heat in Children. *Science Education* **26**, 389–399.
Allen, G. (1966) *Scientific Interests in The Primary School*. London: National Froebel Foundation.

Campbell, J. A. (Nov. 1983) Kinetics – Early and Often (The Blue Bottle Demonstration) *Journal of Chemical Education* **40**, pp. 578–583.

Carle, E. (1970) *The Very Hungry Caterpillar*. London: Hamilton.

Holt, J. (1964) *How Children Fail*. London: Pitman.

Isaacs, N. (1930) Children's Why? Questions in *Intellectual Growth in Young Children* (ed. Isaacs, S). London: Routledge and Kegan Paul.

Isaacs, N. (1958) *Early Scientific Trends in Children*. London: National Froebel Foundation.

Prestt, B. (ed) (1980) *Language in Science*. Hatfield: ASE.

Schools Council, (1972) *Science 5–13 Project: With Objectives in Mind*. London: Macdonald.

Selmes, C. (Sept. 1969) Attitudes to Science and Scientists, The attitudes of 12/13 year old pupils. *The School Science Review* **174**, pp. 7–22.

Stringer, J. (1984) Do Fishes go to Sleep? *Education 3–13*. **12.2** pp. 21–24.

Torbe, M. (1980) in *Language in Science* (ed. Prestt, B.) Discussion in the Science Lesson. pp. 26–49. Hatfield: ASE.

Wragg, E. (March 13 1981) Nothing To Get Excited About. *The Times Educational Supplement* p. 37.

Chapter 3

Developing Science in School

It is a strange paradox that many teachers who accept the importance of primary science, and who recognise the necessity for young children to develop science skills, have the greatest difficulty in teaching science in the classroom.

All of us recognise children's natural curiosity, their desire to handle real things, their wish to experiment safely with machinery, with magnets, with low-voltage electricity, and with 'things that go'. Few primary children are incurious about animals; most become enthusiastic when invited to grow or care for plants. Children, by their very nature, want to discover how things work, what makes them tick. They are full of 'why?' questions. They are even intrigued at second-hand tales of discovery and invention. All this energy and enthusiasm can be channelled into valuable, truly educational experiences, throwing open windows on the world, its natural wonders, and the products of human discovery. But this channelling demands skills on the part of teachers, and many teachers feel insecure about those skills. A few may lack them; most could develop them much further, but many do not recognise that they have the ability to be good teachers of experimental science and may already be practising it with considerable, but unidentified, success. The problem that faces heads of primary schools, post-holders, team-leaders, and science co-ordinators is to identify that success, to define the skills with more clarity, and to develop the confidence of classroom teachers.

Take, for example, a teacher of middle juniors in a small school in a market-town in Warwickshire. One of the authors asked to involve a group of her children in a science project. She was a little perturbed, perhaps feeling professionally threatened. Well, no, she didn't 'do' science as such. She wasn't a 'science teacher', had no training, hadn't the time to go to science in-service courses (and besides, there were other 'priority' subjects), and was very uncertain about the whole area. She did a little nature study, mostly in the summer; the school and its environment invited that, and she had a good knowledge of wild flowers. . . .

While collecting his group of children, her visitor noticed some graphical work, partly obliterated, on the board. What was this? A bit of maths, really. One of the children had had a heavy cold. He'd grumbled when his mother had put unbranded tissues in his pocket that morning instead of the well-advertised 'man-sized' tissues he preferred. The cheap ones were smaller and fell to pieces so quickly. Seizing an opportunity to teach practically a little about area, the teacher had bought a few packs of different tissues from the local shop on her way home that day. The next day, a group of children, including the cold-sufferer, had started a *Which*-style consumer report on the tissues. How many tissues did each pack contain? How many was that to the penny? Did they get close to the 'average contents' label on the box? And the vital teaching point – what was the *area* of each type of tissue? Were some tissues bigger than others, and, using a calculator, what was the area of tissue in each box, and hence area per penny? The results, expressed graphically, seemed to suggest that you got what you paid for; but the question of wet strength had not been resolved, and the investigation slipped across the blurred boundary between mathematics and science, and became a practical, experimental investigation, with sound method, close observation, and careful elimination of variables.

Short of a standard sneeze – though perhaps tissue manufacturers have perfected a method for producing that! – the children could think of no easy way of testing the tissues for their wet strength. But their teacher recalled some work she had seen on cloth and other materials many of which had been shower- or rain-proof. Samples had been stretched across yoghourt pots like drumskins and held in place with rubber bands. Then drops of water had been dripped on the cloth surface (from eye-droppers, but drinking straws would do) until the water had penetrated the cloth by its weight. Translucent pots would help, of course. There had been something about adding detergent, too – but that wasn't relevant to this particular problem.

So samples of tissue were spread, drum-like, across the mouths of translucent dessert pots. Immediately, the importance of marking the samples became apparent. Except for the prettier, and rather more expensive, coloured tissues, one tissue looked much like another. One or two tissues tore on stretching, and were rejected. Torn tissue wouldn't be fair – in scientific jargon it introduced an unacceptable variable. At last the pots were prepared, and water was dripped, by careful finger pressure on the end of a drinking straw, and the drops counted and logged until the sagging paper collapsed under the weight of water. Again the results were recorded graphically, and yielded the surprising results that almost any tissue seemed as good as any other – indeed some of the cheaper tissues performed better in this test than some of the more expensive ones – coarser, perhaps? Or thicker?

The essence of a scientific investigation is a fair test. Indeed it can be argued that the elements of science – class observation, hypothesis, conclusion and the test – are all present in other primary school curriculum subjects – only fair testing is the prerogative of science (and even that, given some practical maths activities, is arguable). Here was a classic example of a complete scientific investigation, and yet the science had passed almost unnoticed by the teacher working with the children. Perhaps the work could be repeated to 'bring out the science'.

There is nothing more dead than a finished primary school project; to try to revive the interest of the children in their handkerchief investigation would have been to court disaster; but the visitor, working with small groups of children on a piece of work to do with children's learning, was surprised to discover that they had exceptional knowledge (compared with similar groups in other classes) of colour and the rainbow. They explained that they were 'doing colour' at the moment. This was confirmed by the class teacher, who explained that a certain configuration of the classroom windows always cast a 'rainbow' across the blackboard edge. This distraction from normal classwork had become a centre of interest in the past week with mixtures of paint being made and a little research done in the library into how rainbows were formed. A suggestion as to how to make a simple light box, and the loan of a few simple lenses and prisms together with a handful of coloured stage-light filters, transformed this work into a rewarding and enjoyable piece of exploration.

And there are many, many teachers – possibly all – who are guiding children into all kinds of scientific investigations every day. Infant teachers inviting children to observe the developments at each stage of breadmaking; Junior teachers showing the children how the beaks of finches vary from species to species. The former certainly do not have an irreversible chemical reaction in mind, the latter are probably not considering adaptation to environment; yet both are working on the margins of science, and it is part of the responsibility of science co-ordinators and head teachers to recognise and nurture the scientific nature of this work, although needless elaboration of scientific terms would not, of course, be helpful or appropriate!

IDENTIFYING PROBLEMS

Why is it then, that so many teachers find science such a difficult subject to teach? Research, such as that of Howard Bradley (1980), would suggest that many teachers find science both unattractive and uninteresting. Some may, for very good reasons, actually find it repulsive. Even well-motivated teachers attending in-service courses struggle to apply their acquired knowledge in the classroom. This is not necessarily true of other curriculum changes. Daily, teachers are taking everything from multicultural education to computer studies in their stride. Yet science still seems to present insurmountable problems to many teachers. The suggested problems are diverse, but perhaps they narrow down to some eight fundamental reasons, which inevitably blur into one another.

1. Some primary teachers are unsure about what science is

Many teachers may have unhappy memories of secondary school science. For them, science may be recalled as confusing, tedious, or difficult. They may have memories of the method–observation–conclusion style of teaching, now much outdated. It has been remarked that science lessons can destroy interest, and then alienate. Some teachers may still suffer the effects of this alienation and feel that science has to do with the proof of what is already known, the demonstration of the apparently obvious, and the repetition of the unsurprising.

Science is tripartite to many. Physics as a subject may have made heavy demands on limited mathematics skills. Chemistry was apparently fraught with imminent danger of burning, poisoning, or explosion. Biology may be equated with dissection, with experiments on plants and animals, or even (improbably) with vivisection!

If our school memories are clouding, adult experiences may have reinforced our distaste. Some adults, paradoxically, appear almost proud of scientific and technological ignorance, a pride which enables others to masquerade as experts because of their superficial knowledge and apparent confidence. Outsmarted by the jargon, outstripped by the accelerating pace of change, they conclude that science – all science – is, and ever will be, a closed book.

It does not help to comfort yourself with a picture of science as basically evil or destructive. Figures suggest that a large proportion of 'scientists' are involved, directly or indirectly, with the development or manufacture of the weapons of war. Indeed, many of us are content with a picture of scientists meddling with the world – encouraging beagles to smoke, putting shampoo in the eyes of rabbits, tinkering with powers and forces they scarcely understand.

So what is science all about? One of the first priorities for anyone preparing a science policy for a primary school is to reach an agreement, or at least some kind of consensus, among teaching staff as to what science actually *is*. *Learning Through Science – Formulating a School Policy* offers a number of possible definitions. Certainly, 'science' embraces a method, a method which, by logical steps, reaches order from disorder. These steps, outlined in chapter 1, include observation, the construction of theories, and their testing by fair experiment. By this means, scientists pursue truth, extend the borders of our understanding, and advance technology. Technology? A field nicely defined by the television commercial catchphrase 'the appliance of science'.

The 'paper handkerchiefs' activities illustrate that many teachers are unwittingly 'doing science'; with encouragement this science can be further developed. By relating the staff development in science to the actual science activities taking place, new work can be rooted in familiarity.

2. Primary teachers are already working under pressure

Perhaps a working definition of an ordinary primary classroom teacher might be someone who teaches the same children on a Friday afternoon as they were teaching on a Monday morning. So many people advising these rank-and-file teachers, who constitute the backbone of the service, are one step – or more – divorced from this simple chalk-face position where the problems may range from how to fill the week to how to fit all the intended activites *into* a week. It is a small step to this 'divorced' situation, and many classroom teachers would say that the step is accompanied by a divorce from reality. Thus, even post-holders 'released' – what a loaded word – from daily classroom contact to a small quota of freedom, may be seen as unrealistic theorists by those whose job embraces the entire primary curriculum. All at high profile, with no peaks and troughs.

Heads are one step further divorced (except perhaps those in small village schools who both teach and administer). They have crossed the threshold of management through a door from which so few ever return. Thus their presence in the classroom may be seen in the context of guest artiste, forever presenting their favourite lessons and freed of the onerous business of producing a balanced diet.

Advisers, inspectors and the like, are so far distanced as to be out of sight. Foraging from school to school, they carry with them their heavy loads of subject responsibilities, or veer wildly in their interests and concerns to reflect the publication of each DES or LEA document. The good are very, very good, and the visits are treasured by those who recognise their input of energy and expertise. The bad are awful, leaving everyone with a sense of inadequacy or incompetence; schools hope that by maintaining a low profile, they may delay their next visit as long as possible. To be fair, the advisers can never win; visit too little, and they are 'never seen'; visit too often, and they have 'nothing better to do'.

What all these – post-holders, heads and advisers – have in common is an axe to grind, and in the view of many sound, hardworking classroom teachers, the axe is ground on them. Where exactly the post-holder and head fit into the development of a science policy in a school is considered later. First, let us look at why many classroom teachers are justified in feeling somewhat jaundiced.

The pressures on classroom teachers have increased enormously in recent years. Aside from children's behaviour, parental attitudes, changing legislation and a developing teacher role, they have been asked to make sweeping changes in curriculum and method. Many of these changes take them far beyond the degree of skill with which their initial teaching provided them. As we shall see, this is especially true in science.

Hardly a day goes by without some blame for society's ills being laid at the feet of teachers. Similarly, hardly a day passes without someone brightly suggesting that this subject or that be taught in schools. Whole areas of education – social, moral, and sexual – once thought to be the prerogative of responsible parents are now the domain of classroom teachers. 'New' areas – environmental education, litter prevention, first aid – elbow forward for a look-in with recognised curricular subjects. It sometimes seems that every charity, every pressure-group, every shade of social and political opinion has its own Education Officer, anxious that his or her faction's voice is heard in the overloaded classroom. And all, with justification, making classroom teachers feel unprofessional or even irresponsible if they neglect them from their teaching programme.

One answer is the retreat to the basics – tried and tested, justified and justifiable. How else to handle the outpourings of all the agencies of curriculum change? Well, many will examine each proposed development from the viewpoint of cost – cost, it should be said, not solely financial but in terms of energy, time, and organisational expectation. What will the returns be on an outlay in these areas, given that we all have limited resources? Will primary science justify expenditure of energy, money, timetable space and classroom reorganisation? Will the gains to the children really be worth while? It is not cynical, in the current climate, to view each curriculum change in this light. It is up to each post-holder, each head, each adviser, each HMI, to justify the subject's inclusion in this competitive atmosphere. And it is not unreasonable to say that in these terms – equipment cost, quantity of expendable materials, the servicing of learning groups, the watchful eye for the foolish or the ignorant, the development of proper progression, assessment and recording – primary science can look very expensive. The enthusiast needs to justify the subject to the uncertain practitioner.

3. Many teachers are either unprepared or unable to think scientifically

Few of us have had the good fortune to be able to explore an individual, personal line of scientific research; in other words, few have had the experience of applying scientific method to problem solving for ourselves. And if we *have* applied a scientific approach to our problems, we may have been unaware that 'science' is one name we could give to that technique. In addition, we can, quite understandably, choose to continue working and developing the fields in which we feel the most confidence, to the detriment of those that would reveal our weaknesses (*vide* Mrs. Doubtful in Howard Bradley's *Times Educational Supplement* article). Indeed, Bradley goes so far as to suggest that there may be a substantial minority of teachers for whom science is, frankly, unattractive. Some may have specific anxieties about their manipulative skills – most lists of primary science resources seem to begin with 'a hacksaw' and 'G-clamps' (yet, until one of the authors began to introduce a craft design and technology element into his science, he had never touched either) and this discourages those who feel that they are unable to 'make' anything. It may be as a result of this that teachers on in-service courses take such a pride in the products of their hands; and may account for one teacher's quite violent reaction when it was suggested that his creation had room for improvement.

Other may have uncertainties about problem solving. For them, lengthy lists of skills, elaboration by scientific method, and the introduction of jargon phrases may be genuinely discouraging. What needs to be grasped is that science is a means of progressing from disorder to some degree of order by means of cumulative experience. Science is organised knowledge. Above all else, it is simple. Anyone who doubts that should be directed to the library to find the *Oxford Primary Science Project* (now sadly out of print), which was so heavily overshadowed by the 'Nuffield Junior Science' books; there, by Redman, Brereton and Boyers, they will find a definition of the Universe in one paragraph, proving this very point. Science simplifies, it does not elaborate. To think scientifically is to think with clarity, but not necessarily clinically.

4. Many teachers lack the training and experience necessary to teach the subject with confidence

A number of people, among them Don Plimmer, quoted in the *Education (Digest)* on primary school science, and the ILEA Science Task Force, identify the vicious circle that develops when ill-prepared teachers have disappointing experiences of teaching science, and so give their own pupils poor preconceptions of the subject.

Despite good curriculum materials available since, and to some extent before, the 1960s, many institutions preparing people for a career in teaching made the subject an optional one, competing with other curriculum areas which might be found more attractive by any aspiring teacher. So it was the exceptional primary school teachers who began their careers with a background in science education. Few schools then put a premium on a science qualification either – and indeed they would have been unrealistic to do so, when, together with an emphasis on 'creative' subjects (Drama, Art and Craft) there were so few qualified candidates for each post. It was a rare junior school, even after the advent of Nuffield Junior Science, that could boast a post-holder for Science. *Infant* schools with a science post-holder were as rare as hen's teeth.*

---

* Plowden (para. 936) remarks that graded posts are often given for 'trivial' duties.
 Paras. 663–675 are concerned with science; there was some objection at the time to the division, within the Report, of subject areas. *Children and their Primary Schools (The Plowden Report)* HMSO (1967)

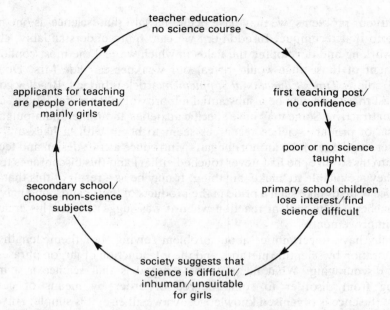

Figure 3.1   The vicious circle of primary science (From *Education (Digest)* with permission)

Thus, teachers trained at this time have little or no background of science experience, and although the Plowden Report laid some emphasis on good science experience, practitioners in the schools may have clung to the kind of book current in the fifties. These effectively filled the timetabled science slot with thinly-disguised comprehension work linked to full-colour illustrations of ice cubes melting and magnets producing improbably neat patterns of iron filings. In this ideal world of book-bound activities experiments never went wrong and questions were never raised that could not be answered.

Given this background, a teacher who ventured into experimental science with real objects was entering an unknown world full of risk and disappointment. It is hardly surprising that they might have felt little confidence in their science teaching, that they might have had poor experiences with classroom control, and that they taught the subject poorly, or not at all.

There were exceptions of course. The Nuffield books from 1963 onwards are illustrated with examples of good classroom practice, and pioneers were experimenting with the activities and approaches currently advocated as 'new'. But for many primary school children, science was an English exercise with little relation to real life. It would be unsurprising, then, if their own feelings towards the subject were cool. Preconceptions were formed – that the subject was boring or difficult, an irrelevant activity more suited to bespectacled boffins than to normal, healthy, curious young people.

Their early experiences at secondary school stood every chance of changing all that. The Nuffield Secondary Science Scheme of the mid sixties presented exciting and relevant activities for the early secondary years; but against them stood the preconceptions of pupils, enhanced by general attitudes that science was very much a minority subject for the reasons described in the first part of this chapter, and certainly not a subject for girls.

As a result, many secondary pupils – and most of the girls – dropped science subjects at the earliest opportunity. Surveys at the time showed few pupils taking science far into their teens. Those that did leant towards the more 'human' biological subjects rather than the physical sciences.

These same young people finished school. Many of them moved on to higher education. Those with an interest in working with people turned naturally to the social sciences, paramedical and medical training, and teaching. Faced with decisions about options, they voted for the cultural, artistic subjects, and the cycle was complete.

Small wonder, then, that so many classroom teachers feel that their background does not suit them for science teaching. And many who have trained in science specialisms may find that their skills – in physiology, say, or geology – need a considerable rethink before they can be applied in the education of young children.

5. Insecurity heightened by the opinion of others

The concentration in recent years on transition between the ages and stages of education has made teachers more aware of the problems faced by those in other areas of the service. There is, perhaps, less staffroom criticism of the education that has gone on before. Indeed, there is a positive move towards matching of curriculum across the phases, in the interests of efficiency and sheer commonsense. This is true in science as in other subjects, and teachers will come across little of the scornful attitude once held by some secondary colleagues towards their efforts in experimental science: 'they're only playing' was one recorded remark by a secondary teacher viewing a primary teacher's science course. Others commented that primary teachers would be well advised to leave the science teaching strictly to them. Such an attitude can be off-putting, especially if a primary teacher already has good reasons for insecurity. It is a welcome change, then, to find increasing numbers of secondary science teachers genuinely interested in primary science, and encouraging primary colleagues from feeder schools to meet together with them to discuss curriculum. While it must be recognised that it is all too easy for well-qualified and experienced secondary science teachers to dominate curriculum planning (one middle-school teacher recorded his own abstention from feeder-school curriculum plans in the Isle of Wight on these grounds) the majority are anxious that their pupils will have developed the appropriate skills and attitudes, so that their 'raw material' will arrive with positive preconceptions.

The opinions and attitudes of primary children themselves can, of course, significantly undermine the confidence of teachers. While it is true to say that the vast majority of pupils at primary age approach experimental science with enthusiasm, a minority can make teachers uneasy because of their apparently superior knowledge.

There is no more unsettling experience than to present a carefully prepared activity only to be told that 'we've done that before'. While this shouldn't happen if a school has a well-established progression in science, it is often true that one or more pupils can exhibit a disturbing knowledge of a subject, putting the teacher's limited knowledge in doubt. Experience would suggest, though, that those who 'have a book about that at home' haven't always read it, and that others who 'saw a television programme about it' apparently gained very little from it. It is important to remember, too, that previous experience is likely to be vicarious, and that nothing compares with practical activity. So a child with an apparently encyclopaedic knowledge about animals will be as excited as any other when setting up a wormery. There are exceptions, however. How would you react to a small, serious, bespectacled child who commented (of an electricity kit) that with just a couple more pieces it would be possible to make a transistor radio? Fortunately for fledgling science teachers, such exceptional children are rare!

6. Changes may be needed to both content and style

In retrospect, it is remarkable how much change primary teachers have assimilated in recent years. Changes have taken place in curriculum content, in the development of new subject areas, in the introduction of technology and in patterns of teaching and learning. Hardly surprising, then, if science is seen as an unwanted child; lacking the status and resources of other curriculum areas, and arriving just when we all thought the family was complete. Arriving, like any new baby, with demands, wants and needs, it seems a drain on the pocket, on resources, and on time.

Most important of all, science teaching might demand that a teacher change both content and style simultaneously. Teachers working an integrated timetable, or grouping their children for a variety of simultaneous activities, may find it easiest to assimilate the subject. A change of content is all that is needed, with a little thought to equipment, direction, safety and monitoring. Effectively, one or more of the routine groups becomes a centre of science activity, and the techniques already in use for organisation and for ensuring progression and proper recording of experiences and understanding, are applied to it.

It is a very different story, though, in a classroom which is more formal in nature. Here, both content and style may have to change to allow experimental problem solving activities to take place. Quite how that can be done is discussed later (Organising Your Classroom for Primary Science, chapter 8) – suffice it to say that to teach a wholly new subject content in a wholly new way may be more than doubly difficult.

7. Many teachers lack a 'feel' for the subject

We have already considered the problems of overcoming suspicion about science; of thinking scientifically; of finding time for science; of the lack of teacher education in science, and of the insecurity generated by the opinions of others. This trial area overlaps all these, and yet has a distinctive nature all its own. It is the problem of the 'lack of feel'.

Given all the drawbacks already described it would hardly be surprising to add that teachers may be 'all-at-sea' with science. Yet this reaction can be understood in part, and a lot of it stems from quite reasonable anxieties. The first is what appears to be the abstract nature of the subject. The skills involved, formulating hypotheses and drawing conclusions from the results of fair tests, may well appear unrelated to real life. The second is that science, by its own nature, may be unpredictable. Prediction is one of the key skills, of course, but even the most experienced of scientists would be hard put to predict the outcome of each and every experiment, while a child, although following careful instructions, can produce results that are both unexpected and (very possibly) not easily explained.

It is this very characteristic that makes science off-putting to many. Alan Ward, co-author of the lively *Sciencewise* series commented to a teacher group that he would anticipate eighty per cent success in his recommended activities producing the desired, or expected, outcome. That, it should be noted, is a very high expectation. In the early stages, a good many activities are not that reliable. There are too many indeterminates: children's carelessness or inattention to instruction; ambiguous direction from the teacher; the failure of apparatus to operate predictably, or of inexperienced children to use it correctly and any number of other variables can result in experimental activities producing inconclusive evidence. Unless you are experienced at handling such open-ended activities, they can present quite a problem.

If an activity is 'unpredictable', can it also be dangerous? Some teachers may be discouraged from teaching science because they feel that there can be risks. Any school activity can be fraught with danger; all of us are conscious of the dangers inherent in pointed pencils, and even rounded-ended scissors. It's a sensible precaution to read the excellent DES booklets on safety, and act accordingly. *Safety at School: General Advice* is a basic text, but it might be worth dipping into *Safety in Science Laboratories*, despite its heavy emphasis on secondary science. While much of the book elaborates procedures for dealing with bacterial cultures and the like, there are clear warnings in both the books against generally popular activities (the measurement of lung capacity, for example) if they are at all hazardous. There really is no reason, providing commonsense applies, with regard to tasting and smelling, heating, the use of appliances on mains electricity, etc., why science should be any more dangerous than any other practical activity – and it is a good deal safer than some. Many of us have memories of lino-cutting, an activity which, however good the intention, often turned into a public blood-letting.

Given these provisions, 'feel' will develop with experience. Experience will always lead to confidence. How that experience is graded and developed is a problem for the curriculum specialist.

8. In-service Education in Primary Science may not be effectively applied to the Classroom

The average teacher's approach to INSET (In-service Education and Training) may be described as the 'credo of unlimited hope'. In other words, INSET attenders are eternal optimists. 'This course', they believe, 'really will make all the difference. My teaching will suddenly become more effective/ easier/ more rewarding, and my classroom will be transformed.' Hard experience on the morning after proves that sound and valid ideas, however relevant, need teacher effort to put them into operation. New initiatives can wither quickly without nurture.

Ideas can be misinterpreted, or poorly applied. Thus, a survey following the launch of Nuffield Secondary Science disclosed that a large proportion of the teachers who genuinely believed they were 'doing' Nuffield Science had in fact modified the ideas so far that the original intentions of the course authors could no longer be identified.

(Note, however, the fate of those who did apply Nuffield as intended. The contemporary education press contained adverts for 'Nuffield Teachers' as if they were something rather special, and a repeat survey of science teachers using Nuffield methods correctly failed because so many had been promoted to other posts).

This sort of problem, besetting INSET providers, is also of concern to the head or post-holder who wants to see science effectively taught in the classroom. How can a head, a post-holder, or an enthusiast advocating experimental science effectively overcome these stumbling blocks? Each problem will be unique, of course, but certain general guidelines can be suggested and chapters 4 and 5 develop these in greater detail.

TOWARDS SOLUTIONS

1. Understanding what science is all about

Any attempt to define science would be fraught with difficulties. Whole books have been written on the nature of science, and for anyone genuinely interested in the subject the Association for Science Education publish an excellent review.

In general terms, though, science has to do with a technique for teaching order by cumulative experience. Test after test, experiment after experiment, lead to the discovery of order where before only disorder might have been seen, to cohesive knowledge where before there was ignorance; and the processes of science – observation, conclusion and so on – are applicable to other content areas than science. Indeed, it could be that the only technique that is uniquely scientific is 'fair testing'.

Fair testing is a principle close to children's hearts. If you suggest, for example, that washing-up with detergent is likely to be a good deal more effective than washing-up in plain water, children will quickly recognise the 'unfairness' of adding the detergent to piping hot water, while washing other plates in cold. By all means try cold and plain against cold and foaming, or hot against hot plus detergent, but the element of fairness should eliminate unreasonable variables.

Indeed, it could be said – and often has been said – that science is a natural subject for young children. Their first discoveries about the world are made by experiment and conclusion. It follows on naturally from an inherent interest in reasons and explanations. What children think about science – and about scientists – is considered later; for the meantime it may be said that teachers who go about answering questions naturally arising in the classroom by simple problem solving (as the teacher did with the paper tissues, or as others have done by wrapping sandwiches in various ways to see which stayed freshest longest, to take only two simple examples) are using the techniques and processes of science.

With experience, science should become relatively predictable. While retaining the capacity to surprise and delight, experiments will often confirm the expectations of the young scientist. And, given the same experimental conditions, experiments, at least at primary level, should be repeatable within limits. That is to say, if we do everything the second time in exactly the same way, the result should be substantially the same as the first time.

Children can have a poor image of scientists (see chapter 2) and need to be shown the evidence for a more constructive view of their activities. It may well be that a proportion of 'scientists' are dedicated to finding ways of killing people more effectively, or are busily occupied with maiming small animals in the cause of advancing knowledge. Children need to be made aware of this abuse of learning, but should also recognise that we benefit enormously from the work of scientists, in understanding, in medical advances, and in our standards of living and material expectations. At some point, the 'science versus God' argument may arise, and needs handling with considerable sensitivity if it is discussed at all; especially if family and child attitudes are strong or fundamentalist. It needs to be noted that many great scientists were also deeply religious, that those who have explored the boundaries of knowledge may have had their faith enriched rather than shaken, and that recent years have seen more than one contemporary scientist enter the established church. The concept of God should not be used as a 'long stop' preventing further argument and investigation.

But this is getting very deep. It may be helpful, in defining what science is all about, to eliminate what is *not* experimental science. Science is not book-learning. We can learn a good deal from books, of course, and there is no other way that we can learn about the lives and discoveries of the great men and women of science except by reference to recorded information. But, fundamentally, the processes of science can only be understood by actively using them. Teachers need to be discouraged from seeing book-learning as a substitute for practical activity.

Science has little to do with what many children would recognise as 'nature study' – the simple collection and identification of plants and creatures. Certain science processes enter this field, of course. Close observation is essential when drawing from life, but drawing from life is not enhanced by giving children access to identification books, when, quite naturally, the ease of working vicariously from the pictures drawn by others is preferred to working from a difficult, and perhaps active, mode. Similarly, the use of a branching key to identify a genuinely unknown plant or animal demands high skills of observation, good vocabulary, careful comparison between specimen and illustration, and other techniques. The relation of structure to function ('Why are giraffe's necks so long?') or structure to habitat, brings in skills of deduction and conclusion. But, despite the fact that one of the finest basic texts for a school staffroom library – *Nature Study and Science*, I. Finch (1971) – is heavily biological in emphasis, many teachers who see nature study as a convenient vehicle for science studies are likely to find this area difficult.

It is, in fact, extremely difficult to apply the techniques of science to biological subjects in the classroom. One reason is that many of the activities are unthinkable. Biologists recently enhanced the learning of small flatworms by mincing some previously conditioned worms and feeding them to 'ignorant' specimens. Whether they actually 'ate' knowledge, or whether the learning had increased the amount of certain related chemicals in the original flatworms, was then debatable. What is definite is that schools are not in the business of putting worms through the mincer, or indeed of chopping up earthworms to see whether heads or tails can be regenerated. There may be a little more leeway with plants, of course, since currently, at least, we do not believe they feel pain; but children who identify with inanimate objects, and are genuinely upset when an old toy is thrown out *because the toy may feel rejection* may find experiments with plants distressing, too. Thus plants starved of necessary nutrients, or of light, may exhibit disturbing symptoms, and these may upset children even more if groups or individuals identify with their particular plant or seed. The unhappiness of a class of children who 'adopt' incubator eggs if the hatching rate is disappointingly low can be imagined. And a small, but moral point, concerns every experiment involving food plants. While we deliberately allow runner beans to shrivel in the interests of scientific curiosity, our fellows in other countries are starving because they are unable to grow and irrigate food crops.

But the chief reason for avoiding the tempting trap of nature study is that biological science is so thoroughly unreliable. If you note the cautions above – that it is unacceptable to harm or abuse plants and animals (significantly described in many primary science documents as living *things*) – then you are left with the area that could be broadly described as 'behavioural'. Thus you look at how animals (and to a lesser extent, plants) behave in certain circumstances. This is undeniably a very rich field. In recent years, links have been established between animal and human behaviour, and the techniques of behavioural observation have been applied to the classroom, with enlightening results. But anyone who has trained a dog will know that modification of behaviour patterns is a long and laborious business, while observation of them in the wild is fraught with disappointment. One example may serve to illustrate this!

In many inland schools it will be recognised that winter brings the seagulls. As they forage further and further afield, they quickly discover that school playgrounds are a rich source of discarded 'tuck' and of accidental losses. These hungry scavengers drop on school playgrounds as playtime ends. At more than one school it was observed that the seagulls were on the ground even before the children were in the building. How were they able to identify the end of playtime? Did they react to the children's reluctant movement towards the doors? Or did they hear, and respond to the school bell? After considerable discussion, it was agreed that one possible 'fair test' would be to scatter a little food and ring the school bell at another time from playtime. One spring morning, the playground was given a few experimental crumbs and the bell was given an untimely jangle. No seagulls came down; they had all gone back to the sea. The sparrows pecked up the feast.

A further disappointment was experienced by a class that observed very astutely, that the scavenging seagulls never landed on or around their well-baited bird table. There could have been many reasons for this; perhaps it was too close to the buildings or in a space too small to allow seagulls to land, or to take off; possibly seagulls preferred to take food direct from the ground; perhaps even the bird-table itself frightened the creatures away. Eliminating all these variables, and producing really fair tests, proved impossible. Experiments could be tried, of course, and that in itself was of enormous educational value; but no real conclusions could be reached.

There are not the same problems with variables in the physical sciences. The anxieties about humane treatment are not there, of course. The conditions are controllable, and reliable. Variables can be altered or eliminated at will. An examination of the strengths of carrier bags, for example, can involve testing to destruction. Plastic bags can be compared with paper, handles can be measured and tested. Does the weather have any effect? What happens when you put your supermarket paper carrier bag down in a puddle? Are the bags of one supermarket chain stronger than another? Will they take more bulk, or weight? Which part gives way first? Where are the weaknesses? In manageable and infinitely variable tests, the qualities of shopping carrier bags can be explored. Technology – the application of science to a real-life problem (getting the shopping home in one piece) can be examined.

Often we can launch into the really unknown with this kind of work. Who would guess, for example, that a paper carrier bag (brown, Sainsbury-type) will lift a junior child between two adults – with care, of course; or that the handles had *nine* separate folds and glueings? Why should the product of one supermarket carry twice the bulk of shopping than the product of a competitor?

This sort of investigation contrasts strongly with the approach that many of us will remember from our own secondary days. The proving of the known – experiment, apparatus, method, observations, conclusion – while outlining in essence the methods of science, contributes nothing in practice to original science. The end result is proof of a fact already known by the teacher, and transmitted in advance to the pupil. And failure to prove that fact is failure of the experiment. If you set out to make oxygen and you do not make it then the science has failed. With open-ended, investigative science, there is always something to learn – more care with the method, better control of variables, closer observation of results.

Properly-handled, scientific investigation should be recognised as a genuine search for truth: a process that can benefit and enrich us.

2. 'I just don't have time to teach science as well.'

The wealth of papers and books emerging from the DES and other sources suggest that four curriculum areas have been identified as of major importance – language, mathematics, religious and moral education, and science. Of these, only science lacks a traditional timetable slot.

To compare science with mathematics is to recognise that maths has all the elements of respectability. It would be unthinkable to imagine a primary school without a mathematics policy, without recognised schemes, without resources or key timetable time (traditionally 'early in the morning, when their brains are clearest'), or without – in the larger schools – a post-holder with mathematics responsibility. By contrast, science is the subject that may lack all of these benefits. Hence, teachers who are understandably reluctant to undertake the subject find themselves able to reject 'low status' science, or to 'integrate it out' of topic work. The 'Science 5–13' team recognised that in application of their materials, motivation of teachers was a prerequisite. If teachers lack motivation, they can avoid the subject only too easily. But a sea change is underway. At courses and meetings, in the educational press and through all the agencies that influence teachers, the message is coming across that primary science has to be accommodated. Post-holders can ensure this development by 'making it easy' in the planning and organisation of all the necessary resources.

Science has strong cross-curricular links. It does not have to replace other subjects; it can positively supplement them. Thus a craft lesson devoted to good model aircraft design can be a good science lesson; lighting a model house can be a part of home economics; charting the stretch of an elastic band can be good mathematics; and aesthetic rather than technical descriptions of bubbles can bring out the best in creative English.

What about the personal costs to teacher and school? Financially, primary science can be as cheap, or as expensive, as you make it. The selection and buying of equipment are discussed elsewhere in this book, but it need not cost a fortune. From the point of view of preparation and planning, science need not be as demanding as other practical subjects – art and craft, for example, or PE. There are methods (described later) for organising the classroom so that the equipment that needs to be prepared can be used as efficiently as possible. A lot in this direction can be learned by junior and middle school teachers from their infant school colleagues. And the return for the investment is genuinely high – even otherwise disaffected children enjoy what appears to be the play element in experimental science; and there *are* ways of using this carrot to encourage them to complete the more tedious and demanding aspects such as recording.

Again and again, a key factor that is identified is the genuine conviction of the headteacher that science deserves priority status. Without this, the post-holder has little hope of persuading colleagues to accept the subject. With headteachers' support nothing is impossible. To be quite cynical about it, the head can resolve the whole issue at a stroke simply by timetabling it!

Science has long had this kind of formal curriculum status in independent and middle schools; perhaps this is one factor in their notable performances in APU Science surveys.

3. Children naturally think scientifically – where do adults lose the knack?

It is not true to say that thinking scientifically necessarily demands higher order thinking skills. So often children's natural curiosity leads on to science. It could almost be said that the great scientists kept their childlike wonder in the world around them. Certainly they had the open-mindedness to accept and develop new ideas, to perceive opportunities and exploit them, and to look for reasons and explanations. As with mathematics, for example, science demands skills from children that include logic, computational accuracy, estimation and measurement, spatial work and pictorial representation. It has been suggested that the one 'new' skill demanded by science above and beyond the expectation of other subjects is fair testing. By contrast, science can develop unique skills related to technical understanding and care for the environment. It has a very special contribution to make to curriculum enrichment.

Many of the great discoveries of science were purely intuitive, however, owing nothing, apparently, to scientific method and logical approach. Thus the shape of a benzene molecule became obvious after a scientist dreamt of dancing snakes. As they swallowed each other's tails, so the story goes, he recognised the natural shape of the carbon 'ring'.

It is this kind of intuitive thinking, which leaps from problem to solution, that it is hard to cope with in the classroom. How do you mark a child's work when they leap from sum to answer without showing any working? How do you handle an answer that a child is unable to explain; where a mental leap is made to a correct conclusion without an apparent train of thought? The answer is that we must recognise, and celebrate, such gifted intuition.

We need, too, to recognise 'mistakes'. Mike Torbe (1980) quotes a secondary teacher's scorn when a pupil responded to a question about removing a stain from trousers with the suggestion that metal polish could be used. He points out that although the answer was specifically incorrect, it was a step along the way to the concept of using a solvent – not metal polish, perhaps, but a dry cleaning solvent, equally pungent, and easily confused.

Chapter 2 also quoted the teacher leading an excellent question and answer session when an eccentric little boy, noted for his improbable answers to general class questions, put his hand up. Asked, if he had seen a flying saucer, how he would prove it to other people he replied 'Ask it to come back next Thursday': collapse of class into general hilarity, and hasty change of direction by teacher. And yet, in retrospect, his answer was as good as any. Of course you ask the flying saucer to come back – the essence of any good scientific experiment is its repeatability.

We have to give children credit for their 'mistakes', as well as for their correct answers; easier, perhaps, when leading a discussion with a small group rather than a class. It is important, though, to value each and every contribution; not to reject one outright, but to weigh it and recognise its importance on the path towards truth. We can recognise (in children's 'why?' questions) the quest for truth and understanding. How best to handle these was discussed earlier, in chapter 2.

4. Breaking the vicious circle

In colleges and institutions all over the country, initial and in-service courses are teaching teachers about primary science. Offered primary science as an Honours option in their initial B Ed, Arts specialists chose the course in dozens. Through a welter of in-service courses, from LEA day-release and evening activities, through DES residential courses, to recognised qualifications (such as the DASE courses: Diplomas in Advanced Science Education, otherwise known as 'Daisy', which are recognised by bodies like the ASE) teachers are being encouraged to embrace and apply science techniques in their own classroom.

While section 8 discusses how this new understanding can best be developed by the INSET provider, we need to consider briefly how the post-holder makes the fullest use of a teacher's in-service experience when the teacher returns to the classroom.

Clear steps can be seen in the assimilation of new techniques by classroom teachers. They can be loosely described in four stages. First is 'it works!' – the recognition that a particular technique produces the expected result. Then follows 'it can work for me', which involves an understanding that the technique is reliable whatever the teacher's own limitations. Then 'it can work for me in my own classroom', with the implication that given particular resources, certain children, and a teaching situation the technique can be successfully applied. Last – and first – comes the assurance that 'my Head will back me in this' – an acknowledgement that the school hierarchy recognises the importance of the planned work.

In these circumstances, it is of key importance that post-holders contrive a 'success situation'. It is no good attempting the impossible; small steps towards worthwhile science are more rewarding since each possesses the facility for small but significant, success. A project on electricity, for example, will stand a higher chance of being completed successfully if the teacher first handles the challenge of simple circuitry and only later approaches the more intricate and sophisticated work. In this way, confidence can be nurtured; one of the drawbacks of science is that teachers can rarely have oversight of it in the way that they can have (real or supposed) oversight of other curriculum subjects. So they can launch into a study of the Tudors or India with confidence, however ill-founded; but their general lack of knowledge means that they are uncertain where a study of the creatures on the school field, or of the uses of plastic, or of heat will lead them. Lacking this oversight, they may enter the field with unreasonable goals – just where do you stop with a study of heat? – or be discouraged by early setbacks – if the first forage round the school field reveals no creatures, what do you do then?

It is at this point that a good curriculum leader could enter and direct them to more reasonable expectations – a whole book could be written on heat alone, so why not just look at candles? And why not start with just a close look at different types of candles, and how they burn? A few words on organisation and safety and the teacher could be aimed at a guaranteed success. The next step might be carefully planned work on candle clocks, and so on (see chapter 7).

Similarly, a gentle word about bush-beating and pitfall traps may help the minibeast hunters to greater success as well as helping to teach the principle that even unpromising environments can be teeming with life if you know where, and how, to look (for more detail, see chapter 7). The next step might be a visit to a contrasting environment, or the construction of a simple identification key but each stage would be successful – and nothing succeeds like success.

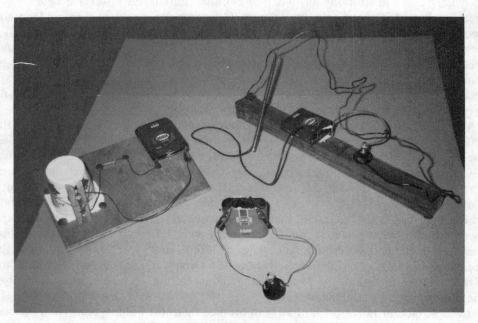

Simple circuit construction can lead to more challenging projects.

Such an approach simultaneously breaks the cycle at two places, giving both teacher and pupil a rewarding experience, and encourages fresh experiments by both. The technique is recognised by INSET providers, as discussed later.

5. The children know more about this than I do, and the secondary school will teach it, anyway

Science teaching in secondary schools is undergoing many profound changes. Not least in the way it is attracting girls to a subject once seen as male-orientated. Examples of good practice abound, and the old adage that if you want your daughter to study science you send her to an all-girls school no longer applies. But for many children it is still true that they will be disinclined to study science beyond the age of options and will 'drop out' with little secondary science experience.

So if we do nothing at primary level, many children will receive little or no education in science at all. Of course, it is incumbent upon us that what we teach is correct: we are wide open to criticism if we teach inaccuracies or untruths. But just as some concepts are taught and re-taught with greater complexity and depth of understanding at secondary level, so we can lay sound foundations at primary level, avoiding always the dangers that over-simplification brings. And we can capitalise on the natural curiosity of young children and the enthusiasm to learn that can be diluted in adolescence.

The knowledge that our children bring is often superficial. Experience of teaching science to young children suggests that they have seldom, if ever, lost their sense of wonder, and that their enthusiasm for practical activities is boundless. One junior boy from a wealthy and well-travelled background was apparently unmoved by any school experience; his sophistication was so great that nothing held freshness for him. One day, a bee-keeper came to school to set up an observation hive. The class watched from the other side of the windows as the beekeeper stripped off his gloves to handle the crawling combs. The blasé little boy watched in wonder. His total fascination with this wholly new experience led him to research bees and bee-keeping accurately and rewardingly. Similarly, the son of a physicist father, so at home among diodes and circuitry, came alive at his first modest experience of pond-dipping.

So we should not be too concerned if the children seem disturbingly knowledgeable; we have had experiences they have never had; we understand dangers they do not comprehend and we can make links between activities and subjects that are beyond their understanding.

6. You're asking me to change what I teach, *and* how I teach it

Once again, the comparison with mathematics is pertinent. Following the publication of *Curriculum Bulletin One*, in the sixties, and the energetic dissemination of the 'new' maths by HMI Edith Biggs, primary teachers took aboard a whole new style and content of primary maths teaching. Now, effectively resourced, supported and organised, it has become the norm for many schools teaching the concepts of mathematics.

What is being asked by way of organisation? Group and pair work is common; many children work individually, or with a partner, from assignment cards; many classes already contain tables for practical activities. Even if this sort of approach is seen more as an afternoon style of working, it is still familiar to children.

Neither is the content 'new' to teachers. Experience with groups of teachers on in-service courses has revealed a remarkable amount of latent knowledge about science content: not, though, always relevant to science with very young children – one teacher could recall the orders of levers, for example, with commendable accuracy. But a cursory examination of some of the lists of fundamental science concepts will show that few are unfamiliar to educated adults. It is the illustration of these concepts by relevant practical activities that teachers find difficult and here they need specialist help.

7. 'I just can't teach science'

'I just can't teach mathematics/ geography/ history/ English'. Is it likely? Most primary teachers have to be generalists so it is probable that they will find any one subject so much more difficult than the others. Behind this 'lack of feel' lies the complex pattern of difficulties described in this chapter. It is the job of post-holder and headteacher to recognise which of the problems is paramount, and to meet it straight on. Is a small amount of success necessary? Does a situation need to be manufactured where the teachers can find their feet and discover the satisfaction of successful science teaching? Is there a lack of resources or time or understanding? All these can result in a poor feel for the subject. Set short-term aims; help the teacher to come to terms with an open-ended activity; ensure success.

One problem is that teachers talk too much. 'Who needs the practice in talking at school; who gets it?' We all talk more when the concept we are handling is a difficult one, on the apparently sound precept that if you say a lot, you are teaching a lot. Hence the attraction of the lecture approach, and the apparent confirmation of this style when a question elicits a right answer. What one right answer proves is that one listener has followed us, or has been there before. But it encourages us to continue with our lecture style.

Other problems that are familiar are those related to teaching the less able, and the 'disaffected'. There a number of ideas current for teaching the less able. The subject's practical nature is attractive, and directly related to the concrete stage of children's learning. Practical activities precede theory, and so follows recognised good practice. Presumptions about normal dexterity should be cautious.

Personal experience suggests that the subject is also attractive to pupils who are otherwise disaffected. Again, the practical and problem-solving aspects have a special appeal.

8. 'It looked fine on the course, but I can't do it now I'm back at school'

The frustration of INSET planners working in the science field has been recognised for years. The 'Oxford' science team, writing in 1963, recognised that application in the classroom left a lot to be desired.

It is essential, from the beginning, to identify the target teacher audience. The needs of outright beginners will generally be different from those of teachers with some experience, those who are post-holders, and heads. Better effect is likely if teachers are assured of support once they are back in the schools; some of the ways of doing this include introductory, pre-course meetings for heads, (which should ensure that the course philosophy is both understood and actively encouraged), the recruiting of pairs, or groups, of teachers (so that the shared experience is supported by the staff), and nurture, back at school, by the course providers.

This combination of approaches has been used with considerable success on local, ASE approved, courses, and by primary science task forces. Teams like those in the Inner London Education Authority flood an area or a school seeing that the subject is not only fuelled and running, but has actually cleared the runway.

Other effective approaches are documented in an ASE article (1984) 'LEA Initiatives in Primary School Science' which lists, and attempts to classify, the documentary evidence for LEA initiatives. Thus, Authorities have produced guidelines for individual school planning, or more official documents aimed at a uniform approach in their schools. Others have organised joint school activities, sometimes centred on feeder schools to a local secondary, or on neighbourhood schools. Secondary schools, for example, have resourced local primary schools with boxes of loan materials, sometimes complete with assignment cards. This can be developed as Local Education Authority loan banks, with boxed and catalogued resources. Directories can list local activities and places where resources can be obtained, and newsletters can update these and spread examples of good practice.

LEAs are producing excellent documents to support primary science.

Yet another initiative relates to Science Fairs, in the British Association for the Advancement of Science tradition, with schools light-heartedly competing to produce the best in ballistas or egg-carrying vehicles.

In every case, the course itself has not proved enough. It may be cynical, but it is true to say that conversion by in-service course alone is restricted to those who were predisposed to accept the change.

REFERENCES

Association for Science Education (ASE) (1979) *What is Science*? Hatfield: ASE.

Bradley, H. (1976) *A Survey of Science Teaching in Primary Schools*: University of Nottingham School of Education.

Bradley, H. (1980) Getting on Course *Times Education Supplement*, 3 October. London: Times Newspapers.

Department of Education and Science, Central Advisory Council for Education (England) (1967) *Children and their Primary Schools (Plowden Report)*. London: HMSO.

Department of Education and Science (1978) *Safety in Science Laboratories*. London: HMSO.

Department of Education and Science (1979) *Safety at School: General Advice*. London: HMSO.

Finch, I. (1971) Nature Study and Science. London: Longman.

Nuffield Junior Science Project (1970) *Source Books and Background Books*. Glasgow: Collins.

Plimmer, D. (1983) *Education Digest*, 9 December: from an original article in *The School Science Review* **62**, June 1981, pp. 641–647.

Raper, G. and Stringer, J. (Dec. 1984) LEA Initiatives in Primary School Science *The School Science Review* **66** 235 pp. 382–388.

Redman, S., Brereton, A. and Boyers, P. (1969) *An Approach to Primary Science*. London: Macmillan.

Schools Council (1980): *Learning Through Science: Formulating a School Policy*. London: Macdonald.

Torbe, M. (1980) Discussion in the Science Lesson in Prestt, B. (ed.) *Language in Science*, pp. 26–49. Hatfield: ASE.

Chapter 4

Developing a Policy – the Role of the Head

Head teachers have to be convinced of the importance of science to their children and their school. It is not enough to sense the pressure and demands of documents like the 1978 HMI report with its criticisms of primary school failings in the area of science. Genuine conviction is necessary, and this takes courage, since it involves the need to learn. The myth of head teacher omnipotence persists, and they are courageous heads who can abandon any pretence of knowing about a subject, and handle both their own insecurity and learning alongside their staff. The commitment of the head teacher to the importance of science is a key factor – perhaps *the* key factor in the successful adoption of science by a primary school. Like it or not, many heads (male and female) are still landed with the 'paternalist' role, and have to lead their staff with this expectation in mind, while still co-operating with external agencies and with other schools. Head teachers have a critical role to play in innovation, resourcing (both human and material resources), encouragement, monitoring and oversight.

HEAD TEACHER RESPONSIBILITIES

To the head teacher, in consultation with the staff, falls the responsibility, especially in larger schools, for planning what approach to science the school adopts. Whatever the size of the school there are key decision areas which are outlined below.

Involvement   Is the subject to be taught throughout the school? Is it to be seen as a class-teacher responsibility or the work of a specialist, or as needing specialist support for class teachers? Will all staff be involved in the planning and execution, or only a 'working group'?

Integration   Will science be seen as a 'stand-alone' subject, with an expertise all its own, or will it be integrated with other curriculum areas – and if so, how will the school ensure that its unique nature is not lost?

Continuity   How will the school ensure that the subject is taught without too great a diversity of style or subject, i.e., that it has a clear pattern in the curriculum, and that it follows a clear . . .

. . . Progression, ensuring that the experiences are graded and developed, enriching the children's science experience as they progress and introducing them to new skills and ideas?

'Course or source?' Will the school undertake a single published course – of which there are many – and thereby ensure that at least the authors' views on structure and progression are reflected; or will the school draw on a wide range of sources – which might include any number of books and cards along with radio and television and the unique experience of the school and its children?

Timetabling Will the subject be timetabled with a specific weekly 'slot', or be integrated into the daily schedule of the children – albeit as a 'science' activity? Additionally, will the school's resources be timetabled accordingly? (This is extremely important if a 'whole school' project is involved.) Similarly, the head teacher takes critical decisions about the allocation of space.

Finance and resources The amount of money to be allocated to science, relative to other school activities, will have a major influence on its character. As the section on resources (chapter 9, pp. 140–153) explains, both capital outlay and maintenance must be budgeted. Will the school spend heavily in the first year, ensuring the resourcing of a wide range of activities; or will the spending be more evenly spread with a gradual building of diversity? A key question, and one seldom answered, is what does the school possess already? Acquisitions from the heady days of Nuffield Junior Science sometimes see their first light, materials bought for early 'nature study' are found to have real value. Search those cupboards!

Fostering specialism Have clear decisions been made about subject specialism, curriculum leadership, possibly graded posts? If a key person has been identified, are they adequately trained and resourced? (Support to curriculum leaders is described below.)

How are radio and television to be used? Key tools, but very proscriptive. Will courses be followed complete or programmes selected – even pre-recorded – appropriately? How much follow-up work will be entailed? How much time between programmes does that mean? How are the video, the tapes, the radio timetabled?

Is allowance made for teachers being a 'mixed ability class'? Some teachers will be further on with science than others; each will need a special kind of help. Has this been recognised? Is the right sort of support being given to the right people?

What sort of help will a curriculum leader need? Curriculum leaders seldom have the in-school time necessary to fulfil their role adequately. Many are only too willing to put in the extra out-of-hours time, but few will have the time to observe the (often transient) nature of the science that their colleagues are actually teaching. For this they need to work alongside them in the classroom: and to achieve this they need realistic timetabling and possibly some release from teaching duties, thus recognising their special contribution. That sort of support helps with relationships – another key area for the head teacher. Recognition of the leader's status will facilitate these activities; and there is nowhere this is more overt and apparent than at staff meetings.

Staff meetings are often underestimated. It is presumed that they are purely business events, where a monologue (or, on rare occasions, a dialogue) settles the future activities of the school. But studies of the staff meeting suggest that here, in a public arena, key issues are resolved, cliques formed and attitudes hardened. The support given to a curriculum leader, to publicise and to enthuse the staff, is of critical importance. A whole meeting given to the science issue will highlight its importance and encourage a sharing of experience.

Monitoring standards   Only the head is charged with ultimate responsibility for monitoring standards. The head's weight behind the more unpleasant criticisms and decisions is essential. Finally, it is the head who is responsible for effective systems for recording children's progress.

INNOVATION – TAKING THE PLUNGE

No school starts science from a completely untouched baseline. Every school has – or has had – science work of some kind, and a wise precaution is to research previous activities. This avoids treading on toes and also helps to meet the traditional argument against innovation – the virtually unanswerable 'we've tried it before and it doesn't work'. This argument subtly suggests that the proposal is not only impractical but passé. Heads have to take a wholly fresh and buoyant approach to the subject to overcome this kind of cynicism. A number of approaches are suggested below; all have advantages and pitfalls. Matching this approach to the school is a key part of the head teacher's role. Alongside this work is the need to define policy; see the post-holder's role, (chapter 5), and the excellent publication *Learning Through Science – Formulating a School Policy*. Without this clear policy, which involves an understanding of what science is in relation to primary schools, and a degree of uniformity of approach, the best-laid plans are doomed.

These are tried and tested approaches; they provide excellent starting points for class and whole-school development.

1. Demonstration lessons and science assemblies

While recognising the 'guest artiste' nature of this kind of work, it must be said that it is hard to refute an argument backed by effective demonstration. There is a world of difference between a demonstration lesson in which a teacher is a passive observer, and actively working alongside a teacher so that both of you have common aims. Most demonstration work will be a continuum: 'I am showing you an approach'; 'we are sharing the work of the class or group'; 'I am encouraging you to take responsibility'; 'I am supporting you and am available as a point of reference.' Like most skills teaching, there will be forward progress and occasional retrogression. There will also be shared disappointments and frustrations; but much can be learnt, even when the science 'goes wrong'.

Influence on a whole school can be exercised by 'lead lectures' of which the science assembly is a practical example. The work should be carefully explained to class teachers and a variety of follow-up activities suggested, at all levels. The shared experience can be enormously stimulating, but there are practical limitations. The science should be on a large scale (a suitable topic is mechanics, with the accent on levers, using PE apparatus, or on friction, using large rollers and wheels) or should make imaginative use of an overhead projector and other visual aids (again, an appropriate topic is light and colour, using transparent coloured gels on an overhead projector).

A whole school, department, or year group can be galvanised into practical work using this approach – with significant demands upon resources.

2. Audiovisual aids

Related, but vicarious, is instigation by visual aids of one sort or another. Excellent films and videotapes are available on loan from commercial companies, from film libraries, and from Local Authority sources like Health Departments. Large groups can have a shared stimulus in this way, but there are the inevitable limitations of commercial materials over which you have little control of content. Thus, the individual needs of a wide range of children cannot be met. Nevertheless, it must be said that the high quality of films of the 'Living World' type is a tremendous stimulus. A source of first-rate primary filmstrips should be mentioned here, since understandably, filmstrips allow a wider range of modification, in the way that you present them and the teaching points that you make. The Philip Green filmstrips are made by a former primary school teacher. Their clear, sharp pictures, simple text, and use of young children's activities as a focus of interest make them excellent for primary school applications at most ages. Topics like 'Holes', 'Flight', or 'The New Baby', are grand project-starters. It is, however, critical, if you accept the premise of this book, to see that the follow-up is practical in nature. It is all too easy to turn to bookwork rather than first-hand experience.

3. Using the school environment

No object, natural or artificial, is without science content. The skill lies in recognising this content, and developing it as a basis for experimental science. Thus, it is possible, even in the most unpromising environment, to find starting points for a whole host of scientific experiences. The stock-room is a practical example. Every school stocks a host of papers for specific needs. They range from newspaper, through exercise and poster paper, to cartridge. Some papers have specific uses – tracing, for example, and tissue. There are various weights of card and board. A whole exercise can relate size and structure to function. More work can take you into paper strength and design, resistance to tearing and to water. Paper can be variously joined – using a variety of glues, pins, staples, and tapes. Some joins are permanent, others temporary. Some damage the paper, others leave it in its original condition. Their strength and efficiency can be tested.

In all these tests, relevance to real life is important. It's very interesting – and revealing – to see how strong paper can be, especially in its resistance to stretch, and its support of weight when folded or curved. But it is relation of this to the everyday – envelopes need to be relatively sturdy and protective; art papers need to take paint well; blotting paper needs to be absorbent and tissue must shrink taut on model aeroplanes – that is the importance of the study.

Once the approach is right, no environment can be said to be without science content. The design and materials of classroom furniture, the structure of the PE apparatus, the architecture of the room itself, can all come in for scientific examination and possible experiment.

The outside environment of the school is a whole new area for study. Apart from the obvious Natural History possibilities, the construction of the building, the main services, the effects of weathering, wear, and vandalism, the use and manufacture of materials all become part of the study. Thus the recognition of concrete lintels can lead to a study of various concrete mixes. A selection of lintels can be manufactured in a home-made mould, and tested for strength and durability.

Work outside the school itself need not be highly elaborate to be successful. You can run a field trip to explore a marine environment or you can make a microstudy of an old stone wall close to home; many of the principles will be the same – and the results can be equally spectacular.

4. Improving the school environment

From exploiting the school's environment, it is a small step to improving it. Books are available outlining every aspect of improvement, internal and external, but one or two independent sources of finance exist, and are worth approaching if you want to develop the natural environment. Oil companies, for example, support projects for tree planting and habitat management, and various levels of local government have schemes; the West Midlands 'Green-up' campaign was one example. If you are a Local Authority school, it is worth contacting your local planning offices; voluntary groups and charitable trusts, like those for conservation and wildlife, may also give you support and labour.

Whatever you plan to do, it is *essential* to contact the agencies responsible for the school grounds and have the plan approved. Without this approval, you may find that your plan is found to be impractical, possibly even a fire risk. You also stand a good chance of having your carefully nurtured plants gang-mown or treated with weedkiller. Given their support, though, it is possible to develop, say, a wild garden or a woodland area, a butterfly garden, a pond – even a swamp! As one head teacher in Wolverhampton put it 'There is a whole new flora and fauna with swampland; and you can't vandalise a swamp!' Horticultural suppliers to local authorities, incidentally, catalogue plants which are wickedly spiky, and vandal-proof, or that survive pulling, breaking and stamping.

Once an area has been established, its potential can be developed, using short- and long-term studies. If classes take turns to be responsible for the wildlife area, they quickly develop a real sense of ownership and responsibility.

The *Bulletin of Environmental Education* will keep you in touch with developments in this field; the Urban Wildlife Group will suggest ways of improving the environment of city and town schools.

5. Visits to places of interest

We commonly use visits to lend life to project work of many sorts but, with the exception of visits to science museums, we seldom use visits for overt science teaching. Yet so many visits have science potential; it just takes a fresh eye to see it. Architectural visits take on a new dimension if you look at the materials and the technology of the structure; wildlife visits can be more than just identification exercises if a little thought is given to ecology – relating the creature to its environment; history visits can be used to highlight the development of human understanding of, and attempts to control, our surroundings.

To give a practical example: many stately homes include an example of a period kitchen. Simple, possibly even crude, implements, contrast strongly with modern tools and devices. An old vacuum cleaner uses a hand bellows; a dolly-tub precedes the modern agitator; a hand-cranked machine sharpens knives. Many use examples of levers, cranks, and gears. All are a significant advance over simple hand-tools. Some can be reconstructed as working models in the classroom.

So give a new dimension to visits by developing the science content.

6. A special visit – the Molecule Club

The Molecule Club is a touring company based at the Mermaid Theatre, Puddle Dock, in East London. Their productions are lively stories with scientific themes; *Sparks*, for example, tells the story of a faraway island where a wicked villain rules a terrified people by the power he has from his knowledge of electricity. Because of their skill and experience, and the tremendous resources they have in the technical knowledge of backstage staff and advisers, the Molecule Club produces memorable theatre that teaches children science in an enjoyable way. Programmes list practical ideas to follow-up the theatre visit. It is worth contacting the Molecule Club to see when they are next in your area.

7. Visitors to school

So many people are willing to give their time and come into school. For some, their profession or occupation is the basis of their visit – the Police, fire service, and railmen are common; Road Safety and Health Education Officers are other obvious examples. But there are many with interesting hobbies – beekeepers, frogmen, breeders of pigeons or birds of prey, model-makers and others. We have experienced enormously successful visits from a watchmaker (small groupwork, of course!) and a piano tuner. There are so many people with an expertise to share. All of them – professional and amateur – can give the children first-hand experience of a unique and exciting kind. The best are very, very good; the worst will need skilful handling; often you can learn from other teachers and schools what their experience has been. All have a potential science input to make; Road Safety Officers will talk about fog and frost, raising questions of light penetration and friction; Fire Prevention Officers explain all the dangers, and preconditions, for fire. Nurses, dental technicians, and Health Education Officers will quite naturally cover scientific topics. Develop the science aspects of the subjects they are covering; advise them in advance of how you plan to use their contribution, so that they can plan appropriately, and look at some of the related books – Macdonald's *Teaching Primary Science*, for example, which covers a wide range of appropriate topics.

8. Loan collections

Do not neglect the loan collections available from libraries and museums. Many libraries will prepare a loan collection of science books, appropriate to an age range and topic. But take the time and trouble to examine the books before using them. Books are no substitute for first-hand experience. And first-hand experience can be gained from museum specimens and materials of various kinds. Models, machinery, and natural history specimens, as well as a variety of non-book materials, are commonly available on short-term loan.

Also available on loan are the videotape, film, and filmstrip productions of a wide variety of companies and nationalised industries. Their catalogues will give examples of free, and low-cost, subsidised materials – posters, leaflets, and books. The Electricity boards and British Gas, British Telecom, British Rail and many other agencies have Education Offices and excellent facilities. Take, for example, 'Understanding Electricity', the educational service of the electricity supply industry. For primary children it produces a selection of booklets, one of which deals with the practice of teaching simple circuitry to infant children. For teachers, this is supported by a video film featuring an infant teacher, Julie Fitzpatrick, and her children. For older children, there are cardboard models of power stations, and films on electricity generation and the uses of electricity.

9. The science content of conventional school activities

Many traditional school activities have science content that goes unrecognised. Bread-making, so common in infant schools, can be turned to science by simple experimenting. Small amounts of dough could be made in many different ways; without yeast, without sugar, in cold and warm environments, with fresh and dried yeast, and the new yeast which is added without 'starting'. Is it true that vitamin C, added to yeast, improves the rising of dough? Will the dough rise more if it is 'knocked back'? And when the bread is made, how does it compare with all the other breads on the market – their shapes, sizes, and variety of crust and crumb? The danger lies in the science being 'integrated-out'. To exploit to the full the science content of many topics, see the excellent Kincaid and Coles' 'Science in a Topic' series. These books, now with a Teachers' Guide, enable teachers to teach traditional topics like Transport, and Clothes and Costume, but ensure that the history and geography content of topics are balanced by the science content.

Look for links with science across the curriculum – to history and artwork for example.

10. The school/team/age group project

If it suits a head teacher's style, then a whole school, or part school, can be involved in a science-based project. This needs careful structuring. The same broad topic – growth, materials, machines – can be taught in many different ways to different age and ability groups. By the sharing and publicising of the work each group is doing, a broader picture of the topic can be developed.

It cannot be emphasised too strongly that the head's role in such an enterprise is to nurture. It is very easy to launch such a topic; it is very much harder to arrange to provide the resources necessary for satisfactory progress – even completion. What is vital, if the whole business is not to go off-beam, or peter out in a series of unrelated activities, is to ensure that the subject is carefully supported, guided and encouraged, and this takes an investment in time by the head teacher.

Take, for instance, a term's project once launched on the theme of 'The Sea'. The whole of a school was involved throughout an autumn term, integrating the subject neatly and rewardingly with Harvest and other traditional themes of the primary school calendar. The integration and involvement of maths strained the topic somewhat, and the connections with Christmas were tenuous indeed. By then the topic was on its knees, the school suffering from a surfeit of fishing nets and sailor hats, with the Bible and contemporary literature ransacked. The careful monitoring of the subject, the guidance through the topics, the redirection of energies, and the ultimate coup de grâce when the subject had run its course were missing. Most important of all, the initial planning had been incomplete. No better, more concise plan for formulating a proper policy can be found than that in *Learning Through Science, Formulating a School Policy*. Answering in straightforward terms the questions 'What is Science?', 'Why do Science?' and 'What experiences do we want to present?' the authors then go on to consider organisation, record-keeping and evaluation. To their formula could be added the lessons of experience.

IMPLEMENTING A SCIENCE POLICY

The head needs to encourage everyone. There is a way in which head teachers, whatever their sex, are viewed paternalistically. One of the most exhausting aspects of the head teacher's role is their need to maintain consistency and enthusiasm, whatever their own feelings. In this respect they need a vast reservoir of buoyancy which it can be hard to maintain. The same is true at every level in the service, but where teachers can draw on experience with individual children, and advisers on the progress or performance of a teacher or school, heads can find themselves somewhat alone, having to draw on inner resources. The role demands an enormous, endless amount of giving, and it helps to recognise this. There are many ways in which this giving can be channelled; here are three of them:

– Only the head can ensure that a post-holder or subject leader, or simply the subject itself, has *adequate attention at staff meetings*. The importance of the staff meeting is often underestimated. It can be seen as a head teacher monologue, or a rehearsal by all staff of ritualised posturing in presenting preconceived ideas. But by its place on the agenda, allocation of time, and their overt support for the post-holder, head teachers can make clear to all the staff the significance they themselves attach to science.

– Only the head, by manipulation of the purse-strings, can ensure that *the subject is adequately financed*. Science is a subject which involves *things*, and even with judicious buying and the use of 'junk' materials, there will be costs to be met. By allocating the school's finances towards the subject, the head can both resource it adequately and indicate yet again that science is significant.

  But money can be further used as a tool to facilitate curriculum change. The simplest example is that of staff or subcommittee encouragement. All teachers are aware of documents which are laboriously prepared in schools for teacher guidance, but which have no bearing on reality. Staff are frequently asked to undertake the preparation of such plans, often at the instigation of external agencies, but in the covert certainty that they will make no significant difference to the practice of a school. This in itself disinclines curriculum groups to make more than a token effort in preparing guidelines. This process is electrified, however, once it has been given an injection of real money.

  First, the group immediately feels that its proposals are going to have real importance. Far from being filed away, its report will actually affect spending. Second, the group restricts flights of fancy; a real sum of money has to be allocated, and good value obtained from it. Third, the spending of money concentrates the mind on reality; without putting a straitjacket on thinking, it encourages the examination of available resources. Last, the inexorable march of inflation imposes a timescale. The meetings must be held promptly, and must be constructive, or the spending power of the group will be quickly eroded.

– Only the heads, by reason of their invested authority, can *effectively monitor standards*. The head has the view across the entire school; the head can demand high-quality work. The head can censure those who fail to achieve the expected standards, can encourage, advise and support. This is the positive side of paternalism.

Schools need, periodically, to evaluate their performance as a whole in given curriculum areas. This is not to identify failing individuals, but rather to recognise, as an institution, those aspects of the school which are specially felt to be priorities for development and to identify ways in which those priorities can be met. This sort of self-evaluation can be undertaken for whole school organisations as in the GRIDS scheme (Guidelines for Review and Internal Development in Schools), pioneered by the Schools Council and the University of Bristol, or for specific subject areas – and here too the carefully structured GRIDS technique can be applied with success in isolating the school's failings in science teaching and correcting these failings in practice.

But heads themselves are subject to external pressures.

THE HEAD TEACHER AND EXTERNAL AGENCIES

The role of the head teacher has been described as one of 'looking out' from the school – having an involvement with external and public relations. (A corollary to this is that deputy heads can be seen to 'look in', to be concerned with internal, staff/staff and staff/child relationships.) Heads are very vulnerable to outside agencies, the more so because their role can be a lonely one, and because, like the neck in the egg-timer, they may be the only medium of communication between the external agencies – governors, Local Authority, community – and the school. It is when they fail to act as intermediaries in the accepted way that the structure begins to break down.

Advisers and Inspectors do much of their work through the medium of the head teacher. An adviser with enthusiasm for primary science can be enormously supportive to a head teacher, and many have developed this expertise even when their initial concern has been with the secondary field. Some are sources of additional discretionary funding – especially to newly-appointed heads, or heads undertaking profound curriculum change. Others are willing to run courses in a school, to work alongside teachers, and to advise post-holders and curriculum leaders. The adviser can, in turn, direct schools to other external resources – local college lecturers, for example – who may be willing to work with the school, lead courses, or work alongside classroom teachers themselves. Some Authorities have set up primary science teams – Oxfordshire, for example – making use of the skills of individual seconded teachers to facilitate curriculum change. The Inner London Education Authority, with the ILEA/JISTT team (Inner London Education Authority/Junior and Infant Science Teacher Training), has made it possible to saturate part of a division with expertise, and nurture schools through the first few critical steps.

Inspectors and advisers are often developing published guidelines, or may be able to direct you to local practical resources. Frequently they maintain a local newsletter, up-dating your work, advising you of local initiatives, and providing you with the practicalities like health and safety advice.

Some authorities have been fortunate enough, most recently, to secure government sponsoring for science by means of the Education Support Grant, a sum of money for which they will have competed against other LEAs. This may provide for the secondment of a teacher or teachers to support and develop work in schools. Since 1978, and the publication of the DES primary schools report, LEAs have made great strides in the support and funding of science in primary schools.

A different form of support can be expected from parents. Many have recognised the importance of science to their children's future, and this importance has been confirmed by the popular press. A number of schools have exploited this enthusiasm by involving parents directly in science activities. One initiative in Coventry begins with a group of parents being shown a number of practical problems which can be solved using 'scientific' methods – bridging a gap, for example, or finding a fault in an electrical circuit. They then assist groups of children to solve the problem under the direction of the teacher. They do not usurp the teaching role, but they are able to direct misguided energies and prevent children reaching frustration point. The co-operation is proving successful, and has been taken up by a number of other schools. Information on the project can be obtained from the Community Education Project in Coventry.

Parental enthusiasm can prove overwhelming, especially if it concerns funding the work. Parents, understandably, like to see some tangible product of their work, especially if they have been actively money-raising. There is a tendency, inevitably, to aim for the more spectacular purchases and heads need to look carefully at the use, storage, and security of equipment before making any major investments. Parents are unlikely to be aware of recent developments in apparatus design and may find it difficult to understand why a head should want to buy mounted lenses when the school could have a microscope! Special care has to be taken over choice of microcomputer hardware and software if early obsolescence and disappointment are to be avoided.

The wealth of printed material aimed at influencing the school's work in science can be overwhelming. An excellent investment is primary school membership of the Association for Science Education, whose services are discussed elsewhere. Their *Primary News* will keep you up to date with developments, and their newsletters describe examples of good practice.

REFERENCES

Association for Science Education (ASE) (1974) *Science and Primary Education Papers No. 3: The Role of the Headteacher*. Hatfield: ASE.

Bulletin of Environmental Education: Town and Country Planning Association (Education Unit), 17 Carlton House Terrace, London. SW1Y 5AS.

Department of Education and Science (1978) *Primary Education in England: A Survey by HM Inspectors of Schools*. London: HMSO.

Schools Council (1978). Teaching Primary Science Project. Diamond, D. *Introduction and Guide*. London: Macdonald.

Schools Council (1980). Learning Through Science Project. *Learning Through Science: Formulating a School Policy*. London: Macdonald.

Schools Council (1984). GRIDS Project. McMahon, A. *et al. Guidelines for Review and Internal Development in Schools: Primary Schools Handbook*. London: Longman.

Chapter 5

Developing a Policy –
the Role of the Post-Holder

SHOULD THERE BE A POST OF RESPONSIBILITY FOR SCIENCE?

In many schools, the question is irrelevant. The number of scale posts is limited, or tied-up apparently irreversibly, or science has not the priority of other subjects. But where responsibility allowances become available, decisions have to be made about allocating one – or part of one – for science. The ASE in 1974 concluded broadly that a specialist science teacher was inappropriate as such. More recent thinking has been that the specialist may have a place, especially in large schools, or schools with older children. The question then arises; if a post of responsibility is appropriate, what is the nature of the role?

The ASE in 1976, looked at the role of the 'post of responsibility'. They reinforced the view expressed in both the Plowden and Gittings reports that 'specialist teaching' was not a good use of a post. The key word, for them, was 'co-operation'. The post-holder would 'co-operate' with head, staff, children and external agencies such as advisory staff.

One contemporary definition of post-holder activity could hardly be bettered; a post-holder:

1. is responsible to the head for planning and assessment;
2. designs and co-ordinates the teaching programme;
3. advises on the planning, organisation, care and use of equipment;
4. advises colleagues on teaching method;
5. is a source of reference;
6. continually educates staff in their subject.

Now what is interesting about this definition is its origin; it comes, in fact, from the Institute of PE Advisers. It highlights some clear similarities between PE and science and more clearly defines the latter.

- Both are essentially practical, activity-based subjects. Sedentary PE would be a contradiction in terms; science needs to be active.
- Both science and PE utilise equipment. This involves financial outlay, maintenance, running costs, replacement and repair.
- Both can lack progression. While PE activities can develop with the changing

demands and skills of maturing bodies, many PE lessons are little different in form at the top of a primary school than at the bottom. The same may be true of science. For example, at almost any age, children may be asked to classify metals by their magnetic or conductive properties. It is to be hoped that the approach and the demands change, and certainly that the method of recording reflects the children's abilities, but the activity is essentially similar.

Both subjects are ephemeral, so that the record, however detailed, can never show exactly what took place and how the activity was organised, or how much direction the teacher gave. This has a profound effect upon the activities of the post-holder (and of the head teacher who wishes to be involved in monitoring). Only by observing actual classroom activity can either PE or science be monitored; only by working alongside a classroom teacher can direct help be given, beyond the provision of guidelines, resources, etc.

We shall examine this definition of responsibility in the context of primary science.

RESPONSIBILITY FOR CURRICULUM PLANNING, IMPLEMENTATION AND ASSESSMENT

Key issues of content, ideas and skills can only be resolved by staff discussion. They will be related to the unique needs and the development of the school's children. Variety is important; so too is a degree of sensitivity. Take for example, the familiar block graphs tracing height and weight. How thoughtful is *that*, given that children can be acutely conscious of extremes, of small stature or excessive weight? A nice example is given by the Learning Through Science team which goes some way to redress the balance. Children attempt to curl up inside the circles of a target (the smallest gets the kudos!) Sensitivity is essential in other areas too – over environmental issues, or children's anxieties; to the anthropomorphism that leads them to become closely attached to the animals they are learning about, and to the variety of home and family backgrounds. One 'Science 5–13' activity, an exercise in genetics related to children's eye colour, was later strongly discouraged after children began to make unhappy discoveries about natural parents.

Post-holders are also concerned with matters of quality. It would not be appropriate to enter into a lengthy discussion here of what 'quality' means in primary education; for a lengthy mind-bending discourse on the subject, see the fascinating cult book *Zen and the Art of Motorcycle Maintenance*. It is, however, necessary to determine good practice; whether the activities are appropriate for the children concerned and what the learners are certainly learning. As emphasised in chapter 1, the HMI Primary Report of 1978 identified science as the subject most poorly matched to the age of the children.

A continuous assessment of the curriculum and how it is functioning in practice, is more or less essential. It is very easy to agree guidelines, put them into practice and feel that the job is over. Subjects are evolving daily and the demands upon many teachers are enormous. No rigid 'tramlines' can respond to changing needs. Revision is part of the job.

Given this fluidity, the post-holder must *design and co-ordinate a teaching programme* that provides a real framework for continuity and progression. This will mean a considerable amount of negotiation between teachers or year groups to develop activities that are appropriate to given ages and abilities, and this in turn highlights certain post-holder qualities:

– The post-holder must be a *model of competence*, and the exemplar of good classroom science practice. This is essential to establish credibility.
– The post-holder must have *enthusiasm*; for the subject, for its rewards, for teaching it to young children.
– The post-holder must be '*an authority*' – if they are not widely read in the subject, they should at least know where to turn for information.
– The post-holder needs *advisory skills*; not just to know when to give advice, but when to back off. As the catchphrase has it, 'a word to the wise can often be infuriating!'

A key part of the role, given the subject's practical nature, will relate to the *organisation of resources*. Critical decisions about storage, access, cataloguing, loan records, repair and maintenance must be made. The Learning Through Science book, *Science Resources for Primary and Middle Schools*, will be as helpful as any.

Clearly, well-planned resources, boxed, perhaps, by subject, activity or skill, marked with contents lists and checked regularly (possibly by responsible children) will be more widely used, or at least open to wider use. A box for breakages is essential, or running repairs can never be done; protection against theft is advisable, especially of small, attractive items – magnets, magnetic compasses, plastic mirrors and so on. Special care will be needed if plants or living creatures are involved. We have a responsibility, not only for the welfare of living creatures, but also to demonstrate that welfare to young people.

Junk materials can be invaluable; and one school solved the storage problem with a well-kept shed, where bins contained the cardboard rolls, yoghourt pots, tinfoil and offcuts that are the stock-in-trade of young scientists. Where this is not practical, other answers can be found – a curtain round a table, for example, hides a considerable bulk.

Post-holders will need to *advise colleagues on teaching method*. This is a sensitive issue. All teachers have a unique approach to their work and it is one of the strengths of the British education system that the diversity is maintained – even encouraged – between schools and teachers. However, a degree of uniformity can provide essential continuity. Clearly understood techniques for handling equipment can prevent abuse and enable children to obtain the most from it. If a binocular microscope is handled in a recognised way, or electrical wires are always bundled, wound or (an excellent storage technique) pushed, bridge-like, into pieces of polystyrene, then a lot of time can be saved by each teacher handling the subject.

Similarly, standard methods of recording will enable the children to concentrate on content rather than technique. A return to the 'observations, conclusions' system is not advocated, but simple decisions about how to mark axes in graph work, or what is expected in children's working drawings, or whether to use plain lines or arrows to label pictures, will help. Similarly, decisions about marking techniques are valuable, not only in science, but across the curriculum. A survey in Warwickshire schools showed that teachers had many diverse ways of noting (say) a spelling error. Some crossed out, others ringed, or underlined, or bracketed, or wrote the work in the margin or at the end of the work. A degree of standardisation would surely help prevent confusion.

Post-holders must be a sound and approachable *source of reference*. For this reason, they should not neglect their own professional development. Teachers turning to them should be sure of up-to-date advice on safety, practical techniques, microcomputer software or simply which book to turn to.

Post-holders need to be aware of their responsibility for *school-based, in-service work*. Whether it is covering a year-group meeting, displaying newly-acquired materials and explaining their use, or leading a whole staff in curriculum planning, they need to take up the normal opportunities that arise to promote their subject.

Only a paragon could fulfil these demands successfully; the curriculum leader will go a long way towards meeting them by helping teachers overcome their uncertainty; by finding the science in what is already happening in schools; by recognising, and leading others to recognise, the rich science associations of the everyday; and by guiding gently towards practical applications and problem solving – technology, the 'appliance of science'.

Two words of warning from experience.

Avoid making too many *demands*, especially in the early stages. The change process is often a slow one.

Avoid the temptation of becoming a 'king-pin'. Nobody is indispensable, but if all the science in the school is dependent upon you and your expertise, then your absence, change of role or interest, move or promotion, will seriously undermine the school's science programme. Remember, a follow-up study of secondary level 'Nuffield Science' teachers proved impossible, because so many had been promoted! That could be you, and your carefully collected resources could be gathering dust on the school shelves.

REFERENCES

Association for Science Education (ASE) (1976) *Science and Primary Education Papers No. 3: A Post of Responsibility*. Hatfield: ASE.

Department of Education and Science, Central Advisory Council for Education (England). (1967) *Children and their Primary School (Plowden Report)*. London: HMSO.

Pirsig, R. (1974) *Zen and the Art of Motorcycle Maintenance*. London: Bodley Head.

Schools Council, Learning Through Science Project (1982) *Science Resources For Primary and Middle Schools*. London: Macdonald.

Chapter 6

Activities, Investigations and Strategies

SCIENCE ALL AROUND

The most enjoyable and potentially profitable science stems from the natural curiosity of the children. There are numerous happenings within the school which can be used by the teacher to develop science skills, attitudes and concepts: 'An observation by one of the children was followed by the spontaneous questions, "Why do we line the tray for our beakers with paper towels?"'

From this one remark, the class teacher was able to involve the whole class in a series of investigations designed to explore and answer the question. This particular class of 35 Warwickshire first school children went on to investigate absorption and, as each stage of the topic progressed, the teacher identified the skills and activities involved (table 6.1 on pages 74–75.)

Likewise, the immediate environment of the school can provide an abundant source of starting points for science. The discovery of a rook's nest led to investigative work by a class of Cheshire juniors; their teacher eloquently recorded their approach:

> The discovery of the rook's nest, its transportation back to the classroom and then a subsequent observation was only part of a wider study of the rook and its gregarious way of life.
>
> It was collected one January almost completely intact at the base of a mighty beech which stood with others forming a major landmark at the centre of a Cheshire village. The vociferous birds left their high perches as we arrived, but soon returned, though still not quietly. The ground was strewn with nest fragments, which cracked underfoot, while the undergrowth was splattered with once viscous remains of the rooks' meals – now preserved as dried but fragmented pellets. Even amongst this debris the fallen nest was conspicuously massive and secure in its framework, yet individual portions were paradoxically fragile.
>
> Having prised the frozen structure from the ground, and awkwardly carried it indoors, it was decided to try to weigh it while it remained reasonably intact. The only successful method involved a volunteer clutching the nest in his arms whilst standing on a borrowed pair of bathroom scales. Although not perfect (without knowledge of the amount of moisture in it) an acceptable recording of mass was achieved.
>
> The nest was installed, not only as an item of display, but also an object to measure, draw and generally inspire. An analysis of the materials was undertaken – sizes of twigs were graphed, the succession of twig sizes down through the layers was recorded and nest linings removed.

Certain invertebrates (living as squatters in the dark tenements, particularly in the unfashionable basements) were sighted. Some were removed for study, although one particular spider remained to spin an elaborate orbital web, and seemed to prosper in its own particularly frugal way.

Feathers were collected from the rookery and were painted in their varying stages of disarray, with special reference to J. S. G. Thomas' poem, 'The Rook' (a study of a roadside fatality). This led to a certain amount of descriptive writing on the roadside accidents of creatures, especially the hedgehogs commonly killed on their post-hibernation journeys.

Although not observed, the phenomena [sic] known as rook-parliaments was discussed, and many varied (mostly unlikely) reasons were ventured.

A large number of pellets were collected and dissected – to reveal mainly seed chaff – but also stones, bones, fur, glass, plastic, etc. Pie charts, using this information, were compiled, showing how rooks from two different rookeries had slightly varying diets.

Throughout, many original, but mostly unsuccessful, visual attempts were made to represent the nest. Some success was achieved with blown paint – this gave some textual requirements but was difficult to control. Finally, an ancient tactile medium (charcoal) was used. It echoes the 'bible blackness' of the nests, birds and trees; and being wood-based seemed exactly the right medium to represent the seemingly illogically constructed nests.

The nest suffered in the time it remained a centre-piece – the edges fell away continually, it became over-measured and in the doing lost much of its shape and finally it snared an unsuspecting pupil who landed noisily amongst its brittle twig pile. Soon after it left the school carried by four young 'pall-bearers', who disappeared into a March mist and distributed it in the local wood. Perhaps fragments were collected that year by the other eager nest builders and have been re-cycled in a 'Phoenix-like' way.

From *Primary Science Guidelines*, Cheshire LEA (1982).

As a result of the children's practical problem solving – how to transport, weigh and measure the nest, how to record their findings using a variety of media, and how to establish the bird's feeding habits – a range of skills and concepts were developed. Opportunities for careful observation of the range of life forms dependent on the nest, opportunities for a range of discussions, and opportunities for creativity were all afforded as a result of the study. Most of these children would have seen birds' nests before without appreciating the complexity of their construction, the range of materials used and their varying purposes. These children will now look at their environment with enhanced perspectives.

Of course science is enjoyable. A series of walks in Fife by Class 3 of Guardbridge Primary School opened their eyes to many hitherto unobserved wonders; the class would certainly agree that *science is fun*:

Class 3, which consisted of Primary 4, Primary 5 and some Primary 6 pupils, followed an uncharted path in the summer term. Under the guidance of Dr. Ian Strachan, the Countryside Ranger, we set out to discover a little, or even a lot, about life around the Eden Estuary.

The first outing took the children on to the shore near the Paper Mill. There they learned how to use binoculars and found, to their amazement, that right there in the middle of their village were at least eight water birds – waders and web-footed. They discovered the differences in their footprints and shape of beaks, and how they used these in the hunt for food. The tufted duck dived for its food and caused much excitement because of the length of time it stayed under water. The swans were preening, and the cormorant sat motionless on a pole so that everyone could see his shape and colours.

On another Thursday we set out to walk through the village, across the main road and down to the edge of the river. This was an area which the children thought they knew

Table 6.1 *Absorption – seizing an opportunity*

Organisation	Materials Used	Activity	Skills involved
Whole class grouped together with teacher	Beakers for soft drinks on a tray lined with paper towels	Discussion to try to answer the question: 'Why do we line our tray with paper towels?', 'What else could we use?', 'What might be totally unsuitable?'	Identifying a possible problem Drawing on past experience to suggest suitable materials
Children working in small groups or singly on prepared activity	Variety of materials suggested by children, and others at teacher's discretion (ready labelled to facilitate easy recording) Hoops or enclosing circles to make sets	Investigating suggestions Sorting materials into sets Prediction: Those that will absorb/those that will not This activity lasted for about two weeks	Comparing and sorting Recognising similarities/differences Looking for patterns and relationships Making predictions based on observations of patterns Sharing experiences Making permanent records of sets, charts, graphs, etc
Whole class grouped together	Charts made by children Tank of water Materials under investigation	**Discussion:** How do we know who has sorted the materials correctly? How can we find out? **Suggestions from children:** 1. Get a tank of water and put each item in singly 2. How can we tell if the items have absorbed water or just got wet outside? Break the items open and see if they are wet inside – not suitable for all items 3. Water level in tank will drop if item has absorbed water – problem of small difference in water level visible (to be followed up)	Comparison of results Identifying problems Suggesting suitable investigations to answer questions Modifying investigations in the light of experience Recognition of variables

Organisation	Resources	Activity	Skills/processes
Small groups or pairs	As above, plus balance measuring equipment Junk	4. If you can squeeze water out then water has been absorbed – not suitable for all items 5. Items may increase in size if water is absorbed – time factor to be considered 6. Weight increase 7. Softer if more absorbent Investigate one of the suggestions made above Choose two items which will absorb/two which will not	Selection of suitable materials to set up investigation Controlling variables Predicting
Small groups	Selection of four types of material	Weighing each item Immersing in water for controlled time Re-weighing Recording results	Consideration of variables Setting up a fair test Measurement of time/mass Computation, recording Proposing further investigation from observations
Individual children	Selection of four types of material	Drawing round each item and measuring perimeter Immersing in water for controlled time. Re-measuring saturated materials and noticing any difference in size	Setting up a fair test Consideration of variables Measurement
Class discussion	Results from all investigations	Which test appears to give more accurate results? Why?	Consideration of further variables, *i.e.* size, thickness, suggested more accurate ways of measuring, ways of testing

Adapted from: *Science Guidelines for Young Investigators* Warwickshire LEA (1983)

Science walks and visits can be rewarding. (Reproduced with the permission of Janine Wiedel.)

well, and were astounded to see teeming life in small pools on the saltmarsh. Even two small bodies sitting down in the grey, smelly mud didn't seem to dampen their spirits, though it did make for a hasty retreat to school.

As a contrast, our next trip of discovery was down to the grassy triangle between the football pitch and the reservoir. The children's lists of plants and insects seen, examined and returned to their own habitat, covered sheets of paper. Dr. Strachan encouraged them to discover for themselves why the plants on the football pitch were much shorter than similar ones growing wild. Even if they only remember one quarter of what we saw it was a worthwhile experience. We looked at trees, trying to remember weather rhymes about oaks and ash, while some quick eyes noted a reed bunting and a blue-tit. The most exciting moment for many was when they saw a strange spider, caterpillar or fly moving about in these wonderful little bottles with a magnifying glass end.

Our final outing was to St. Andrews to look at what was in rock pools along by the Maiden Rock. The crab was the biggest any of us had ever seen, the sea anemones waved their tentacles gracefully in the water, while the hermit crabs and water snails moved rapidly under seaweed or overhanging rocks, What did it matter if the icy east coast wind did make our teeth chatter while we ate our lunch? We'd had a fabulous time.

The main thing the children learned was how to observe and compare, to appreciate and protect. They began to take a pride in their own area – so much so that one morning we went down and did a clean up of all the rubbish on the land beside the reservoir. The children were thrilled to collect and bring back to school three plastic bin bags, a cardboard box and assorted small containers, all brim-full and spilling over with left behind junk.

We learned to enjoy the music of Smetana when we listened to The Moldau while we worked. Our language work benefited enormously, as even less articulate children found clover whose leaves 'looked like clubs on a playing card.' Another child wrote of some mallard ducks 'swimming gracefully', while others were 'waddling funnily.' A third was fascinated by the ragworm we found in the mud because it 'looked jagged and zigzaggy.'

Our most successful project in years enjoyed by all the children (and the teacher) – after all who can complain when a normally rather unenthusiastic Primary 6 boy was amazed at the sound of the bell ringing at the end of the morning! 'Isn't it amazing how the time goes when you are enjoying yourself?' – this from a boy who normally found three lines and a chewed pencil enough work for a morning!

From *Making Tracks*, Fife LEA (1983). Elizabeth S. Thirkell.

Clearly then there is no shortage of starting points – a paper towel, a discarded, fallen rook's nest, a nature walk; in each case opportunities were seized and the science developed. There is no pressure to initiate large, long-term projects: from small beginnings the teacher can gradually extend and widen the science experiences of the class.

BROAD AREAS OF INVESTIGATION

We have already discussed the nature of primary science as a concern for the acquisition and development of a whole range of skills and attitudes; not only for work in school, but also essential for life outside. Primary science is also about the formation and reinforcement of concepts or ideas. Happenings in the classroom or during fieldwork become vehicles for development of these attributes and, indeed, are occurring in many schools without being labelled 'science'.

In order to enrich the curriculum science-wise, there must be an awareness of what science is and where it is already happening in school, as well as an acceptable structure to enable us to translate our definitions into classroom practice.

Fred Ogden, General Adviser for Tameside, defines this 'acceptable structure' as:

An organisational approach that YOU feel relatively at ease with and which will enable you to implement work of a scientific nature . . . i.e. enquiring . . . finding out . . . investigating . . . observing, predicting and experimenting

It is also necessary for children to receive a balanced science experience; and even though it is understandable that those teachers (and they are a majority) with a 'non-science' background probably feel happier when dealing with the science of 'living things' – plants, animals, ourselves, etc., a balanced programme must, even for the younger children, include components which might come under the label of 'physical' rather than 'biological' science. The DES documents already referred to, mention four very broad areas or aspects of science that children should meet in their early years:

The study of *living things* and their interaction with the environment.
Materials and their characteristics
Energy and its interaction with materials
Forces and their effects

This obviously allows a school to select almost any topic or area of investigation. However, there are two important principles which should guide our choice:

- There needs to be a balance of activity between 'biological' and 'physical' topics, and within these two areas.
- Thought should be given to any sequential development of ideas through the school, and to the depth of approach appropriate to particular groups of children.

DEVELOPING A SCHEME OF WORK

A scheme of work need not imply an inflexible syllabus which must be rigidly adhered to at all costs. On the contrary, the class must be able to respond to developments – starting points such as the rook's nest which might present themselves; avenues of investigation which children might wish to follow arising out of a particular activity or topic; the need to allow different groups of children to work on diverse aspects of a theme according to their interests and abilities.

However, a scheme will enable the school to consider progression and breadth of concept development, the depth of approach, and an overall balance in content areas. Such a scheme will not be static; it will evolve over several years as experiences of success are incorporated, disasters rejected, and resources slowly built up. The whole staff, under a co-ordinator, will be involved.

For the less experienced teacher, clear guidelines will help initiate science in a particular class – there is nothing wrong with a prescribed science activity *if that is the most efficient way of ensuring good science practice*. There are, of course, several commercially-produced primary science schemes available (Appendix III) and, if a school has little experience of science, they can be invaluable in providing a bank of ideas and starting points which can be modified to suit individuals. Most are flexible in that activities can be geared to particular situations – time available, resources, patterns of working, etc.

Those LEAs which have produced their own guidelines for primary science show a remarkable similarity in the broad areas of work recommended. Thus, common topics include the science aspects of:

Ourselves, animals and plants
Water, air, light and sound
Time and weather studies
Materials
Energy and forces, including electricity and
    magnetism
Rocks and soil, the solar system

These content areas, as has already been stressed, are vehicles for the development of ideas and skills and attitudes, and a scheme might well begin by listing those attributes which science can help develop or reinforce. No doubt different groups of teachers will produce different lists, and arguments can always be made for and against individual components. This is how a scheme should develop. Starting points are legion and are mentioned throughout this book.

Two typical broad areas which might be covered are *living things* and *energy and forces*, and after discussion, a range of basic concepts which children might reasonably be expected to meet, in one form or another, is established. In chapter 1, an example of how a simple card system could be used to order our ideas and add or reject items was mentioned. In each of the lists illustrated, one of the broad basic concept areas has been expanded in order to indicate some of the actual activities children might base their investigations on: reproduction in the case of *living things* (table 6.2 opposite), and electricity from the *energy and forces* list (table 6.3 on page 80).

Table 6.2 *Living things – some broad/basic concepts*

1. The variety of living things have different food requirements

2. Plants use material from the soil, from the air and sunlight

3. Water is essential to life, and living things contain a substantial proportion of water

4. Living things are components of food chains: some animals eat plants, others eat animals which in turn eat plants

5. Green plants can make food, animals cannot

6. Food is required to promote growth and provide an energy store essential to support life

7. Living things produce waste materials

8. Oxygen is taken from the air or from water

9. Pollution can be harmful to living things

10. The life cycle is repeated each generation

11. Plants and animals reproduce by a variety of methods

12. Living things depend on each other in various ways

13. Man makes use of animals and plants for food, transport, raw materials, etc

14. Many living things need care and protection in early life

15. Some animals are warm blooded

16. Many living things are usually well suited to their environment and over long periods can adapt to changing environments

Reproduction – some related concepts

a. What are the parts of a flower?

b. How are seeds dispersed?

c. What are the conditions for seed germination?

d. Can parts of plants grow into new plants?

e. How do birds build a nest?

f. Are all birds' eggs the same?

g. How long before a hen's egg hatches?

h. How do caterpillars change?

i. Parts of the human body.

j. How do babies develop?

k. The need for fertilisation.

Thus we begin to develop a basis for classroom or fieldwork. Further discussion with the children themselves, bearing in mind available resources, their past experiences and their capabilities (which should not be underestimated) will allow their work to develop. Likewise, if certain skills are to be encouraged, the scheme of work might include examples of general or specific skills which can be developed by the science experiences (see table 6.4 overleaf).

There will be overlap, but useful guidelines are being established. The scheme is not prescriptive; it can and should be modified and extended. Some form of record keeping and assessment might be implied – this is dealt with later (chapter 9). It is a basis for an approach.

Table 6.3   *Energy and forces – some broad/basic concepts*

1. In order to move something it is usually necessary to push or pull it	
2. Energy is used when something is caused to move	**Electricity – some related concepts**
3. Energy can come from a variety of sources	a. A balloon, when rubbed on a woollen jumper, sticks to a wall
4. When energy changes its form it does something useful	b. A needle, stroked with a magnet, becomes a magnet
5. Energy is not 'lost', it changes its form	c. An electric current, flowing through a coil of wire, will magnetise a piece of iron inside the coil
6. For electricity to flow, a complete circuit is necessary	d. Some materials conduct electricity
7. Gravity is a force pulling everything towards the centre of the earth	e. Some wires become hot when a current flows through them
8. Friction is a force which tends to oppose motion and produce heat	f. Electricity can be produced by various methods
9. Certain structures can resist forces better than others	g. An electric current affects a compass needle
10. A substantial amount of energy originated in the sun	12. Coal was originally plant material
11. Insulation can help save energy	13. Oil was originally animal material
	14. Machines help us do work

Table 6.4   *Examples of skills which might be developed*

practical skills	process skills	attitude skills	language/maths skills
use a: hand lens simple microscope thermometer	observe classify	work in an organised manner	weigh and measure with increasing accuracy
handle tools safely	use a simple key	appreciate need for safety	build up a word bank
work safely generally	identify a problem and propose ways of tackling it	ability to work independently/ co-operatively as appropriate	keep diaries/records
grow plants from seeds/cuttings	draw conclusions		give factual accounts
make collections	collect information		record appropriately
care for animals	appreciate fair testing		discuss/debate
pour liquids			use reference books
			descriptive writing
			use graphs

Constructions using rolled paper tubes can be related to real life structures. (Reproduced with the permission of Janine Wiedel.)

TOPIC WEBS

In order to clarify ideas and to see at a glance the variety and extent of possibilities inherent in a particular theme or topic, a *topic web* construction has much to recommend it. Some topics can be very open-ended and it is advisable to begin with a large sheet of drawing paper!

One school decided that several classes, through the age range, would look at *the wind*. A complex topic web evolved (see figure 6.1). Here we emphasise the science aspects of the theme, but in many cases such topic webs will include a much wider perspective: language, maths and craft work, music and drama.

The organisation can be made manageable by identifying those aspects more appropriate to infants (as shown in figure 6.2), or to juniors (figure 6.3) and then deciding what might be accomplished by particular classes or groups of children.

At this point reference can be made to our concept and skills list and we can formulate ideas of why we are doing particular things and what we hope to achieve.

It is unlikely that the whole spectrum of possibilities outlined in these topic webs will be covered. As the work progresses, new ideas will evolve, new areas for investigation present themselves. The topic web is a skeleton of the theme, very flexible and adaptable. Hopefully it will enable the science work to be balanced by, and integrated with, other curriculum areas, avoid needless repetition from year to year without adequate progression, ensure a balance of science activities suitable for all the children, and yet still allow for the development of the unexpected.

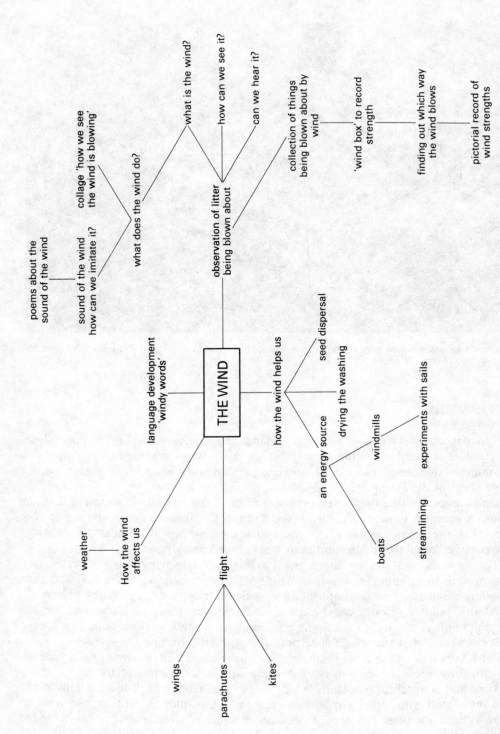

Figure 6.1 Developing a topic web based on 'the wind'

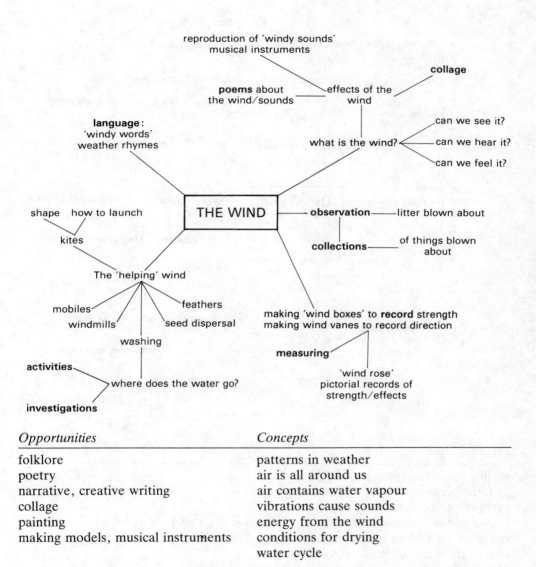

Figure 6.2 An infants teacher might extract from the overall topic web those aspects most suitable for a class of younger children

Opportunities	Concepts
folklore	patterns in weather
poetry	air is all around us
narrative, creative writing	air contains water vapour
collage	vibrations cause sounds
painting	energy from the wind
making models, musical instruments	conditions for drying
	water cycle

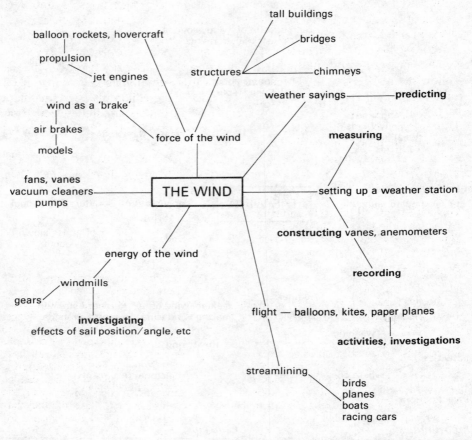

balloon rockets, hovercraft

propulsion

jet engines

wind as a 'brake'

air brakes

models

fans, vanes
vacuum cleaners
pumps

structures

tall buildings

bridges

chimneys

force of the wind

weather sayings —— **predicting**

measuring

THE WIND

setting up a weather station

constructing vanes, anemometers

recording

energy of the wind

windmills

gears

investigating
effects of sail position/angle, etc

flight — balloons, kites, paper planes

activities, investigations

streamlining

birds
planes
boats
racing cars

Concepts

air fills the space around us
patterns occur in weather cycles
paths of projectiles
in order to move something it is usually necessary to push or pull it
energy is used when something moves
energy can come from a variety of sources
when energy changes its form it does something useful
certain structures resist forces better than others
machines help us do work

Figure 6.3 In the junior school, the classes might decide to look at other aspects of 'the wind'

PLANNING INVESTIGATIONS AND SOLVING PROBLEMS

[handwritten: → direct link with maths – solving a problem]

An investigatory approach, where children solve problems engineered by a teacher or, better still, which arise from their own observations or questions, is fundamental to science in the primary school. However, it need not be a daunting experience for teacher and pupil, requiring expensive equipment to undertake complex 'experiments'. We have already seen how a pupil's spontaneous question following an observation of a tray of beakers of soft drinks led to a range of science activities involving the whole class; how small groups or individuals work towards a common goal, having seized an opportunity. *What?* and *where?* and *how?* and *why?* are children's questions that can be used to initiate investigations, encouraged by an understanding teacher who can guide their discussions and approaches and, far from needing to know all the answers, can find out alongside the pupils.

The selection and management of investigations is a concern of teachers which has been anticipated by the West Cumbrian Advisory Team in their booklet, *Primary Science West*, and they discuss some of these concerns:

> 'To what extent can the children be given their head?'
> 'How many blind alleys can they be allowed to follow?'
> 'Shouldn't they get a real "conclusion"?'
> '. . . but I don't know the answers'

> These and related issues are a real concern. As ever, teacher skill and thought is at the core; the knack is variety, balance and knowing your children. Teachers on many occasions will need both to stimulate and to guide investigation, but again without totally stifling initiative. No child can be allowed too many dead ends and failures; not every investigation (maybe a very few) produces nice clean answers and absolute truths – to experience such limitations is in itself important, though a constant lack of success kills motivation and enthusiasm. The teacher's skill is encouraging and drawing out those questions which can lead to profitable investigation. The match with the children is critical. Remember too that conclusions are not everything – many lessons can be learned, skills acquired and experience widened along the way. At the end of the day the children may not have proved (and written down) Newton's Law of Motion, but they may well have measured, timed, counted, handled, thought and talked – an acceptable start!

These last two activities are possibly the most important. Pupils need time, individually, with their classmates, and with their teacher, to think through their work and talk about it, and to discuss it at length.

This time is not always given

A group of Oxfordshire primary teachers advising their colleagues on investigative approaches to primary science gave their guiding principles for such work:

'Make maximum use of the school buildings, grounds and surrounding environment.' In stressing this they quote the story of a particular class in West Africa being taught about bees from a biology chart, when overhead in the roof a swarm of bees was building its nest unobserved!

'Have freedom to engineer a situation to provide learning experience.'
'Know where you want to go, and anticipate children's needs.'
'Bring the right things into the classroom to provide a stimulus.'
'Have materials, equipment and a wide range of "string and sealing wax" items.'

To illustrate what they mean by investigatory activities in science, and how they can be organised, they present a case study of work on vegetable dyes.

This was a term's work carried out with a vertically grouped class of 32 pupils aged 9 to 11. There was a complex mixture of ability. The investigations were carried out by small groups of children, while others were engaged in a variety of other activities across the whole curriculum. From time to time the whole class would become involved simultaneously, especially when discussion about the next stage of the work took place. There was some degree of practical direction once the groups had decided on their course of action. This was necessary largely because of safety and the complex nature of the investigation. Once a routine had become established, the work went forward smoothly.

The Experiments

After a few initial attempts we established fairly obvious facts. Colours varied according to dye material used, the type and amount of fibre being dyed, and the time that fibres were in the dye bath. We learnt from books that wool mordanted with alum took up and retained dye better and more evenly. We decided to incorporate this into a series of experiments to see how many different colours we could obtain by dyeing using vegetable materials.

Some children decided their own course of experiments and used any type of plant material, ranging from broom flowers through a great variety of leaves to different barks and roots. Apart from this, four main groups evolved, using –

1. Blackberries (from a deep freeze)
2. Onion skins or shallot skins
3. Elder leaves
4. Lichens

Once the dye material was chosen it was decided that the different fibres – mordanted, and unmordanted – of thick Aran wool, thinner white wool, white nylon, and white acrylic fibre, accurately weighed to the same amount, could be incorporated into the same dye bath for each experiment, and the results displayed on a large shade card.

Time was the first factor that was changed, allowing the materials to simmer in the dye bath for a quarter, half, one and two hours. This alone, without counting group 4, gave us 96 different samples of yarn. The longer the fibres were dyed, the deeper the colours became, but an optimum time, beyond which little change occurred, was found for each dye.

The children knew the tap water we had been using contained 'chemicals', so rainwater which would be purer was also used. The colour results for some dyes, especially blackberry, were very different. Salt and vinegar added could also make a difference. So the groups began to diverge.

Elder leaves of different ages, from different localities and soils gave different results – well illustrated by leaves gathered at the same age from the same garden but with one bush near a permanent bonfire site giving different colours.

Different wall and tree lichens from different areas used immediately, or after steeping in ammonia and water, gave different colours. In this group the mordanting with alum made little or no difference to the results.

Other mordants were used, by a small group, after this first series of experiments, using different barks. The same dyebath and conditions produced very different colours for wool mordanted with different chemicals. One mordant with each bark produced different colours but all with the same tone. It was easy to pick out all the samples where an iron-based mordant had been used, etc. This showed that the type of mordant had as great an effect as the type of bark.

Organisation was very important with so many experiments going on. The wool was mordanted in bulk, although there were a number of batches, and then weighed into small samples. The mordanted and unmordanted wools were tied with different types of thread to distinguish them. The different types of yarn could be easily identified. One skein of each type of yarn and wool was tied loosely together with strong nylon. Three old saucepans were used as dyebaths, large enough to contain sufficient samples of yarn for a complete set of different yarns to be removed at the end of each time period. Each batch was thoroughly rinsed and hung to dry. A label was attached, with full details of the dyeing process, immediately afterwards.

All this was essential to prevent muddling. All samples dyed with the same dye material, when labelled, were kept together, hung on strings and displayed.

We had a cooker with two hotplates and a small electric boiler to take one saucepan. These were in continual use once the project was fully under way. The boiling dyebaths were closely supervised. With common-sense precautions, and a discussion on safety factors, the children quickly became aware of the dangers involved, checked each other and immediately reported when they needed help.

The children worked in small groups, many in pairs, but no more than four in a group. They compared results and were interested in what others were doing. The more capable, sensible, children helped the less able, and all obtained good results.

As there were so many processes involved, once started, the project did not really have any bottlenecks, although the sink and the cooker were always the busiest areas. The processes had to follow a set order, so a natural flow developed, and the children became systematic and methodical.

We had no accidents, or disputes about the use of equipment or facilities. Everyone enjoyed the project and was anxious to do an experiment and go on to another one. The end of term came and we ran out of time before the children had run out of ideas: there was always another colour to be found or made.

We produced, under quite strict experimental conditions, hundreds of different colours. After large shade cards explaining how each colour had been obtained were made, and results compared and analysed, the coloured yarns were used for embroidery and collage work.

From B. Cumming (1978) 'Vegetable Dyes' in Oxfordshire LEA
Science Work in Primary Schools.

This approach lends itself to individual or small group work. There are occasions – when introducing a theme, or discussing findings relevant to the whole class, or winding up the project – when whole class involvement will be necessary. Once again, the need for adequate time for reflection and discussion is stressed.

Investigative work, of course, requires some selection and control; a truly open-ended approach is not realistic. Children need experiences which are not too complicated for them to unravel, and the situations must not be so loose that no guidelines are given, nor so highly structured that childrens' initiatives and enthusiasms are stifled. The type of questions asked of the children is crucial. For our purposes we can regard pupil activities as being *closed-ended* or *open-ended*, the particular nature of the activity being, to a large extent, conditioned by the type of question posed.

Closed-ended questions often result in convergent thinking, children focussing on a particular aspect, such as simple recall of facts. If we wish to illustrate a concrete idea, a closed-ended approach is often used. Thus we might wish to show the class how to prepare a plastic-covered length of wire for fixing to a battery terminal. If there are enough equipment and materials available the whole group can participate and so master a specific technique. Such activities will provide children with a range of skills and knowledge which can subsequently be used in their problem-solving activities.

However, although the importance of closed-ended activities is acknowledged, primary science (and indeed any science) is best served by an open-ended approach.

Open-ended questions are divergent in that they often lead to other questions and initiate tasks of a truly experimental nature, requiring positive thinking and planning of investigations. A range of responses or solutions is possible to questions such as:

'How could you tell if . . .?'
'Do all flowers take up water at the same rate?'
'Is our sense of taste affected by our sense of smell?'
'Is it a fair test if . . .?'

The pupil is allowed to think and to come to personal conclusions.

Broad questions, not directly related to the experiences of young children, overawe them and produce little or no response.

'Which materials rust?'

can be narrowed down to a more manageable:

'Will an aluminium pan rust?'

This will help the children organise their thoughts, find out and later answer broader questions:

'What other objects might rust?'

The questioning technique can also be used to differentiate between reasonable and unreasonable responses. A lead must be given as to the types of investigation initiated – misconceptions can easily become established if enough people repeat them. Even correct responses can be evaluated:

'What is the evidence?'

can lead to better understanding than merely a simple affirmation.

Implicit in the forementioned is a practical approach to problem solving. Real-life problems rarely have unique solutions and are often much more complex than might appear at first sight. Usually we are obliged to settle for an optimum solution, having first considered the pros and cons of particular solutions. The process of problem solving is iterative; if one proposed solution is found wanting, we backtrack and try another, until an acceptable outcome is found. Diagramatically, the process might develop along the lines shown at the top of the opposite page.

The problem-solving process is illustrated by the experiences of an Oxfordshire school:

Which is the stickiest tape?

It was not known how long this topic would continue, or how the children would accept it. The idea behind the lesson was to get the children to *act* and *think scientifically* about a problem, rather than being concerned with the *content* of the work, or finding a *right* answer to the problem set. It was hoped that good *attitudes* be developed to scientific process, and that the children would acquire a number of scientific *skills*.

Experimental problems that arose in the work induced the children to develop *fair tests* and the children were encouraged to raise objections about their investigations, and then to try and put them right through discussion.

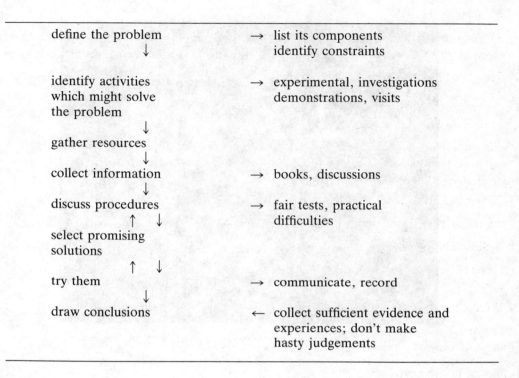

The children were also instructed to record their findings themselves. This proved very useful, as it raised their own problems through some groups obviously needing more gentle guidance than others.

Materials: A wide range and sizes of different types of sticky tapes, Sellotape, insulating tape, coloured tapes, Bandaid, etc. The rest of the equipment was suggested, built, or obtained by the children, depending on their particular line of investigation.

Aim: To try to get the children to think and act scientifically over the solving of an open-ended problem.

Duration: The work outlined actually lasted for three weeks and was continued in the year base, though in some cases the children had gained all they could from the work after two sessions.

Position in curriculum: This acted as an introduction to *materials* as a topic.

At the start of the lesson we discussed the various uses of sticky tapes and the question was put as to which one was the stickiest. The children offered their ideas as to how this could be tested, and these were discussed by the group as a whole. This was very useful as some children were able to envisage the problems that various methods would produce, and so these could be rectified by discussion. The children were then left to their own devices to carry out their own investigations and to record their own results.

Children's suggestions

1. Sticking pieces of tape to different materials, paper, wool, etc. then pulling off the tape, and using as a measure of stickiness the amount of material on the back of the tape.

The choice of adhesives and materials for modelling can be informed by problem-solving experience.

Problems arising:
(a) how could we standardise the length of the pull?
(b) how could we standardise the amount of pressure exerted in sticking the tape down?
(c) as far as the wool was concerned, how do you gauge the amount of material pulled off?

2. Immersing the tape, stuck to different materials, in water. They used silk, cotton, velvet, rayon, felt and skin, equal sizes of tape, and timed how long it took for the tape to become detached from the material. It was suggested that temperature may also have an effect on stickiness – and the experiment was repeated using hot water.
Problems arising:
(a) standardising size of tape
(b) keeping the temperature of the hot water steady to enable fair testing
(c) some tapes seemed unaffected by cold water.

3. Sticking the tape (equal lengths and widths) to the wall or side of the benches and hanging weights onto the tape until it pulled away.
Problems arising:
(a) how to arrange apparatus
(b) most tapes broke, but still remained sticking to the surface
(c) 'creep measurements' were too difficult.

4. Using tapes stuck to different surfaces with elastic bands, the elastic bands were pulled and, using a ruler, when the tape came away from the surface they measured the height of pull as a measurement of stickiness.
Problems arising:
(a) accuracy of recording (3 or 4 tests had to be done on each)
(b) standardising size of tape
(c) rubber band fatigue (one also had to use the *same* band with *every* test!)
(d) different surfaces had to be tried as it was pointed out that different tapes had different jobs.

Other methods were tried, many unsuccessful. It didn't matter; at least the children were able to see why their ideas didn't work.

All the way through these investigations children were encouraged to discuss and compare results and methods. This was a valuable start, the door was then opened for other similar investigations on strengths of different materials, glues, plastics, forces and elastic band investigations. Not really planned, but because of the interest generated, plus the benefit gained by the children, the other work was postponed until we had exhausted our ideas.

From *Middle School Science*. Oxfordshire LEA (1983)

TECHNOLOGY IN THE CLASSROOM

Science and CDT (craft, design and technology) have a unique relationship to each other and can serve each other in a very special way. Craft, design and technology can pose problems which can only be answered by scientific investigation, and CDT can provide an application for scientific concepts which would otherwise be abstract and theoretical. Craft, design and technology is a practical, problem-solving process that often results in 'working', three-dimensional products. While it uses simple, commonly available materials like card and paper, wood or metal, it can range into plastics – especially those cut or joined by heat – or other, more exotic materials as appropriate. This demands the informed use of a modest range of tools and these need to be introduced together with the appropriate safety precautions (chapter 9).

Perhaps a good way to consider approaching CDT is to plan what, ultimately, you would like to see your children building. *Ideas for Egg Races* compiled by the British Association for the Advancement of Science, is a source of ideas for all age ranges and *Problem Solving in Primary Schools*, published by Durham SATRO (Science and

'Technical Lego' is one way of introducing technology into the classroom.

Technology Regional Organisation), is an excellent introduction for primary school teachers to the problem-solving approach, providing many starting points.

It might be that you aim for ten- and eleven-year-olds making a motorised model, perhaps with lights, as a response to the problem 'make a vehicle to carry a maths book across a dark classroom'. To expect children to make it, from scratch, without a considerable amount of teacher help, is to anticipate the impossible.

Preparatory work will be needed through the preceding years. Break down the problem into individual tasks. There is the construction of the vehicle body, the choice and mounting of the power source, the appropriate gearing, control and direction systems and many others. Take each task and subdivide into skills; at every stage remember safety factors. Now, for each skill, list the necessary tools and materials. Now it is possible to consider the work that builds up the children's experience towards the chosen problem.

An example may make this clearer. The vehicle body will need to be constructed. A number of materials would be appropriate – wood, metal, plastic, even heavy card. Others would not be suitable (clay, fabric or plaster of Paris). Suppose wood to be most appropriate – sturdy, relatively easy to work, capable of taking a good finish. The task, then, is to build a wooden vehicle body. Appropriate experience could be provided by simple wood modelling – boats and aeroplanes for example. These, too, can be a response to a problem. (Find the 'fastest' boat shape along a plastic gutter test tank, pulled by a standard weight.) Now consider the skills – how can wood be marked out, cut, shaped, fixed and finished? Nothing can be assumed; it is no good giving young children tools and materials and expecting them to master all these techniques unaided. Take a single skill – cutting wood. A craft knife, for older children carefully supervised, might be appropriate to soft wood – balsa or obeche – while a junior hacksaw or a coping saw might be more suitable for larger-scale work. A good vice is essential. Safety advice must be stressed at every stage.

Only *now* can individual skills be related to the children's abilities. This is dependent upon their understanding that the wide range of available materials has a range of properties; that these properties determine the techniques necessary to handle the materials, and that each problem can be better met by one material rather than another.

All this may seem very discouraging. Two things need to be borne in mind. One is that much of the work is closely related to familiar science; another is that modest projects can be successfully completed without a vast range of tools and skills. Some excellent little magnetic games were devised for infants by a group of lower juniors – 'park the car in the garage'; 'arrange the features to make a face'. Older juniors produced simple quiz games using electrical circuits – 'join the question with the correct answer to make the bulbs light'. Children experienced at balsa work enthusiastically devised their best flying models using the standard wood provided to each.

At every stage, the scientific implications are clear. Every power source – clockwork, motor, twisted rubber band, electric motor, even model petrol or steam engine (care!!) has advantages and disadvantages. Chief among these considerations are power output, weight and controllability. Experiments with electric motors will raise questions of circuitry, control (what sort of switch is appropriate?) reversibility, and even variable speed (with commercial or home-made variable resistances). To apply electric motors successfully, they will have to be understood. A frequent source of frustration is the electric car incapable of carrying its own batteries – a microcosm of the real-life problem! Answers range from improved gearing, through models running on long wires, to models pursued by children crouching low over them to carry battery boxes!

The process of CDT

There is a generally recognised structure to the process of approaching CDT problems, not unlike a version of the 'Scientific Method'. First, it is vitally important to identify the problem accurately. If it is, for example, to build a 30 cm paper bridge capable of holding a 100 g mass at its centre without buckling, then it is no good using the wrong materials, bridging too narrow a gap, or only supporting the weight distributed across the bridge.

Next comes the 'ideas' stage. A number may be proposed, many may be appropriate – an electric burglar alarm could be operated by a moving door-handle, an opening door, a tripwire, a sensitive 'doormat', or a number of other triggers. To build all these as prototypes is clearly impractical, and a design stage follows when some of the proposed solutions are drawn out on paper – an acid test of their feasibility.

Some of these 'design books' can be among the most valuable pieces of language work the children complete in school. Because they are directly addressing two audiences – themselves, as they clarify their thoughts, and their teacher, as adviser and experienced guide – rather than completing cold and irrelevant paperwork, the design has an immediacy and importance not found in other communications. If the design is initially faulty, and neither designer nor teacher spot it, the construction may have no hope of success. Modification in the light of experience can be anticipated; but total failure is hard to take.

Only then comes the construction stage, when the chosen structure is made. At this point, all the previously learned skills are brought together to resolve practical problems. Lack of understanding of elementary scientific principles can undermine the project – one of us, for example, found a boy painstakingly wiring up a mapping game with bare, uninsulated wire. The idea of the game was to show the capital of an EEC country when that country's 'button' was pressed; as it was, every city in Europe came alight. Conversely, well-understood principles can be applied rewardingly – the reduction of friction, for example, can be achieved by fitting moving parts with wires and beads, or allowing dowel rods to turn in old pen-tops.

Finally, one must face up to the bitter truth – does the chosen solution really meet the problem? It will be necessary to return to the problem as defined, and to evaluate the response. It may be that the designers have to admit, albeit reluctantly, that the problem has not been solved. A lot has been learnt, and this valuable experience can be ploughed back into the 'ideas' stage, and a fresh solution found. More likely, the solution *has* been found, but a certain amount of modification and improvement has been necessary. Thus a group of juniors, faced with giving a slow parachute descent to a plastic soldier, applied their experience and observations of real parachutes, to cut and trim their prototypes until the toy descended without spinning or swinging. For a fuller account of this process, called by them 'Investigations; Invention; Implementation; and Evaluation', see the 1980 APU document, *Understanding Design and Technology*.

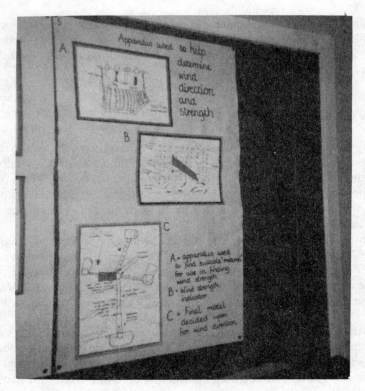

Several different approaches may need trying before a correct answer is found.

CDT and girls

There has been growing awareness that primary school girls are at least as interested and often more successful than boys in their science work. This may be one aspect of their greater relative maturity at primary age. Certainly there can be few teachers who still hold the opinion that science is strictly a subject for boys; and few girls who still believe that to express an interest in science is somehow unfeminine. Publications like *We Can Do It Now*! from the Equal Opportunities Commission draw attention to the high quality of work in science and technology by girls and boys of all ages. The DES publication *Science 5–16: A Statement of Policy* is generally known by the significant title 'Science for All'. Girls are no longer out of place in science laboratories; but they may not always handle craft tools in primary classrooms, or middle and secondary school workshops.

A lot can be done at primary level, before children's attitudes and opinions harden. Primary boys and girls, for example, are genuinely interested in younger children, their abilities, limitations and welfare. Both will respond to a project involving them in designing and constructing for small children – toys or games, for example, or safety locks which cannot be operated by a toddler. Similarly, they will enjoy an activity involving animals – again, a toy, or a cage allowing a discreet observation of small creatures.

The design and construction of commercial products appeals to both sexes. An examination of items as everyday as lunch boxes shows that basically their materials have been curved or flanged in such a way as to give them rigidity, while thought has been given to making them hygienic, possibly airtight and easy to clean. The construction of purpose-built packages is rewarding to girls and boys, and can follow the examination of the boxes used to pack fragile objects like china and Easter eggs.

Another popular project for girls and boys is the design and construction of musical instruments. Making the range of *percussion* instruments is a commonly tackled activity – from yoghourt-pot shakers to xylophones. Rubber-band instruments are popular, too, and a lot can be done with wind instruments, especially if you allow children to use the 'reed' end of an old recorder, or a brass instrument mouthpiece, as the basis of the design. These activities will appeal to all young children and may be less orientated to boys.

A wealth of such suggestions and ideas for involving girls in CDT work can be found in the publications of the Equal Opportunities Commission.

CDT and schools broadcasts

BBC Schools Radio first presented in the spring of 1983 a unit of five broadcasts called 'The Bicycle Programme'. This series, based on a Coventry Schools Project, has one teacher broadcast and four children's programmes, and is designed for tape recording and 'stop–start' use. It takes the bicycle as the starting point for work to heighten technological understanding. Road Safety Officers can provide a wealth of visual materials that will support work on and around road transport, and posters on bicycle maintenance are especially valuable.

BBC Schools Television has a service for primary teachers and pupils (5 programmes for each) called 'Up and Down the Hill'. It is ideal for stimulating 'egg-race' activities, as it deals with designing and constructing model vehicles.

Fitting CDT into topic work

CDTs place in primary education will almost certainly be seen as integrated with other work, rather than as a 'stand-alone' subject. It may actually stimulate other work, in that the other topics – geography, history, science or whatever – are related to the original CDT project. Work in CDT to produce a camera stand, for example, might lead to science work with photosensitive paper, and reference work on the early history of photography.

Alternatively, other subjects can lead *to* a related CDT topic. In some ways this is more difficult, since the teacher needs the experience to recognise where a good piece of CDT work can arise naturally from the children's interests. When you are already working within the constraints of limited resources, children's skills, and your own confidence, relevance to a given subject is a further demand upon the imagination. In reality, the connections can be either rather strained (a history of transport project resulting in an egg race) or fairly mundane (a Natural History study of birds leading to a roomful of bird trays).

Any CDT work will lead to a wealth of communication, spoken, written, drawn, and through models. It provides a practical application for mathematics and is of direct relevance for science studies.

REFERENCES

Department of Education and Science (1983) *Science in Primary Schools: A Discussion Paper by the HMI Science Committee*. London: HMSO.
Department of Education and Science (1985) *Science 5–16: A Statement of Policy*. London: HMSO.
Department of Education and Science (1980) APU *Understanding Design and Technology*. London: DES.
Everley, B. (1981) *We Can Do It Now*. Manchester. Equal Opportunities Commission.
British Association for the Advancement of Science (1983) *Ideas for Egg Races*. London.
Stoker, A. (ed) (1986) *Problem Solving in Primary Schools*. Durham: SATRO.

LEA Documents

Cheshire (1982) *Primary Science Guidelines*. p. 21.
Fife (1983) *Making Tracks* (No. 4) pp. 8–9. 'Science is fun', Elizabeth S. Thirkell.
Oxfordshire (1978) *Science Work in Primary Schools*. pp. 4–5. 'Vegetable dyes', Betty Cumming.
Oxfordshire (1983) *Middle School Science*. pp. 21–23. 'Which is the stickiest tape?'
Tameside (1980) *Primary Science: The Need for an Acceptable Structure*, Fred Ogden.
Warwickshire (1983) *Science Guidelines for Young Investigators*. pp. 16–17.
West Cumbria (1982) *Primary Science West*. p. 7.

Chapter 7

Developing Practical Activities in Schools

Several activities are suggested here that develop as 'mini-topics', with minimal science equipment and relatively few demands upon the teacher. It must be emphasised that pieces of work like these should not be seen in isolation, but rather in the context of a *whole-school policy* that recognises a hierarchy of skills and the development of attitudes. Age-ranges suggested for the activities are those learnt by experience; schools, and children, vary, and work that one group finds demanding on their manipulative and intellectual skills may not stretch another. Nevertheless these examples are, in the best possible way, 'foolproof', and may provide satisfactory starting-points for an uncertain teacher.

CANDLES

A whole book could be written about candles and their associated science, and indeed one title in the Macdonald 'Teaching Primary Science' series is an excellent example; but we can only provide an introduction to half a dozen simple activities that have been 'proved' in many classrooms.

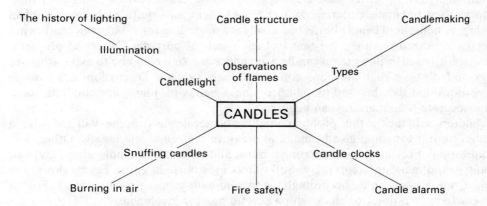

Figure 7.1   Developing a web of activities based on candles

Burning has a fascination for children, but it need not be fatal, or indeed dangerous, with a little care! Fundamental rules concerning tying back long hair, not carrying candles around and that only the teacher should light the candles are essential. In practice, children are very aware of the dangers – real and imagined – of flames, and take considerable care. A last word about fire safety after each activity can help to develop good long-term attitudes and habits.

Observing a candle

Michael Faraday wrote a lengthy treatise about the candle flame. Observe that melting wax forms a tiny pool in the cup or the tip of the candle, and the excess runs down the side, while burning gas appears first blue, and then shades of yellow and red. The wick bends over, and is consumed *outside* the flame, where it is exposed to air.

Children do not always recognise that they are left with *less* candle after burning. Weighing the stub, the trickles and runs, helps to persuade them. Candles for this, and other activities, should always be stable. Night-lights have natural stability, but cake candles are better for clocks, and can be supplied with a roll of Blu-Tack curled around the base. They are best pushed into aluminium cake cases. Water in the base of the cake case will add to the safety of the activity.

Candle structure

Candles are solid fuel, which is why they are safer for children than spirit or oil lamps. Carefully cutting a candle from end to end will demonstrate that the wick is continuous, and also that it is curved. Only the wax holds the wick out straight. The curved wick, invented in 1825, slows the rate with which the wick is consumed, and so the speed with which the candle burns. The same-sized candle can last longer.

Candle clocks

Traditionally, King Alfred had a hand in inventing candle clocks. Whatever their history, they fascinate children, and can lead them into quite elaborate problem solving. A household candle burns too slowly for rewarding tests, but cake candles are effective, and reasonably consistent in their speed of burning. Overhead projector pens (spirit-based) will write on candle wax, and a first step could be to mark arbitrary rings and observe that they are consumed, one by one. Discussion will lead to suggestions that they be used to measure time, when, with junior age children, some quite accurate time marking can begin.

Children will tackle this problem in three general ways. Some will measure a candle, burn it for some given time, and measure the remaining length. Others will avoid formal measuring by comparing a burnt and an unburnt candle after (say) two minutes, and marking accordingly. Still others may burn an entire candle down and then divide a new candle accordingly (a 'five-minute-candle', for example). For all these activities, a timer or clock with a second hand is invaluable.

Candle alarms

From the candle clock, it is a short step to a candle alarm. A pin pushed into a candle holds washers by a thread. When the candle burns down to the pin, it falls out, releasing the washers to rattle down onto a tin tray. Other groups may simply knot a thread round the candle – beware smouldering threads! More sophisticated is a 'progressive alarm': Support a household candle horizontally over a tin tray, and drape washers along it on threads, at intervals. As the candle burns the washers fall.

Types of candles

An attractive display can be made from a variety of candles – plain, coloured, moulded, and decorated. Their origins and uses are all of interest. Candles *can* be made using kits from craft shops, and colour and decoration can be added, but all these activities need considerable heat, and must be demonstrated by a teacher. A few candle factories and craft workshops may welcome visits.

Candlelight and the history of lighting

You might like to explore, practically, the different types of lamps that have been used in history. Various fats will burn, usually with a smoking flame. You can dip and make rush lamps. Tiny amounts of spirit or oil can be used to make lamps, and different wicks can be investigated. Almost any museum will provide examples of lighting through the ages. The connections with the festival of Diwali and other festivals of light can be developed.

Snuffing candles

While blowing fans flames by providing extra air, a sharp breath carries the burning vapour away from a candle or match and so puts it out. That is, the heat is blown away from the source of fuel; compare dynamiting burning oil wells! Children have some difficulty in understanding the role of air in burning, and may need several examples of how deprivation of air extinguishes a flame. Experience has shown that the relationship between (say) the capacity of jam jars put over candle flames, and the length of time before they extinguish, is not a simple one. Factors that come into play include candle height, rate of burning, the shape of the jar (which may prevent circulation) and the extinguishing effects of carbon dioxide. Similarly, the way water can rise to take the place of consumed oxygen is an abstraction that young children find difficult, should you choose to show this classic test.

Fire safety

A vital part of all this work is to engender simple ideas about fire safety. If you are uncertain about tackling this subject, invite an officer from the local fire service. His visit may well be spectacular; it will certainly be sobering.

For other ideas on using candles, see Irene Finch's excellent book *Nature Study and Science*.

COLOUR SEPARATION

Analysis by colour separation is fascinating and attractive. It links well with work on paper or food (see figure 7.2). The separation of colours as described here is called chromatography, but there is little need to bother children with the word; more important is *how* it works, which is, simply, that some soluble dyes and pigments move faster through paper, when carried along by a solvent (e.g. water), than others.

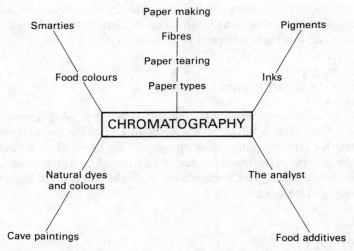

Figure 7.2   Developing a web of activities based on chromatography

Paper types and characteristics

Paper is the stock-in-trade of school. A collection of paper samples – tracing paper, blotting paper, drawing paper, paper towels, and so on – can be related to their function, and an interesting chart drawn up. Paper towels, for example, may be rough textured, tear unevenly, are heavily pigmented, but highly absorbent. Typing paper is very strong (one sheet, looped into a tube, will support a child hanging from a pair of broom handles), smooth-surfaced, and non-absorbent. Whatever we may think of their adequacy for drying hands, the fact is that if paper towels were larger or smoother, they would be cumbersome, expensive, and more difficult to dispense. If typing paper were softer, it would produce smudged print.

An investigation of how they tear will show that papers have a fibrous structure; in newspapers, many of these fibres lie parallel, facilitating straight tearing. Loose structured papers like blotting paper tear unevenly; they have masses of air spaces that absorb water – or ink. Greaseproof paper has crushed fibres that mat together so closely that they give a translucent, grease-resistant surface to the paper. Tests will show that it is not waterproof.

An interesting test is to cut two equal squares of newspaper and support them horizontally to explore their degree of 'droop', and hence of strength. Clamp the edges of the squares between a couple of rulers, one square with its print parallel to the rulers, the other with the print at right angles. One square 'droops' more than the other; children's explanations for this phenomenon range from the effect of draughts to the weight of print or pictures. A hand lens will show that the linear fibres give the relative stiffness to the paper. A drop of ink on the paper will form an *oval* blot rather than round, again because of the fibres.

A food processor will be found enormously helpful in paper-making; use it to make a suspension of soft, fibrous paper in water, and add boiled starch. Spread the resultant sticky mass across a fine meshed frame by dipping the frame into it. You can make your own frame using nylon mesh, or buy a commercial one. After letting the liquid drip off, turn the paper over onto an absorbent cloth. You can stack several sheets like this, with absorbent cloths between the layers. Press or weigh down your stack, and then peel it apart, letting the paper dry thoroughly before use.

Separating inks

Bottled inks (except Indian ink, which is not water-based) are made of one or more pigments which can be separated using loose-textured paper. Filter paper is frequently recommended, but other papers – blotting, or newsprint – are cheaper, and nearly as good. Put a single small drop of a good quality fountain pen ink in the centre of a piece of paper, and drip water on to it very slowly – a drinking straw will do for this, but plastic droppers can be bought from chemists. Do not hurry this stage – the ring of water should not grow faster than the ring of ink. As the blot grows, so the individual pigments of the ink will separate (unless, as with most *blue* inks, there is only one pigment!) Quink permanent black ink, for example gives a succession of concentric rings ranging from blue to yellow. The further the blot spreads, the clearer the separation.

The process can be automated by making two cuts into the centre of the paper to produce a 'mushroom'. Put this on top of a jam-jar, put a tiny drop of ink at the top of the 'stalk', and dip the end of stalk in water. The water will rise and the ink will separate.

Less paper is used by cutting it into fingers, and putting the ink drop close to the tip of the finger. Dip the finger, blot down, into water. Bulldog clips will suspend the paper, with the 'blot' just above the water level, or you can simply fold the top of the paper over the edge of the receptacle.

Good quality water-based felt pens (Berol, for example) will produce the same effects, and lead on to other investigations. A simple matrix can list the available Berol felt pen colours down one side, and pigments across the top. Which pens contain which pigments? Can you identify a pen given its chromatogram? Can you mix two pen colours and then separate them?

An enjoyable extension into 'forensic' science is to 'find the writer of a poison-pen letter' – or a Valentine card if you prefer more innocent anonymity! Collect several water-based pens of different makes, label them for identification, and use one to write a short message in secret, and then cut the message into pieces. The children run the pieces as chromatograms alongside tests on the suspect pens. Which blots – which patterns – match? Which pen wrote the message?

Separating food colours

Official lists can be bought of the approved food colours, and a number of current publications will also help you to decipher the E numbers on the food you eat (and may also query whether these chemicals do us any good). Bottled food colours can be bought in a wide range from grocery shops and chain stores, or in an unlimited variety from specialist cake-decorators, but three or four colours are enough to start with.

Running a chromatogram will show whether the food colours are made up of one or more dyes; a couple of colours can be deliberately mixed, and given to children to separate, with 'pure' colours for comparison and identification. Up to three colours can be identified in this way, but where they share dyes they can be confused easily.

The classic 'food activity' is the separation and identification of the colours of the candy coats on the chocolate beans marketed as Smarties. These are manufactured in a range of colours, and the colours – red, yellow, two shades of brown, and so on – are made up from a number of identifiable dyes. The dyes can be extracted by simply dropping water gently onto a sweet laid on a sheet of absorbent paper. (Licking the Smartie first softens the candy coat.) When all the dye has been washed out, the Smarties are grey and unattractive, but that seldom prevents their being eaten!

A simple matrix can chart colour against dyes; which is the most commonly-used colour? If you then make the assumption that all the dyes are used in equal quantities, it is possible to calculate how many arbitrary 'barrels' of the various dyes (red, yellow, and so on, and a rich red-brown colour one child dubbed burgundy) will be needed by the chocolate factory.

Grass, leaves, and many fruits and vegetables can have their colour extracted by crushing, and be run as a chromatogram. These natural dyes – like those of blackberries and red cabbage – can be very strong and attractive.

There are wide curriculum links here, with dyeing and colouring, and the use of natural colours for painting. Connections could be made with the spectrum, the colours of light, and with eyesight. A number of books deal with 'colour' as a specific topic; a rich diversity of ideas can be found by referring to the index of 'Science 5–13'.

Chromatography and analysis

The application of chromatography in the analysis of foodstuffs, in ensuring that only permitted colours are being used and that the foods comply with regulations, may interest some children. It will certainly be news to many that someone tries to ensure the safety of the foods we eat; and a discussion of shelf life, sell-by dates, and storage times in refrigerators and freezers can lead into a major study on food storage and preservation.

The analysis of pathological samples to help diagnose illness is not relevant to small children, but teachers could note it as another example of the application of chromatography.

Analysts use other solvents as well as water but experience has shown that only water is practical in a primary classroom.

MAGNETISM

Magnets are popular with children and teachers alike, yet few seem to get beyond the experience of 'playing' with magnets, and fewer still apply that experience to a practical use.

The wealth of experience and understanding that can be gained from activities with magnets can be appreciated by examining this list, which is by no means exhaustive:

- Magnets can be found in many different shapes and sizes
- Magnets attract certain metals
- The centres of attraction can be found by hanging pins or paperclips along the magnet's length
- Since magnets attract many objects, the only true test of a magnet is repulsion by another magnet
- When two magnets are joined, pole to pole, they behave as a single magnet
- A magnet, supported but allowed to move (on a floating cork or in a paper stirrup) will be affected by bringing another magnet close
- A magnet supported as above, may align with the North–South line of the earth
- Magnets are surrounded by a force field. This field declines with distance
- The force field can be demonstrated by sprinkling iron filings on a paper over a magnet
- A permanent record can be made by sandwiching the iron filing pattern with damp blotting paper; a 'rust' picture results after a few days
- The effect of magnets over a distance can be demonstrated by clamping a strong magnet over a table: tie a paperclip to a thread, and put it to the magnet. Now pull it gently away from the magnet, towards the table. A gap appears; tape the thread to the table to maintain the gap
- Repeat the 'Indian Rope Trick' as above. Pass objects through the gap. Some pass through without disturbing the paper clip, some do not
- Make a magnet by stroking a piece of soft wire, end to end, with one end of a magnet
- Test the new magnet with iron filings
- Destroy the new magnet's power by heating, or banging
- Recognise the connections between magnetism and electricity by putting a small magnetic compass in a loop of electric wire, and passing a low-voltage current through with a battery
- Make a temporary magnet by wrapping a suitable 'core' – preferably iron, since steel will become permanently magnetic – in a coil of insulated wire, and passing a low-voltage current through
- Test your temporary magnet with small metal objects. Do not leave it wired up; it gets hot, and runs the battery flat

– Demonstrate one possible explanation of magnetism by sweeping a strong magnet across a group of small 'mapping' compasses. They tend to develop a common polarity
– Make a crane or breakdown truck, and wire it up with a temporary magnet. Wire in an 'operating light' to protect the battery from total discharge
– Make a magnet game using washers, a board, and magnet on sticks
– Make some small boats with a metal 'cargo', affected by magnets
– Fix up a couple of model soldiers with magnetic bases, so that they 'fight' or 'flee'
– Suspend a lodestone. It should face North/South
– Examine both cheap magnetic compasses, and the more expensive, oil-filled 'Silva' type. Note the advantages of the latter
– Examine a luminous compass, intended for night use
– Identify the compass points in relation to your classroom or school. Mark them clearly in your room
– Identify the intermediate compass points – NW, SE, etc. mark those
– Lay a simple trail or treasure hunt using compass directions
– Use two ring magnets on a wooden stick to demonstrate how trains, or loads, can be carried on a magnetic force field.

These, together with the statements listed under 'Ideas' in chapter 1 of this book, can be used in the card game you will find described there. By putting these statements onto cards and organising them into a hierarchical list – or a branching web – it is possible to plan the ages and stages at which they would be most appropriately taught. The topic of magnetism presents a wealth of work and opportunity for discovering that is seldom explored in the primary school. There are many possible approaches to ordering this work but one method is to ask:

1. Are these new ideas, or simply skills?
2. Are the new ideas actually true, or are they half truths and fallacies?
3. Which ideas and/or skills need to be understood or mastered before later ones can be tackled?
4. Can the work be ordered on that basis?
5. Which ideas and skills are most appropriate to which age and ability ranges?
6. Can the work be extended into technological applications?

Far from losing its exciting play dimension, work on magnetism will be given a fresh lease of life by this careful planning.

A SENSE OF TASTE

Work on the five major senses is perennially popular, combining as it does immediate relevance to young children (who never cease to be interested in themselves) with a variety of simple and reliable tests. A further dimension to the subject that always proves interesting is work on sensory deprivation; hence the attraction of stories about people like Helen Keller and Louis Braille.

It is generally true to say however, that it is the 'star' senses – hearing and sight – that receive the major attention. Some senses (the kinaesthetic sense, for example, which enables us to recognise where our limbs and bodies are in space) are seldom considered at all. And 'lesser' senses, like taste, are frequently glossed over. Yet there is a wealth of work that can be tackled on this subordinate sense, teaching us more about ourselves and others.

Taste and smell

These two are very closely related. Smell makes food attractive; some smells are so strong that we can 'taste' them. Children can explore their skills at identifying food by taste alone when they are holding their noses, or when they have a heavy cold. Who is better at identifying food blindfold, an adult smoker or non-smoker?

Similarly, taste can be related to sight. The unattractiveness of 'blue food' can be confirmed by colouring mashed potato or milk. Does instant mash actually taste different if it is dyed with food colour? All mashed potato looks pretty disgusting when coloured, in fact. A far more attractive range of coloured foods can be made with a little preparation – blancmange, for example, or arrowroot and sugar, with added food colour. Either taste better than instant mash.

Identifying tastes

Another popular activity is the identification of tastes, blindfold. Does texture help? Does smell? Can texture and smell clues be eliminated? Can we present 'pure' tastes?

A couple of problems arise here because some particularly strong tastes – peppermint, for example, or onion – are to a large extent the result of their pungent smells. And further, so much of our food is processed and flavoured that onion is far more likely to be identified by children as 'beefburger', or vanilla as 'icecream' that a range of possible 'correct' answers has to be allowed.

In all these tasting activities, special precautions need to be taken to ensure that the foods are palatable and safe, and that the risk of spreading germs (by, for example, using a common spoon) is prevented. *Children must also be discouraged from random, unsupervised tasting, at school or at home, of course.*

A further, moral, dilemma is presented by our use of foods just for testing, in a starving world. Samples should be kept small, waste minimised, and the opportunity taken to make this aspect a positive teaching point.

Classifying tastes

Ultimately, most tastes can be identified as a combination of four – bitter, sour, salt and sweet. These correspond with four types of sense organ, scattered but found in distinct areas on the tongue. Using lemon juice, instant coffee, sugar syrup, and salt solution, it is possible, and important to other work, to identify these four tastes, and ensure that children are quite certain which is which. It is interesting to explore the effect of heat on these tastes. Do they have a heightened smell and/or taste, when they are warm? Again, their strength can be explored by testing them in various dilutions.

Try a tablespoon of instant coffee in a teacup of warm water, a teaspoon, a half teaspooon, and so on. It is usually necessary to try the weaker solutions first – the stronger tastes dull the senses to the weaker ones.

Tastes and people

A survey of favourite tastes can be revealing. If you can ask a wide range of ages, you can find a general trend to popular tastes at particular ages; sweet, perhaps, among small children; salty in the early teens; savoury in middle age. Do elderly people like peppermint? Do adults who smoke heavily lose their sense of taste?

An opportunity for multicultural work arises here, especially if your children come from a wide range of home backgrounds. We have been fortunate in the parents of our pupils: Asian parents have provided chapattis and samosas; Cypriot mothers have prepared sweet honey cakes; an Iranian parent let us try 'real' natural yoghourt. A wealth of opportunity to taste, test, and explore the food of other countries and cultures can be exploited to introduce children to differences and similarities. Celebration and festival meals are interesting, too; few have the wealth of meaning and symbols present in the Jewish Passover meal – the boiled egg, horseradish, salt water and so on all have a deep significance.

Tongue 'maps'

The tip, base, centre, and edges of the tongue all have concentrations of taste buds. For most children, these concentrations are sensitive to a particular taste at a particular location. If you apply drops of sugar-water, with a cotton bud, to these areas of the tongue, you should find that one is specifically sensitive to each major taste. Great care should be taken to ensure that there is no cross-infection from child to child; cotton buds cannot be re-used. (You can make your own for these tests, very cheaply, from cotton wool and pieces of plastic drinking-straw.)
Once again, it is essential to ensure that children do not get the idea that they can safely taste unknown substances unless you have approved them.

'MINIBEASTS'

The term 'minibeast' was coined by the 'Science 5–13' team to describe all those creepy-crawly animals brought to school to shock and intrigue others. Things of beauty – like ladybirds and woolly caterpillars – are treasured, while things that frighten or disgust – slimy, yellow-and-black slugs, for instance – may be seen as enemies to be destroyed. Minibeasts make a fascinating study in themselves; but it is in the development of children's attitudes to living creatures that they have a major contribution to make. And it is as an unexpected gift – usually in a matchbox or jamjar – that they first put in their appearance in the classroom as a rule. No starting point could be more spontaneous and intriguing. If the creature is to be kept, even temporarily, then information about its habitat and food must be answered and reference books come into their own.

Many minibeasts will successfully complete their life cycle in captivity, given the right conditions. Snails are easy to keep, needing damp soil in an aquarium or covered plastic lunch box and a diet of vegetable matter. Woodlice are easy, too, using the shelter of rotting wood, and eating grated carrot. Ladybirds are attractive and popular in the summer, but need to be fed on live aphids. A 'lemonade bottle cage' is best for ladybirds; few children know that the adults can fly. Worms can be kept in a home-made wormery, constructed from two small sheets of double-glazing plastic (Crystalite) sandwiching a simple wooden frame filled with damp earth. Thick rubber bands will hold the whole device together; it should be kept upright and covered. Fallen leaves put on the surface of the soil will help feed the worms.

Alternatively, minibeasts can be introduced to the classroom as a topic starter. Blowfly larvae, sometimes known as 'gentles' or less attractively as maggots, are far less appalling to children than they are to some adults. They can be bought, in season, from fishing shops, and provide lively and responsive small creatures for some simple and harmless experiments on animal behaviour. Gentles are the larvae stage of the blowfly, an active, tapering white worm, which crawls vigorously, and, after a short and hungry life, pupates as a brown chrysalis from which the adult fly emerges. The pointed end of the worm is its head. A few children will not handle gentles at any price, and those who will *must* wash their hands afterwards. Plastic disposable spoons (kept expressly for minibeasts) are a good way of moving the creatures.

The behaviour of gentles can be related to their preference of environment – dark, damp places. If you place the creatures in front of a lamp – a torch will be ideal – they respond by crawling rapidly away from it. This can be tested as an objective experiment by taking a number of gentles, say, ten, and putting them, one by one, on a cross marked on a sheet of paper. Lay your torch to shine along the paper horizontally, and 'track' the minibeast with a pencil. This is easier if you use squared paper and mark the places where the gentle crosses a line. When the creature finally crawls off the paper, retrieve it and put it in an empty pot – its 'run' is over. If you now join your marks, you have the track of the creature. By using a new gentle every time, you confirm that the behaviour is that of the *species* and not of a single individual. This precaution is one that should be discussed with the children – and ideally, drawn from them – before the activity is attempted.

When ten gentles have been tried, the pattern should be apparent. All the creatures flee from the light, a response that can be linked with hiding from predators and from the drying effects of the sun. (In fact a careful examination of the gentles will show that they have two dark spots on their tail. These are light receptors, not 'eyes', and they do not *see* with them, they only recognise a light source and naturally try to balance the light falling on each receptor. This automatically results in movement away from the light source.)

A second test is concerned with choice of substrate. Using a 'choice chamber' ten test gentles are observed to see to which substrate they choose to move. Use plasticine to make a circular wall on a board, and then divide the disc up into chambers with plasticine walls. Leave the middle open, so that from it, the creatures have access to – and equal choice of – the three or four chambers. Now prepare a number of substrates

– dry, damp, and wet sawdust. Perhaps a chamber should be left empty, as a 'control'? Ten gentles, introduced to the centre of the choice chamber, can be allowed a given time to choose their preferred conditions.

But do children recognise the importance of excluding other influences? Would the creatures respond differently if the light – with an effect that has already been recognised – is excluded? If the creatures are placed in the choice chamber, and a sheet of card is used to keep it dark, do they react differently? The numbers choosing the various substrates with and without light can be counted and compared.

Some groups of children have moved on to giving food choice to the gentles. Flour, bran, and other dry foods – in tiny quantities – have been placed in the choice chambers. These children have claimed that their results have been conclusive – but what do *you* find?

Somewhat more attractive than gentles are elegant stick insects. Most commonly obtained varieties eat privet leaves, but care must be taken not to throw out eggs with droppings, or the tiny young with stripped food plants. Stick insects have interesting behaviour, some of which enables them to camouflage themselves most successfully; they 'quiver', for example, when the leaves are gently blown, or if they fall to the ground. Their slow, hesitant advance enables them to move without (presumably) attracting unwelcome attention from predators.

The third approach to minibeasts is the organisation of a study of a convenient outdoor area. If there is nothing else to be learnt from such a study, it is that no environment is completely without life; indeed, once you have learned how to look, outdoor environments, however unpromising, will provide a wealth of life to study. Older walls have lichens and animals living in the cracks; an untended corner filled with grasses and weeds can also contain a variety of small creatures, and discarded stones and wood have their own population of minibeasts. With a little planning and care, an organised minibeast hunt can be enormously successful.

Try gently beating bushes in summer. Shake or lightly beat leafy bushes over a newspaper, and collect the creatures dislodged. A 'pitfall trap' in a neglected corner can be successful. Sink a yoghourt pot, or the plastic pots that chemists store tablets in, into the ground. Cover it to prevent it filling with rain, using a slate, file, or piece of bark. This should be slightly raised on a few stones, so that animals can wander into the pot, fall, and be trapped. Nocturnal creatures can be caught in this way. Open the trap *every day*, and remove it altogether when the activity is over, filling the hole.

Areas of open water have their own fauna, which can be collected using ordinary kitchen sieves, and are best seen by shaking them gently onto white plastic trays or plates. *Children should be discouraged from visiting open water, however shallow, alone; and the water must never be tasted.*

Small creatures can be moved about using disposable spoons, soft paintbrushes, or 'pooters' as described in the equipment appendix.

Collecting for collecting's sake should be discouraged; once the first flush of excitement about the variety of the finds is past, attempt to relate what is discovered to the habitat; and consider the ways the animals and plants are adapted to survive, and thrive, in their environment.

REFERENCES

Faraday, M. (1962) *Chemical History of a Candle*. New York: Collier.
Finch, I. I. (1971) *Nature Study and Science*. London: Longman.
Schools Council (1975) *Candles*. London: Macdonald.
Schools Council (1980). Learning Through Science Project. *Learning Through Science: Formulating a School Policy, With an Index to Science 5–13*. London: Macdonald.

Chapter 8

Organising your Classroom for Primary Science

One of the major objections to starting or developing primary science is that the subject sits uneasily on class teachers' 'style'. They find it hard to combine with an 'integrated' or a 'classwork' approach, or whatever style they have evolved. The special demands of science teaching seem to clash with their usual class planning. Teachers have been known to use the organisational difficulties of science as an excuse to ignore the subject.

The situation is further complicated if some specialist teaching is available – in middle schools for example – and they are attempting to integrate the science with the classwork of their once-a-week class 'at a distance'.

It is worth while examining the various organisational methods open to both class teachers and specialists. Some adapt easily to 'shared classes', 'setting' and other teaching situations; others do not. Ultimately the choice must be made by the class teacher facing the problem. Only they can know all the constraints. But in making this critical decision, it is worth bearing a number of criteria in mind. Apply them to the methods suggested here. How do they measure up?

CRITERIA TO BEAR IN MIND

(1) How demanding?

Some techniques, while apparently superbly effective, can be unreasonably demanding of teacher time and energy. If you find yourself running from place to place, or beseiged by frustrated children, then the learning cannot be at its best. Beware hectic activity at the expense of 'crisis management'.

Ideally, as we all know, children should all be stretched without frustration. Similarly, teachers should be working hard without being frayed to the point of exhaustion. A little thought on the provision of equipment, on the presentation of ideas, techniques and safety precautions, and on the system of checking and recording, will save a great deal of wasted energy.

(2) How effective?

Most methods of teaching primary science will motivate children. With motivation comes interest and involvement. Care must be taken, though, to ensure that the activities are relevant and appropriate to the age group of the children concerned. While this is relatively easy with teaching experience, it is not always possible to ensure progression – that concepts and techniques, key ideas and practicalities are taught in a logical and hierarchical way. This is one of the criticisms of some of the methods described below.

(3) How efficient?

Any method that it is difficult to control and regulate will not be efficient. A careful balance must be struck between (say) an open-ended investigation and teacher direction. One of us remembers spending long hours as a small boy, trying to control an electric car without either wires or a radio transmitter. A few words on the need for a conductor for low-voltage electricity transmission would have saved a lot of frustration.

(4) How stimulating?

A good piece of science should involve and motivate. Even an indifferent practical activity can often, apparently, achieve that purpose. But we should be looking for science work that genuinely stimulates a need to report and to record. The widest variety of recording techniques may be appropriate, of course; writing, drawing, tape-recording, photographing, model making, and on many occasions, the experiment itself or its results, displayed so that the observer can clearly understand what took place and what was achieved. Some activities – e.g. photographic and darkroom experiments – lend themselves perfectly to this technique.

(5) How appropriate?

The method to be used has to be matched both to what is being taught, and to the children who are learning. Some activities are ideally suited to simultaneous group activities, especially when a wide variety of related results may be produced. A whole class, for example, may do work concerning snails, choosing their own techniques of recording the shape, structure, and movement of the creature. Later, all the results can be compared to see which most clearly expresses the essential nature of the creature, and of the children's experience. But equally important as matching to content is matching to children. It would not be surprising if a class experienced in whole-class 'chalk and talk' teaching had difficulties in adapting immediately to a circus of experiments. They have had no experience of organising themselves, of moving purposefully, of finding the materials they need, or even of clearing up efficiently. They will need a gradual introduction to this style of working and clear direction, at first, to prevent chaos. On the other hand, certain techniques can, of themselves, produce valuable learning. On in-service courses, for example, the authors plan varied practical work for teachers that overtly introduces them to new ideas and processes, and organise it so that, more covertly, they gain experience of working in different ways, alone or with colleagues, on one long-term study or a series of short-term experiments, and so on.

(6) How specialised?

Often this is a decision for the head teacher or curriculum leader, in consultation with staff. It arises particularly in middle schools, where specialist staff can work in purpose-built rooms in some cases. Is this appropriate? Various answers could be given, but commonly the degree of specialist teaching increases with the maturity of the pupils, so that younger children experience classroom work, and older children use an equipped laboratory. But it might be appropriate to work in classrooms throughout, with the specialist as peripatetic 'adviser', collaborator, or substitute teacher.

(7) How structured?

As mentioned elsewhere, Roy Richards, in planning with colleagues the 'Learning through Science' cards, was always keen on allowing what he called elbow-room. Thus, although much of the work-card is fairly prescriptive, a proportion is open-ended, allowing pupils to explore their own ideas and curiosity. This highlights a major constraint when considering method – how much structure will be needed in the work?

The nature of this structure is nicely illustrated by the British Association 'Young Investigator' Bronze Awards, which are presented for success in any of three styles of investigation. The *first* describes very precisely the nature of the exercise, the apparatus to be used, and the way to observe and record results. The *third* presents only a problem – 'you need 36 straws, rubber bands, a marble, and some sellotape. Build as high a structure as you can to support a marble as high as possible. Say what you did.' The *intermediate* style gives more advice and help, but with plenty of 'elbow-room'. Some styles are appropriate to some children in some circumstances – others to others. To present inexperienced children with the marble activity without help and support is to invite frustration.

To precisely prescribe (beyond obvious safety precautions) children's activities when they first experience electric circuits is to invite trouble; within the constraints of safety and commonsense, a free request to 'Get the bulb to light' is possibly better.

Within the physical constraints of room, resources, teacher confidence and experience, these seven criteria, and others, will help you to determine whether your method is really the 'best' one. While not exhaustive, the list below outlines many of the methods open for science teaching. Note that the methods to which our children will commonly be subjected in the secondary school may not be so varied.

Whole-class lessons
{
'Chalk and talk'
Vicarious experience
Demonstration lessons
Whole-class activities
}

Group work
{
Assignments
Integration
Thematic
Circus of experiments
}

Individual work
The 'Science Table' (and the Craigie Kit)
Team Teaching

WHOLE-CLASS LESSONS

'Chalk and talk'

This is still a common teaching method, and it has advantages for the teacher (and disadvantages for the learners). Whatever teaching technique is used, there may well be a period of 'chalk and talk' to set the scene or to draw conclusions together; the maximum effectiveness of this method can be achieved by close attention to the use of language – see, for example, chapter 2, or, for much more detail, the ASE book *Language in Science*. Preparation work is minimised, of course, and classroom organisation is straightforward but, perhaps, it is increasingly quite demanding on the teacher. Teachers can no longer anticipate a placid and receptive audience – if they ever could. The maintenance of children's attention is very demanding, and effecting their involvement in true dialogue is a considerable skill. The larger the group the less certain the degree of involvement. Nevertheless, there are economies to be made by this approach in, say, task-setting or drawing general conclusions. And there are examples of very good practice in this traditional method; the gathering of infant children around a teacher, for example, which inspired the production of large discussion books for the Longman 'Scienceworld' series.

It is the children who may feel the limitations of this method. While it is, of course, easy to ensure progression, there is no guarantee that each step in that progression is being grasped by every pupil – indeed it seems most unlikely. Absence, lack of attention or understanding, can break the sequence, however skilfully presented – and individuals at both ends of the ability range are likely to feel a degree of frustration, for very different reasons. The method also goes against the very nature of science as a practical activity offering first-hand experience. Its use in the science field is somewhat limited, but it should not be discounted.

Vicarious experience

Both the BBC and Independent Television offer excellent primary science series; the BBC has good radio examples as well. A number of companies offer science-based videorecordings and movie films for hire or free loan; others present filmstrips and slide sets. There are even science cassette tapes, which claim to teach science by story, and there are microcomputer programs.

The common factor in all these resources is that they teach at second-hand, whether or not they go on to encourage emulation by first-hand experience (and most of them do). There is not space to review them all here, but it is worth considering one or two of the more notable examples of which we have personal experience.

Both the television series currently available are quite excellent. Television has several valuable dimensions, of course, which make it able to complement, rather than substitute for, first-hand experience. Television cameras can visit factories, laboratories, and workshops. Many workplaces *will* allow personal visits, of course, and some – potteries, for example – are especially geared to visitors. Others, like newspaper offices and presses, will accept visitors by appointment, and one or two workplaces – a disused coalmine is one – have been adapted to visitors' centres now that their useful life is over. But the remarkable processes that go towards manufacturing, packing, and testing everyday articles are rarely seen by the public, least of all schoolchildren, who will commonly find that the lower age limit excludes them, understandably, from all but the very safest workplace visits. So films of the manufacture and testing of clothing, or the processing of canned pineapple (both to be seen in current 'Science Workshop' programmes) are all the more valuable because they show activities otherwise inaccessible to our children.

Secondly, television can introduce us to unusual guests. Visitors to classrooms are not uncommon, of course; Road Safety Officers, police and firemen, train drivers and parents with unusual work or hobbies are general; but a 'dowser' finding water (successfully) with a forked twig, or the 'fastest window cleaner in the world' are unusual. People practising their skills are always fascinating – it is part of the appeal of 'holes in the road' – and children are always engrossed by guests whose work – or hobby – is closely related to the programme's subject.

Even more engrossing to children are other children. You can experience a noticeable heightening of attention and interest when the programmes go – as they commonly do – to other schools to watch children busy with science activities. This is doubly valuable – reinforcing the programme's subject matter and giving the children ideas about the organisation and direction of their own practical work by example.

Many teachers will recall the 'Science All Around' series produced for some years by the BBC. These excellent programmes found and exploited the science content in everyday surroundings. When they were superseded, the BBC wisely used the same series adviser, Irene Finch, and produced an excellent weekly programme, 'Science Workshop'. One of the problems with 'Science All Around' for class teachers was its weekly nature. A week was hardly enough for adequate follow-up. Before you had investigated one topic, another was introduced. It was just too rich.

Science Workshop overcomes this problem by producing its programmes in pairs. The first of each pair (the core programme) introduces a topic. A second (development) programme follows a week later, extending the subject. Taken as a

Books support primary science programmes.

whole, the series provides a science course with related practical work (the importance of which is emphasised). This practical work has been carefully chosen to be 'safe and suitable'.

Another advantage of the series is that it covers *two* years, which is especially helpful if you teach a mixed-age-group class or for other reasons you may have the same class for more than one year. There are 12 topics in each year, and two children's books complementing the series – Red and Blue. (The Longman publication *Nature Study and Science* which can be used for any science work, or for background on the series, is recommended.) The whole nature of the series reflects attention to detail – in a hierarchy of science skills, for example, and emphasis on classroom discussion. The series is an excellent one for junior children from nine to eleven.

Complementary to 'Science Workshop' is the Independent Television product 'Starting Science', for children of eight years and over, made by Central Television. The early programmes had a lively, almost circus-like style about them, and many bold ideas, including poetry and aesthetic experience, related to the science themes. The newer, remade programmes are less adventurous, but perhaps more effective. They currently comprise fourteen programmes, presented fortnightly, to allow for practical work as 'Science Workshop', and on broad termly themes of 'Ourselves', 'Transport' and 'Design and Technology'. The approach is a problem-solving one, and the aim is enjoyment of science activities and the shaping of good attitudes. 'Starting Science' does not stand alone, but should be used to enrich a school science theme. Two books supplement the series and are available from Books for Students Ltd. in Leamington Spa. Current topics in the programmes include 'Car Design' and 'Mysteries', the latter taking the work to the borders of understanding and towards the inexplicable.

The programmes meet the criteria of valuable vicarious experience: one, for example, on sensory deprivation, effectively demonstrates what it must be like to be deaf. They also contain excellent sequences in school – often of very ambitious work (take, for instance, a programme on energy where a bicycle is used to drive a dynamo, work power tools and a pump) and engage children's fascinated attention. They are short, sharp and stimulating. The teachers' notes presented with the series are excellent, showing lots of acceptable practical ideas arising from each programme. A completely new Independent Television series, 'Science – Start Here', will be replacing 'Starting Science' in September 1987. 'All Year Round' complements 'Science – Start Here' for younger children.

There are two current radio programmes of note – 'Introducing Science', soon to become 'Science Scope', for the nine to twelve age group, and 'See for Yourself', for infants. 'Introducing Science' is a two-year series based upon children's own experiences. It has some simple activities involving minimal preparation and is acceptable as a teacher or pupil demonstration. A topical programme invites pupil contributions, and 'Introducing Science Extra' deals with basic electronics using an ingenious, but rather fiddly, low-cost kit. The electronics programme should be taped. The pauses can be extended for teachers to ensure that all their pupils have wired up the neat little baseboards correctly – a time-consuming exercise with anything but a fairly small group. The programmes adapt well to headphone sets, where small groups of pupils can control the speed and development of their own activities. A sandwich box (as recommended in the programme notes) is ideal for keeping the kits; a small block of expanded polystyrene on which you can spear them and retain them for future use is excellent too. Soldering of parts is eliminated, and the whole kit is virtually indestructible; a spares service is available for replacement of lost parts. The last programme in the series of five, used with a Radiovision filmstrip, shows the practical application of the electronics the children have learnt.

This section on junior electronics has been described in detail by the authors since the MEP/DOI (Microelectronics in Education Programme/Department of Industry) sponsored initiative really does cross the boundary from passive viewing or listening to active participation and cannot really be called vicarious. The new 'Science Scope' series will have similarities, especially in stopping points for discussion.

'See for Yourself' is a radio series for six- to eight-year-olds stimulating science and maths activities. The lively, ten-minute programme is best recorded and the sections used one at a time, to allow for discussion and response. Whether or not children remember the factual information involved they should have a grasp of the key ideas; and the attractive Radiovision filmstrips that support the series, the simple computer programs, and the practical activities will all enhance the learning. A full-colour book, the *See for Yourself Science Book*, is available from the BBC, and is based upon the series. It includes lively original verse and music, further suggestions for science work, and some attractive discussion pictures. Altogether, 'See for Yourself' is an interesting package for infant and lower junior science and maths; well worth closer examination.

The programmes of 'See for Yourself' are constantly being updated, a process that goes on throughout all broadcast material as programme matter is brought up to date or renewed. The programmes described here may not be current when this book is published, but the products of both the BBC and the Independent Television Companies, which are commonly made at the request of a National Body, the Schools

Broadcasting Council of the United Kingdom, are always of a very high standard indeed.

An interesting and unusual example of vicarious work is a series of six audiocassettes published by KK Tape Services. These are the 'Science Through Story' tapes, devised by Bill Bailey, described as 'a practising teacher of great experience'. He claims to have personally used all the material in the teachers' notes, and aims the tapes at teachers with no equipment and only their own classroom, who believe science teaching to be beyond them. He is confident that they will find the scheme 'offers a way through this seemingly hopeless morass'.

The teachers' notes are direct to the point of naïvety – the appeal to non-specialists would lie in their simplicity and the way that they make scientific principles understandable. They are a little cavalier on occasion: 'it may not be wise for children to know the proportions of the constituents of gunpowder', for example. Others are questionable, both practically and morally – 'It might be possible to imprint a young bird that has hatched in the classroom', they suggest. But some of the ideas – speeding up rusting by 'putting fine steel wool in a little water and adding a Steradent tablet' (the oxygen released from the tablet oxidises the iron) – are fresh and original, and have the stamp of genuine experience.

The stories are about Bimba, a bush-baby, and his adventures at a village school. The method is described as 'second hand discovery'. The cassettes are to be purchased one at a time. You might try one and see.

Mention is made elsewhere in this book of the excellent filmstrips by Philip Green, which include a number of familiar science topics – 'Holes, gaps and cavities' for example. They have a good clear text, allied to high-quality pictures and sound teachers' notes. There are other sources of filmstrips, of course, including the 'Radiovision' programmes already mentioned, and some of the commercial science apparatus suppliers.

Videotapes and 16 mm films are available for purchase or hire from a number of suppliers, including the nationalised industries. These are usually well-made but need previewing to avoid disappointment should the film not match its description precisely. Appendix IV lists some of the sources of material, but reference should be made to guide books and catalogues, too.

Audiovisual materials should never be seen as an alternative to practical activities.

Demonstration lessons

There is a long and respectable tradition behind the demonstration lesson. There are a very few activities, even in primary schools, which are best undertaken by a teacher, either for practical or safety reasons, or because expense precludes repeating them for a whole class. Simple extension to the Craigie Kit (qv) allows for demonstration using a wooden frame. As a general rule, however, children's own experiences will have far more value for learning; the Nuffield Maths books made much of the Chinese proverb 'I hear and I forget; I see and I remember; I do and I understand'. Primary science is not creating a new thinking! An uneasy compromise between class and teacher activity is reached when a pupil performs the demonstration activity for the class.

While this can set up strains and tensions from jealousy, it does help to hold attention. As a general rule, even a fairly mundane individual or group activity beats a demonstration lesson.

Whole-class activities

One of the authors on teaching practice in 1965 observed in a junior classroom the first primary science he had experienced since nature study at school. Using a dozen washing-up bowls (these were the days of forty-odd to a class) all the children examined sinking and floating with a variety of everyday objects. The forward-looking young class teacher was beginning to put into practice the principles learnt from the Nuffield books and from Plowden, modified to suit a classroom style where everyone had always done the same thing at the same time.

This classwork approach has its points. Schools still buy small apparatus in quantity to allow simultaneous working. But the style of classroom has changed, and with that change has come the recognition of each child's uniqueness. The spread of ability that many teachers face in their unstreamed, mixed-age group, shrinking schools, as they attempt to teach children coming from a wide variety of both indigenous and recent immigrant backgrounds, makes a nonsense of many whole-class activities. Only where there is a very high degree of common background and experience can it be at all appropriate; and even then the learning that each individual experiences may be quite unique. Nevertheless, by this method (not uncommon in secondary schools, where the practical activities, while perhaps not identical, can be very similar across the class) a properly structured progression can be ensured.

At first sight the apparatus requirements look easy, too. Providing you have enough, you have only to set up duplicate trays or tables to the number of the class, or the number of groups. But remember that one lesson (if you are teaching weekly science lessons by this method) will probably suffice to use up all the possibilities of those materials, and the following week will need fresh preparation. Contrast this with the circus approach, described on pages 119–20.

Despite these doubts, teachers using such methods can teach science remarkably efficiently. What is questionable is whether they are also teaching effectively. The whole-class method makes it almost impossible to meet the needs of individuals, and this drawback is compounded when the children have a wide ability range, or a wide variety of mother tongues.

GROUP WORK

Assignments

Probably the most demanding way of teaching science – for the teacher – is by individual, or group, independent assignments. It is certainly the ideal recognised by the Nuffield Junior Science Project, and a number of experienced teachers can use it with outstanding effect. Given free range, the breadth of group activities can be devastating – from pollution to genetics, from chemical energy to static electricity. It needs considerable nimbleness of mind, not to mention a wide variety of resources, to handle this sort of work proceeding simultaneously. Children need to develop the confidence and responsibility to handle classroom materials, to explore beyond the classroom, to involve outside agencies, experts and other sources of information. Above all, they need to be able to plan effectively in the face of disappointment, to use their time constructively, and to be motivated to record and report. Assessment of such work can only be effective with constant monitoring; and class records of progress will need to take account of whether children are using their valuable time constructively.

In a sympathetic environment, children working in this way can be well motivated, and can pursue individual interests with success. Since each assignment is unique, the work will be open to the achievement of children's full potential, but experience would suggest that the disenchanted will still need motivation, and the less able will still need a lot of individual attention, while the most able will also make their unique demands. In other words this is no easy road and teachers will still need to work as hard as ever.

It is more important with this method than with some others to ensure that there is a proper framework of skills within which the children work, or it is very easy to neglect some altogether.

Integration

This is a variation on individual assignments, in that science activities are pursued by groups of individuals, alongside groups busy with maths or language, or other classroom work. It is more economical with resources and teacher time, since fewer materials will be needed at any one time and the work of the other groups can be planned to involve the consolidation of skills previously learned, and thus be less demanding of teachers. The ability to perform mental gymnastics when faced with the varying needs of groups or individuals will still be there of course. Nevertheless, many teachers apply this approach with success.

Thematic work

With this style, small groups work on independent but related assignments. Thus the class may be involved on a general topic related to electricity. While groups explore and make practical applications by constructing little electrical devices, others investigate current electricity, or discover something about static charges, and still further groups work on an appropriate computer program, or view a tape-slide presentation on related subjects.

The approach demands a lot of apparatus, with resulting demands on setting up and putting away. A lot of the apparatus will be very similar, and this means duplication and expense. There are organisational demands, especially in providing appropriate work for groups which have completed assignments, or wish to explore beyond the limits of the planned activities.

The circus of experiments

This method has proved to be consistently successful once children have grasped the rules of the game. Based upon the traditional rotation around fixed PE apparatus, the circus, when properly organised, can be an effective method for teaching science. It adapts well to the demands of most primary-age children.

Imagine a room prepared for simple work on current electricity. The tables or desks have trays or boxes of materials ready, together with work cards and equipment for recording the activities – whether pencil and paper, camera, tape-recorder, or whatever. The setting-out of the tables can be deputed to a group of children – since the same materials will be needed in the same places for a series of lessons. The classwork is outlined by the teacher, together with safety warnings about the dangers of domestic electricity and advice on using the apparatus wisely. (One tip here is to insist that all electric circuits include a bulb – this serves the dual purpose of showing when the circuit is completed and, when it is left completed, of ensuring that a battery is never left connected back to itself so that it overheats, bringing danger and the probability that it will quickly run flat.)

The aim of the work cards will commonly need outlining – the need for this lessens with experience and growing confidence, but at first it helps to explain exactly what your expectations are. Even when the cards are carefully matched to the reading skills of the pupils there can be confusion.

Now the groups start work, using the cards to guide them. They will need teaching as they work – and this will go beyond 'servicing' with routine advice and apparatus repair, to the principles behind the activities. One by one, they reach a completion point; this may be within the timespan of one lesson, or it may be longer – there is always a danger that activities may be rushed in an effort to complete them before the bell rings. Careful and accurate recording must be encouraged. Completed groups should show their records to and discuss them with their teacher; only when the teacher is satisfied should they move to a new, vacant, activity.

This move is facilitated if a few extra activities are planned beyond the total needs of the class, especially towards the end of a lesson series when many groups will have completed most of the activities. There are practical problems. There is a natural tendency to rush if children see a popular activity become vacant. It is not easy to arrange a feedback to the whole class. And it is difficult to build in the potential for individual exploration beyond the confines of the 'long-distance workcard'. Most important of all, there can be little chance of progression from easy to more demanding activities; indeed, children may have to begin with the higher order work before descending to the simple. Nevertheless, the circus can be a valuable method for encouraging young children's science activities.

INDIVIDUAL WORK ON CHOSEN TOPICS

Clearly individual work is the purest form of science study and the most closely related to how an academic scientist might work – although, increasingly, scientists work in teams and co-operation with others must be reckoned high on the list of science skills and attitudes. Children pursuing their own studies may be uniquely motivated but will also need direction, advice and guidance to information sources if they are to avoid some degree of frustration. All this puts pressure on the teacher to provide resources and some information where necessary. This method, of course, should ensure that children are working to their own potential and in areas of immediate interest and relevance to them.

THE SCIENCE TABLE

This approach is one that many teachers, especially those new to science, have used with success. It is well-suited to work card assignments, with their inevitable limitations on individual initiative. It is easy, however, to organise and control and no unreasonable demands are made on teachers.

It is important to differentiate between a nature table, which often invites positive interest, and a science table, which is for active involvement. The best of nature tables, of course, can be beautiful and rich, well-displayed and labelled and a stimulus to the work. By careful use of lenses and other magnifying aids, the nature table *can* involve children actively in close observation, but the science table is to the nature table what the lively and participative science museum can be to a glass case.

On a classroom table a weekly activity is displayed. A comprehensive set of apparatus is provided (only one to provide, resource and supervise), and a work card appropriate to the children (only one card to explain to the class, to decipher and support). The 'work card' can be provided by the imaginative use of audio-visual aids – 'Language master' cards, for example, or a short cassette tape, or a computer display.

Pupils take turns at the table – individually or in pairs or groups (thus introducing co-operation on a task). They complete the assignment and record the work as is most appropriate – perhaps with a choice from a selection of recording techniques. The teacher checks, supervises, advises and maybe suggests appropriate extension work. One by one; or better, two by two, the children take their turn at the weeks's assignment. When everyone has completed the work, there can be general discussion, conclusions can be drawn and new work presented. Progression is assured and control problems are minimised, while assessment of the approach of individuals and/or groups is simplified. How far this method goes to meeting the individual needs of children depends to a large extent on teacher skill in adapting the work appropriately. By the end of a term, however, a class of children will have completed a progressive series of science activities and the teacher can be certain that they have been exposed to various skills and experiences.

Description of the Science Table would be incomplete without mention of the Craigie Kit. Devised by Ian McLellan, this large science kit was marketed until very recently by Oliver and Boyd and spares can still be obtained from McLellan. Buying one was a major investment – towards £100 by the end of its availability – but it is worthy of discussion because so many schools were tempted to acquire one as an all-in panacea for science problems and many are gathering dust on stock-room shelves. The Craigie Kit was biased towards physical science and had some of the traditional disadvantages of science kits in general in being somewhat limiting on original work and was an expensive way of buying polythene bags, syringes, etc. But the Craigie Kit has a number of unique qualities, not least an ingenious apparatus construction system based on special split pins and a perforated baseboard. (A kind of perforated scaffolding – an optional extra – converted it to a class or group demonstration apparatus, as previously mentioned.)

Together with very complete apparatus provision, the kit had a number of activity books on key physical science topics – air, water and electricity for example. These led the children through carefully graded experiences. The tendency to rush to the teacher when problems were first encountered was discouraged by the provision of a clue book (reading ability was assumed throughout). At the end of a unit of activities a quiz book and answer book could be used by children in pairs, to test the ideas understood. A teacher's book gave the background to the work.

The Craigie Kit has been described in some detail because it adapted so well to the science table; but if one is not available to you, its ideas still translate well to home-grown science. A 'panic envelope' can be provided to help when the science becomes difficult; and a few searching questions for which answers are available can be used to ensure that the work is understood before progressing to the next stage. The Craigie Kit proved sturdy and robust in use. It contained sufficient apparatus for three pairs of children to work simultaneously. While some of the apparatus (notably the battery boxes for electricity work) was fiddly, most was very straightforward. It proved a boon to small village-size schools seeking a single purchase physical science scheme. Perhaps a revival of interest in the Craigie Kit might bring it back on the market.

TEAM TEACHING

It is not uncommon – especially in older junior and middle school classes – for teachers to exchange groups in order that a specialist teacher may take the class science. The pros and cons of this method are discussed elsewhere. By team teaching it is intended to consider the system whereby two or more teachers (one, possibly, a science specialist, or with at least designated responsibility for the science education of the children) share a large group of pupils. Various methods are used, and some may be seen in the DES curriculum film on primary science.

One, using a specialist room, fully-equipped, on a timetabled whole-class basis, sees one teacher directing the activities, but both or all the teachers working alongside them to ensure that the room's facilities are fully-used. Another involves the specialist withdrawing a class-sized group – or smaller – to a special room and working with them, in isolation but towards the agreed aims of the year group. A third sees the specialist advising colleagues on using the science room, while taking no personal part in teaching science to any pupils beyond his own class group.

Where a science room is not available, a specialist can still teach in isolation alongside, or simply advise. Some schools have developed the idea of the lead lecture where a specialist teacher prepares the whole team and introduces the subject to all the team's children, perhaps with audio-visual aids or some demonstration. The groups then split with the team's teachers and develop the work with the support of the specialist. In these and other examples, the specialist teacher is seen by both adults and children as a source of reference. The allocation of the year group, school, or part of school, can be on a variety of criteria – whether pastoral groups, interest groups, or setting, – by interest, experience or ability. Team teaching offers many advantages. Wherever possible, the active involvement of all the team in sharing the science teaching should be seen as the ideal. Only by this approach can teachers, as well as children, genuinely develop their own skills and understanding of the subject.

REFERENCES

Finch, I. (1971) *Nature Study and Science*. London: Longman.
Prestt, B. (ed) (1980) *Language in Science*. Hatfield: ASE.

Chapter 9

Practicalities

SAFETY AWARENESS

In a general text such as this, the aim is not to produce a comprehensive and all-embracing guide to safety in science activities, but rather to promote an awareness of some of the hazards implicit in science in the primary school. There are specialist publications which give greater detail and expand the areas of safety mentioned here. Concerned practitioners should be aware of guidelines produced by their own Local Education Authorities (and in case of doubt should ask for advice from the Science Adviser), by the Department of Education and Science and other government agencies, by professional organisations such as the Association for Science Education, by the Schools Council, by CLEAPSE (Consortium of Local Education Authorities for the Provision of Science Equipment) and by manufacturers, suppliers and their organisations: *Plastics in Schools – Safety and Hazards* (issued by The Plastics Institute, London), is a typical example. Many of these will be referred to in the following paragraphs and some useful references and addresses are included.

John Creedy in his *Laboratory Manual for Schools and Colleges* lists four essential ingredients of accident prevention:

- Good Housekeeping
- Knowledge
- Good Storage
- Safe Working Procedures

Although the Manual is directed in the main to the secondary and tertiary levels, these four 'ingredients' are very relevant to the primary phase and its science involvement.

A DES inspired publication which offers invaluable advice and guidance on safety education is *Safety in Practical Studies* which includes many useful references and is sectioned to deal with the practical aspects of art; craft, design and technology; home economics; dress and textiles; music and rural science.

In 1981 the DES also introduced an occasional bulletin *Safety in Education* to supplement the advice given in the department's safety series of booklets, which will hopefully 'help teachers to be more aware of the kinds of hazards they are likely to meet and to refer to the expert advice that is available'. *Safety at School: General Advice* (DES Safety Series No. 6) emphasises:

124

The natural instinct to explore and venture must not be suppressed, for only through experience can independence be developed. To remove all possibility of accident would be to prevent the child learning how to recognise and deal sensibly and confidently with hazards which are sure to arise in later life.

Safety awareness in general, and during science activities in particular, is an essential attitude to be developed in young children and one which can be applied and extended throughout their lives.

The desirability of involving a range of local contributors to school science has been mentioned elsewhere in this book. The visits of the fireman, police and road safety officers can provide an ideal starting point, not only for science, but also for safety education.

For example, 'science and colour' might involve the children in an investigation of road signs and how various colour combinations affect our perception of them; another popular investigation is to devise ways in which the safety aspects of the various car colours might relate to accidents in fog or during darkness. It is easy to envisage such a project developing to include the road safety implications of children's clothing when walking to school or when cycling.

Work involving bulbs, batteries and electricity has obvious links with safety. Although, at this level, mains electricity should not be used by pupils for their investigative work, electrical safety should be discussed, possibly in the context of safety in the home, and the potential hazards as well as benefits of mains electricity can be identified. Once again, outside agencies are only too willing to offer advice, assistance and resources. Every teacher should be aware of the excellent resources provided by Understanding Electricity, the educational service of the electrical supply industries. Its stated aim

is to improve the knowledge of young people about basic electrical principles and their practical applications

To this end, a substantial catalogue of the resources provided is produced annually. Safety is paramount and considerable thought and care has resulted in the availability to teachers of an impressive array of booklets, posters, cartoons, films and videotapes, and teaching packages for use in school. Education officers are available for consultation and for school visits.

Some hazards associated with the natural environment

The natural world provides a fertile environment for the primary scientist working with plants and animals. Anyone planning a substantial involvement in this area could do worse than refer to the books produced by the Schools Council Educational Use of Living Organisms Project.

The primary teacher might like to consider the aims of keeping animals in school and whether there is a valid reason for keeping animals in the classroom on a permanent or long-term basis.

Certainly, pupils should be discouraged from handling wild mammals and they should not normally be brought into school; they can transmit disease to man. Likewise, wild birds, including pigeons and re-captured budgerigars, should not be brought into school. The examination of dead specimens also includes the risk of disease and, although a source of scientific investigation already mentioned, birds' nests and owl pellets brought into school from the wild should be handled carefully; it is recommended to wear rubber gloves and preferably some form of protective clothing. In any case, the hands should be thoroughly washed afterwards, as they should be after any outdoor science, such as work with minibeasts.

The aforementioned *Safety in Practical Studies* has several very relevant sections on this whole area, including a list of diseases associated with animals kept in schools.

One of the most important and desirable aspects of the primary science curriculum is the study of plants. Providing a few simple rules are adhered to, the safety problems should be minimal. Unless involved in particular science activities involving taste – undertaken only after a discussion of basic safety rules including cleanliness and the use of very small quantities – children should be warned against the indiscriminate eating of plant material. Some plants are naturally poisonous or have poisonous components, whilst seeds may have been treated with fungicides. In their book *School Science Laboratories*, Archenhold, Jenkins and Wood-Robinson include a list of some of the more common toxic species of plant material (see table 9.1).

Some hazards associated with the physical environment

Many of these hazards are concerned with the materials being used or investigated and also with the apparatus or tools required during such investigations.

A working knowledge of first-aid can be invaluable to the teacher and courses are frequently organised. The DES suggest that

> it is also desirable that some teachers should have attended a course of training and taken a certificate in first-aid issued by the British Red Cross or the St. John Ambulance Association (*Safety in Practical Studies*)

Such teachers might be responsible for the maintenance of a first-aid kit in school and also for a kit to be available during field work. Local Education Authority medical officers should advise on items to be included.

Eye protection should be considered during any activity that might cause damage to the eyes of practitioners or other children in the vicinity. Extra care should be taken during work involving tools, saws, hammers, etc., which might cause particles to fly from the work area. The testing of plastics can be particularly dangerous; bending them or striking them with a hammer can cause sharp-edged pieces to be propelled long distances – wrap them in a cloth when bending them, or cover them when hammering in order to minimise such risks. The CLEAPSE School Science Service produce an excellent booklet on eye protection (L135) and although many of the hazard situations are more likely to be found in the secondary school, the primary teacher should be aware of particular activities which might conceivably cause problems with younger children.

Although much primary science work can be carried out using relatively simple equipment of the 'string and sealing wax' type, it is sometimes necessary, and desirable, to use commercial apparatus. There are few occasions when glass equipment need be used. Many of the more common glass items are now produced

Table 9.1 *Some Poisonous Plants*

Common Name	Botanical Name	Poisonous Parts
Garden flowers		
Aconite (winter)	*Eranthis hyemalis*	All
Christmas rose	*Helleborus niger*	All
Foxglove	*Digitalis purpurea*	All
Iris (Blue flag)	*Iris versicolor*	All
Larkspur	*Delphinium ajacis*	Foliage and seeds
Lily of the valley	*Convallaria majalis*	All
Lupin	*Lupinus* sp.	All
Monkshood	*Aconitum anglicum*	All
Narcissus (daffodil, jonquil)	*Narcissus* sp.	Bulbs
Garden vegetables		
Potato	*Solanum tuberosum*	Green sprouting tubers and leaves
Rhubarb	*Rheum rhaponticum*	Leaves
Shrubs and trees		
Broom	*Cytisus (Sarothamnus) scoparius*	Seeds
Cherry laurel	*Prunus laurocerasus*	All
Laburnum (Golden Rain)	*Laburnum anagyroides*	All
Rhododendron	Species: Azalea American laurel Mountain laurel	Leaves and flowers
Yew	*Taxus baccata*	All; seeds lethal
Snowberry	*Symphoricarpus albus*	Fruits
Hedgerow plants		
Black nightshade	*Solanum nigrum*	All
Buttercups	*Ranunculus* sp.	Sap
Deadly nightshade	*Atropa belladonna*	All
Privet	*Ligustrum vulgaris*	Berries
Thorn apple	*Datura stramonium*	All
Marshland plants		
Hemlock	*Conium maculatum*	All
Hemlock, Water dropwort	*Oenanthe crocata*	All
Kingcup, Marsh marigold	*Caltha palustris*	Sap
House plants		
Castor oil plant	*Ricinus communis*	Seeds
Dumb cane	*Dieffenbachia* sp.	All
Hyacinth	*Hyacinthus* sp.	Bulbs
Poinsettia	*Euphorbia pulcherrima*	Leaves and flowers
Woodland plants		
Cuckoo pint (wild arum)	*Arum maculatum*	All
Mistletoe	*Viscum album*	Fruits
Oak	*Quercus* sp.	Fruits and leaves
Poison ivy	*Rhus toxicodendron*	All
Toadstools	*Amanita muscaria* (fly agaric) *A. pantherina* (the panther) *A. phalloides* (death cap)	All

Reproduced with permission from Archenhold, Jenkins and Wood-Robinson, *School Science Laboratories*, 1978.

from materials less hazardous to the young investigator. Thus acrylic plastic prisms, virtually unbreakable magnifiers, transparent beakers, measuring cylinders, bendable mirrors which can be cut with scissors and plastic tubing are all readily available from a range of suppliers including Osmiroid.

The primary teacher involved in science-type projects in school occasionally requires a source of heat for particular experimental work. If such work is to be attempted by pupils, very careful supervision is essential and, in most cases, it is advisable for the teacher to carry out the procedure either alone or with pupil assistance or participation.

Once again, the science can be a vehicle for more general safety awareness. The Science 5–13 team recognised this and gave an example in the unit *Change*. Relating the general safety awareness of children at risk through clothes catching fire they suggest flammability tests of small samples of various fabrics. A candle might be a reasonable source of flame, the samples being held by wooden clothes pegs (plastic ones being much more hazardous because of melting, burning or emitting fumes). A ready source of water and a bucket of sand might be advisable.

Candles are probably the safest form of naked flame heating for the primary school. They should be secured firmly on a surface free from paper or other combustible material; surrounding walls should also be cleared of decoration which might conceivably ignite. Other naked flame heat sources have increasing safety hazards and the authors see no case for spirit burners or portable gas burners in the primary classroom. Another fuel to be avoided is the solid fuel briquettes commonly used for camping stoves, etc. They evolve harmful fumes that are dangerous in confined spaces.

For most heating purposes at this level, hot water is adequate. Children are more familiar with such a source and many will have observed the use of kettles or gas rings in other situations. Heating in the classroom is another activity for which advice from the LEA and its advisory team might be sought.

There are two other areas where practical science activities can cause problems to particular children. Often children are required to provide data personally. If the pupil has a medical history including conditions such as asthma or lung infections, physical exercise such as running or blowing can obviously cause distress. A second area, although not strictly concerned with safety, to which the teacher should be sensitive is in the type of activity which might cause children to question family ties, for example, surveys of eye colour. Knowledge, not only of the children themselves, but also of inherent hazards in all kinds of pursuits, and of safe working procedures can combine to make science safe, enjoyable and instructive.

Hand tools in the primary classroom

The use of hand tools by young children should be encouraged. It is desirable and useful, and as craft, design and technology is increasingly interrelated with science, children of all ages are likely to be using hand tools in the classroom – the saw, hammer, screwdriver, hand-drill and wire-strippers. An uncluttered workspace is essential and careful supervision and guidance in correct working procedures will help prevent cuts, bangs, and distress.

Safety Measures
- Loose clothing should not be worn and long hair should be tied back as both can get in the way.
- When working with, for example, wood, the materials should be firmly held in place using a vice clamped to the work surface, or by G-clamps; the hands should be positioned so as not to be in direct line of the tool, e.g. the saw or hammer.
- Children should be encouraged, when sawing, to do so slowly, using an even, non-forced action, preferably keeping the wood horizontal. For most cutting needs, a junior hacksaw is adequate or a coping saw, although the fragile blades do not last very long!
- A hand drill will suffice for hole boring.
- If nails are being used, round nails with large, flat heads are best as they can be held in position between the teeth of a comb in order to protect small fingers.
- Tools should be kept in good condition – loose hammer heads can be particularly hazardous – and it should be insisted upon that tools are only used for their intended purpose.
- Good storage is especially relevant in this type of work. Collection and transportation of tools by children must be done in such a way as to be safe for them and their fellows. Storage of materials should be tidy and any stray nails removed from stored pieces of wood.
- Sharp knives and chisels are particularly hazardous and the recommendation must be that children should not use them.
- Care should be exercised when using adhesives. Cyanoacrylate adhesives should not be used in school. They can bond skin to skin and involuntary wiping of the eyes can be particularly dangerous. In general, skin contact with adhesives should be minimised, the hands being cleaned as soon as possible. Liberal use of adhesives in poorly ventilated rooms can cause irritations and they should not be used near naked flames.

ANIMALS IN SCHOOL

'A dog is for life, not just for Christmas': the car stickers correctly identify our responsibility to all animals, not just to dogs. So often in schools the acquisition of classroom animals seems to come from a chance incident – an animal found, or donated, an unwanted pet, or an interest created by a story or television programme. Classroom animals need to be thoughtfully anticipated – their origins, care, and possibly ultimate disposal, must be carefully planned in advance. This sounds a little cold-blooded but it is essential, for the children's well-being as well as the animal's. Ultimately, responsibility for an animal in school – whom it bites, whom it infects; and its own health and condition – lies with the head teacher, and the head should always be consulted before animals are introduced into school – even as visitors.

It is not possible in a book of this length to cover all aspects of animal care. Many excellent books, such as the publications of the ILEA Centre for Life Studies, contain explicit information. The ASE can help, too, and the SNSS, as can the Universities Federation for Animal Welfare. All may answer your questions.

The first concern should be 'Why keep animals in school at all?' One answer is that, fundamentally, teachers are aiming to inculcate in their pupils healthy attitudes to the welfare of *all* living beings, humans included. Experience of animals can increase children's respect for them, and deepen their understanding. Much more mundanely, animal-keeping can open children's eyes to the understanding that living creatures need constant care and attention; that they do not thrive on neglect. This lesson may be better learned at school where others *can* take on the responsibility of feeding the gerbils when some children lose interest; the consequences at home might be tragic. Many animals – especially mammals – have a therapeutic effect on children, particularly those who are disturbed, anxious, or neglected. Conversely, these children can identify very strongly with the vulnerable, dependent nature of small animals, and can feel very deeply their mistreatment, disease or loss. Another aim can, indeed, be to develop understandings of the life-cycle, of birth and death. For this purpose family groups are ideal, of course, rather than individual animals. But this raises natural problems of population growth. Certainly the children will learn far more about parental care for the young and the growth of independence from observing the development of young animals.

Animals are a stimulus to creative work and aesthetic appreciation, especially when their behaviour is experienced at first-hand. More clinically, they provide strong motivation for close study and observation, for investigation and measuring, for prediction and planning socially. They enable children to co-operate on management and maintenance; and in the long-term, they provide an opportunity for the development of caring qualities, perhaps for lifelong interests.

The case for keeping animals in school on these grounds may seem overwhelming. By contrast, however, the practicalities are demanding – increasingly so over the past few years as the amount of advice, and even legislation, surrounding the keeping of school animals has increased. If you are satisfied that you have good educational reasons for choosing to keep classroom animals, you need to decide very early on what creatures are most appropriate to your situation. Many invertebrates are both fascinating and easy to keep. While they are hardly pets to cuddle or walk, they can fascinate children with their beauty – or superficial ugliness! – and stimulate a lot of fine close observation work. Simple experiments on their behaviour can be performed without causing them discomfort; and their life cycle can be short enough to be completed in the span of a class study.

Wild 'minibeasts' *can* be kept for a short period, of course. Many books contain plans of formicaria and wormeries. A wormery fitted with alternative layers of sand and earth will show how worms act to mix the soil. Rotting leaves lying on top will be drawn down for food. At the end of the period of interest, minibeasts can be returned to the wild. The weather and provenance must be right for this, of course.

A little more ambitious is the keeping of butterflies and moths. These creatures can be provided by recognised butterfly farms, and can include the familiar species, or exotic, even foreign, insects. Native insects are to be recommended; again, they can be released when the study is over. Simple butterfly cages can be made from fine netting; plastic lemonade bottles adapt beautifully into covers for potted food plants bearing caterpillars. Most insects are very specific about food plants; all will need cleaning out, especially at the caterpillar stage, very regularly. Stick insects are perennially popular and easy to keep; common examples may eat privet. Their camouflage and behaviour are extraordinary. They are all too easily thrown out with discarded food plants. They also escape with regularity, being able to move very quickly on occasion. They seem to migrate upwards and will usually end up on the ceiling. Stick insects are relatively cheap and other schools may welcome excess stock. Do not confuse baby stick insects with ants or mites.

A more demanding, but very exciting, project is keeping desert locusts. These can be obtained from local secondary schools, or from some colleges, and should be kept in a large aquarium with a tight-fitting metal gauze lid. They need a good temperature which can be maintained with an electric light bulb. Commercial locust cages have a bulb operated intermittently by a bellows thermostat. (Do not place this near a window; the nocturnal flashing has been known by the authors to attract passing policemen.) The failure of the light bulb may not be disastrous. As their temperature drops, locusts become more and more lethargic and finally immobile. They then cease to eat and so may eventually die – but this does take some time. Indeed, turning out the bulb some minutes before changing the food plants is to be recommended, since it makes the creatures easier to handle. Locusts eat exactly as might be expected: they will decimate large tussocks of grass and, if starved, will cannibalise each other.

Provide, in the cage, a tall, preferably transparent, container filled with damp sand. Females will lay egg-tubes some ten or twelve centimetres long in it. They are shaped a little like vanilla pods. Newly-hatched locusts are small and black and appropriately called hoppers; they go through a number of skin-splitting stages before emerging as winged adults capable of reproduction. Some children will find locusts particularly repulsive; nobody should be made to handle them alive or dead. Special care should be taken to keep locust cages where children are *not* going to be in close proximity to them for long periods. Public areas, like corridors, are best. Children, especially those inclined to asthma or breathing difficulties, can react to the dry, dusty nature of the creatures.

A fascinating experience may be provided by the loan of a strobe light from (say) a visiting secondary school teacher. This regularly pulsing light can be synchronised with the wing beats of an adult locust suspended from a tiny thread halter. The wings appear slowed down, and their grace and beauty can be fully appreciated. That a creature so apparently unattractive can possess such qualities is a valuable lesson for young children who may destroy creatures because they see them as ugly. Precautions must be taken when using stroboscopic lights. Moving objects, such as wheels, can appear stationary and the flashing light can also be disturbing to some children, especially if they are prone to epilepsy.

Honey bees have been kept in schools, with many of the strictures outlined above and more besides because of the dangers of stinging. An observation hive (glass-sided) ran successfully for a full year in a junior school without a single sting because commonsense precautions were taken. The hive was screwed to an old table that was in turn bolted to the floor so that it could not be tipped over. The bees entered and left through a metal tube drilled through a window-frame opening on to a rarely-used side of the school, and the fields beyond. The hive was set up and started by a skilled beekeeper, and he also provided advice on feeding bees and on sensible precautions. When the study was over the hive was corked shut, at night, and removed complete with contents. It provided a unique experience, and, with the beekeeper's co-operation, the children were able to sample their own honey.

Vertebrate animals are the most commonly kept in schools. Aquaria are attractive, and food blocks can make daily feeding unnecessary (in the holidays, for example). Do not underestimate the weight of a full aquarium – it may not be something for the nature table – or neglect fish diseases like white spot and fin rot. An altogether more natural environment can be provided in a pond or lake. Ponds can be constructed within school premises – in quadrangles or school gardens – using brick, stone, concrete or plastic liners. Small nature ponds can be made using heavy-gauge plastic sheet. In either case, care should be taken to prevent children falling in – either by constructing a low wall or fencing around the ponds, or netting its surface. Ponds are very vulnerable to damage, and some Wolverhampton schools have developed swamp areas – yes, swamps – which are virtually vandal-proof, yet rich in both small wild-life and birds.

Amphibia and reptiles are interesting animals for study, but should only be obtained from reputable dealers and never from the wild. Frogs can only be kept by providing a source of live food – e.g. blowflies – but some other creatures can be kept quite easily in purpose-built vivaria or in modified aquaria. Consult the appropriate books before acquiring even a humble tortoise; and remember that many reptiles live in the sort of dry, arid conditions that can affect children's breathing.

Closely-caged birds are inappropriate, if the hope is to develop children's sensitivity to animals' welfare. Birds, too, can be heavily parasited, and some bird diseases can be transmitted to humans. Nevertheless, a well-constructed aviary can be an attractive and stimulating feature, and once again, specialist books on the school environment can help you to construct and stock one successfully.

Mammals are, for primary school children, the most commonly kept group of animals. Small mammals are warm, furry, and attractive. They form family groups. They are active, and show a wide range of interesting behaviour. Handling and care of small mammals can be especially rewarding to children who find human relationships difficult. As with any other animal, the fundamental questions need to be asked – 'Why are we keeping them?' – 'Can we care for them adequately?' – 'Can we cope with an increase in numbers?' – 'What happens to the creatures when the interest is over?'.

If you decide that the answers to all these questions are positive and optimistic, then approach a reputable supplier – not the corner pet shop. Accredited breeders are listed by the Laboratory Animal Breeders Association (LABA). Not all reputable companies are accredited under the scheme, for instance some major biological suppliers, but you can still anticipate carefully-bred animals from them. Their address is: LABA, c/o Charles River (UK) Ltd., Manston Road, Margate, Kent CT9 4LT.

Do not take in unwanted pets. The dangers of disease apart, you can never be certain what you are accepting. A colleague fell for two small, grey rabbit kittens. Within months they had outgrown anything except the largest hutch and could kick so viciously that the children were unable to handle them safely. A reputable dealer will know the potential size of the adult animal and will advise you accordingly.

The following advice is based on personal experience of keeping small mammals in the classroom; certain specialist guides will give a far wider view.

Mice are extremely smelly animals and need daily cleaning if you are to avoid their characteristic odour. They are also very quick – too quick for young children – and can bite, even when handled daily. They are interesting to observe as family groups, however, as they breed prolifically and have a variety of coat colours.

Rats are much more rewarding than the name might suggest. Again, they need regular cleaning, but are attractive – even affectionate. They breed rather too well, but are available in a range of beautiful colours and patterns. Their behaviour supports the commonly-held view that they are intelligent animals.

Hamsters are slower moving, and less rat-like. They are relatively tidy and smell-free, if kept clean, but can disappoint children because they are most active at night. If kept alone, they can fight others – of either sex – fiercely, and this is one reason why they are hard to breed. This fierceness can cause them to nip fingers even when tame. Hamsters are natural escapers, perhaps because their bodies appear so fat we are surprised to find how small a gap they can squeeze through.

Guinea-pigs are popular creatures, with a wide variety of coat colours and fur patterns. They are quite large animals with a corresponding appetite and need for space. They are messy if fed on vegetables and are cleaner on appropriate dry and pellet food, but as they are unable to make Vitamin C they need either some fresh food or Vitamin C added to drinking water. They breed easily from a very early age and the young are miniature adults whose eyes are open as soon as they hit the ground ready to start running around, which is essential in their wild, open-country existence. This means that quite young guinea-pigs can be handled without fear of adult animal rejection. From experience, guinea-pigs would be personal classroom favourites if there is adequate space.

Gerbils are probably the best choice if space is more limited. They are tame and easy to handle and groom themselves against and through the hands that hold them. Because they are desert animals, so producing very little urine, their cages stay relatively dry and smell-free. They breed only occasionally to produce rather unattractive, blind, pink babies. If disturbed the adults may eat these naked young. An exceptional gerbil may nip fiercely without reason, and become untrustworthy, but most show lively, attractive behaviour. It is not easy to mix established groups, or introduce individuals to them. Nevertheless, they are still the best bet for a first classroom animal.

Rabbits can vary widely in size, colouring, and nature. The tiny dwarf rabbits are attractive and easy to handle, and need smaller hutches, but they do not always breed easily and can miscarry their young. The larger rabbits need substantial cages, and, preferably, runs (as do guinea-pigs). They eat large amounts and can be very messy. Frequent cleaning is essential. The larger species breed exactly according to their reputation. Big rabbits can be very strong and may give scratching kicks that can hurt small children badly. Long-haired rabbits (and guinea-pigs, too) can cause allergic reactions in some children.

The suggested list of science equipment describes the laboratory-type cages which are the most hygienic homes for small mammals. Some are translucent, and others (polycarbonate) are transparent. The barred lids or fronts are made of stainless steel, and the whole cage is easily cleaned. Hoppers are supplied for dry foods, and plastic bottles with stainless steel ball-valve nozzles are also available. These products, from suppliers like North Kent Plastic Cages and Biotech Consultants, are quite excellent, but unattractive to anthropomorphic adults, who see them as scientific, and not appropriate for pets.

If you choose a more homely cage avoid the pressed-metal varieties that rust and leave rough, dirty edges. Water bottles are vastly preferable to bowls; the youngest of animals, providing they can reach them, can cope with the ball-valve immediately. Some animals – guinea-pigs especially – deliberately soil open water, and while this may serve some biological purpose such as reinfecting them with intestinal bacteria, the result is fairly horrible. Peat, softwood sawdust and shredded white paper make good litter. Only hay is ideal for nesting – not hard, sharp straw. Thorough cage cleaning, including a prolonged soak in a suitable disinfectant, is important. There are many different pelleted foods, and the appropriate one should be chosen and supplemented with seeds, nuts, and fresh fruit and vegetables in small quantities. In general, food sold by pet shops and greengrocers from *open* bins should be avoided.

Children must wash their hands thoroughly before *and* after handling small mammals to prevent spreading infection. They must be shown the correct way of handling and supporting the weight of such animals to prevent panic and possible abuse. Children often get scratched at the crucial moment of introducing the animal to its cage, especially rabbits, which can rip into clothes and forearms. The wild scrabble can be avoided by putting the animal in *backwards*.

Reputable suppliers will be able to sex animals accurately, while even pet shops make mistakes, and the authors have known female guinea-pigs to give birth at a very young age – ten to eleven weeks – because they were left in mixed groups by a pet shop. If you plan to breed the animals, take advice on introducing them to each other and on separating them after mating or birth. Note that many mammals come on heat immediately after giving birth to ensure a new litter should the first be lost. If you want to avoid a large number of young this is a time for separation although some pairs may be difficult to re-establish.

Classroom animals should not be 'lent' for the week-end or holiday. Contact with, and infection from, other animals cannot be prevented, and animals can be allowed to 'play' with others of their own species with predictable results. If interest wanes, or a teacher changes schools leaving the animals without an interested adult you may find that a neighbouring school will welcome the unwanted aninmals. Beware 'good homes', and on no account attempt to kill the animals yourself; apart from reflecting a callous attitude to the disposability of living creatures, it can so easily go wrong and cause a creature suffering. Instead, approach one of the animal organisations (RSPCA, PDSA) for advice.

Lastly, always remember that only rodents and rabbits from approved sources are allowed in schools, and that tests and experiments on them are forbidden, especially if they involve deprivation of food or vital parts of their diet. Ultimately all the animals in the school are the responsibility of the head teacher, who should be consulted on their acquisition and welfare.

PLANTS IN SCHOOL

Providing the children can be patient and not expect instant action, plant growing in school is fun, informative and relatively inexpensive.

With imagination an almost endless range of containers can be used so long as a few basic conditions are met to ensure success. Traditional clay pots, with the drainage holes partially covered to prevent loss of compost, or plastic pots, seed trays and ornamental tubs; or adapted yoghourt cartons, cut-away plastic bottles, metal pie cases, etc. are all perfectly acceptable. Remember to pierce drainage holes in the containers, which can then be stood on a suitable tray lined with gravel, peat or absorbent matting which can be kept moist. For more serious work you might consider a commercial *propagator* in order to stabilise humidity and temperature and so aid the growing process. Of course, covering your plant pot with a plastic bag after an initial watering should be sufficient to begin germination.

In parallel with the number of growing containers is the number of growing media available. Basically water must be retained and air allowed to reach the roots, especially in impervious pots. Ideally the growing medium should be free of weed seeds, spores and insects. Nutrients will eventually be needed, but can be added once growth is established. Large seeds such as peas, beans and peanuts, as well as bulbs with their own food supply, avocado stones, acorns and conkers can be grown in a great variety of environments, including water – possibly a science investigation in itself.

Common rooting media include washed silver sand, vermiculite peat and bulb fibre. These are all suitable for bulbs and for cuttings. They can be gently shaken from the plant to show root development. Children can make their own rooting mixes, using equal parts of loam, leaf mould, peat and silver sand. Such a mix is suitable for plants and seeds, although it can contain spores and insects. There are several commercial preparations available. The John Innes mixes are partially sterilised and plants and seeds have the benefit of added nutrients. More expensive are the soil-less composts, e.g. Fisons Levington, which are loamless and free from disease. The best results are obtained by germination in seed compost and subsequent transfer to potting compost.

There are many ways in which plants can be grown:
1. Before sowing *seeds*, fill the container to within 1–2 cm of its rim with damp compost. Small seeds can be sown on the surface while larger ones can be more easily spaced. Very large seeds such as peas and beans are best soaked for a few hours first. Cover the seeds with compost to a depth about twice their width. Watering is preferably done from below, before the whole system is introduced into the propagator or covered with a polythene bag which is left tied until germination begins.

   Once the seedlings are visible, ensure adequate light and ventilation and turn the container frequently. After three or four leaves appear, transplant if necessary by carefully lifting with a nail file, or similar tool, before the roots become entangled. When transplanting, the root-stem line should be just below the surface level. Again a polythene bag will help ensure growth.

2. Many plants can be propagated from *stem cuttings*, especially during the early part of the summer term. Select a healthy young shoot. Remove the cutting just above a leaf joint and trim it to the next leaf joint. It should normally be about 7–14 cm long. After removing any flower buds and lower leaves, dip the bottom of the stem into rooting powder and insert into the compost. Firm the compost and water well.

3. Plants forming clumps can be *divided* using a sharp knife and then re-potted.

4. Many trailing and climbing plants with long pliable stems, such as ivy, can be *layer propagated*. Pin a healthy stem into a pot using a hair pin and leave it attached to the parent plant until it begins to root.

5. Pronounced leaf veins on plants such as Begonia can be cut with a sharp knife and the *leaf cutting* laid on moist compost and pinned down, the whole being enclosed in a polythene bag. New plants grow from the cut veins.

6. What must be cheapest of all is to simply cut the leaves from carrots or beetroot, cut off the *vegetable top* and place it in a saucer of water. Watch the green fern begin to grow.

In consistently *warm* classrooms plants will thrive. However, at night, weekends or during holidays, the temperature may drop to less favourable levels and late frosts should be anticipated. Beware, also, of draughts. Window *light* is usually adequate, but do not leave your plants in direct sunlight, especially if they are covered with polythene bags which can magnify the sun's effects. The *water* requirements of plants vary, especially with temperature, light and season. During the main growing period, keep the compost constantly moist, but during cold weather or in the winter months keep watering to a minimum, almost allowing the compost to dry. Once growth is established regular *feeding* is beneficial, providing you follow the instructions and are not tempted to overfeed.

Inspect the *health* of your plants on a regular basis. If a plant appears to be ailing make sure that it

- has sufficient water
- does not have too much water which will cause root, stem and leaf rot
- has sufficient light
- has sufficient warmth
- does not require feeding
- has not been overfed
- has room to grow – should it be re-potted?
- is free from pests which will cause spotted leaves

Finally, remember the safety aspects:

- if you use any 'chemical' – e.g. rooting powder, insecticides – always wear gloves, and do it in a safe place, preferably out of doors, where children are not at risk
- many seeds are treated with fungicides – warn children not to eat them and to wash their hands after working with plant material
- read the instructions carefully
- store fertilisers, etc., in a safe, secure place
- dispose of empty containers safely
- wash hands and equipment after use

SOURCES OF INFORMATION AND SUPPORT

The projects

Nuffield Secondary Sciences
To neglect Nuffield Secondary Sciences (and Nuffield Primary Mathematics) would be to miss out important roots of the primary science movement. Nuffield Maths, in the

sixties, paved the way for the projects to follow, with the development of Teachers' Centres, local curriculum groups, and teacher involvement in the development and application of materials. Alongside this, Nuffield Secondary Sciences – although dividing the subject into three clear disciplines of Physics, Chemistry and Biology – radically changed the way that science was taught to some of our secondary children.

As with many projects, Nuffield Secondary Sciences elicited three broad types of reaction among the teachers at whom it was aimed. One group took it aboard, lock, stock and barrel. Another, larger, group accepted a proportion of it; some used it quite commonly, others less frequently. More importantly, a number *thought* they were using it, although in fact it made little difference to their practice. A third group rejected the project, misunderstood it, or were simply fearful of it. Contemporary advertisements for 'Nuffield Teachers' did nothing to enhance its popularity: it was not intended to produce a whole new breed of science teacher.

Nevertheless, Nuffield Secondary Sciences brought with it a change of climate. It introduced a high degree of practical activity to science teaching, and it had a seminal influence on other texts. Most important of all, it provided a forum for teachers to discuss science and science teaching; it helped to break down barriers, and encourage teachers to share problems and solutions. But the project had its weaknesses, too. It looked different from traditional ideas of science books, and used language in new and different ways. Though it was certainly demanding, especially in the concepts and key ideas, it lacked social relevance, and omitted many of the aspects of technology. Nevertheless, the ice had been broken, and in 1967 Collins published a crucially important and influential project.

Nuffield Junior Science

Two teachers' guides, an *Apparatus Sourcebook*, a book on Animals and Plants, and a number of small booklets comprised the (teacher) materials of the Nuffield Junior project, aimed at teachers of children aged from five to eleven.

Nuffield Junior Science recognised that questioning was a natural activity for young children, and that both teacher and child could learn from open-ended discovery, with 'a beneficial effect upon teaching'. It encouraged a breadth of experience, both in and out of the classroom, appropriate to the age and development of the child, and the growth from that experience of 'lines of enquiry'. The whole concept was child-centred and intended integration with other subjects. To this end, it was unstructured in approach (although within each interest topic it encouraged flow diagrams to plan and record). Unlike Nuffield Secondary Sciences, which presented fairly radical ideas within the framework of traditional conservative practice, Junior Science proved very daunting, since it had high expectations of teachers' organisational skills that few felt confident to fulfil. This approach has been vindicated by subsequent projects, and Nuffield Junior Science must be regarded as a major, trend-setting work, effecting a sea change in the direction of primary science. It will be seen on many school bookshelves, but may not receive the attention it deserves.

An Approach to Primary Science – The Oxford Project

Contemporary with the heavily funded Nuffield Schemes came this modest, shoe-string project from a small team – Stewart Redman, Anne Brereton and Peter Boyers, based in Oxford. It is unusual to find this small, concise book on any staffroom shelf –

especially today, as it is out-of-print. But it is remarkable in that it paid a great deal of attention to content – in terms of 'main ideas' – rather than processes. An excellent review may be found in the article by Norman Booth (sometime HM Staff Inspector for Science) in *Education 3–13*. This examines the 1969 'Oxford Project' and its four key ideas – Energy, Structure, Chance and Life. It proposes that many of the day-to-day events in the classroom relate to one or more of these four ideas, and that science gives us one way of looking at them. This 'way' is scientific method, observations leading to inferences, and verification by experiment. The book, in eight short chapters, outlines in pairs the theory and practice of its four key ideas. These chapters give enough work to immerse a child for six years in the offered experiences. Many of these 'experiences' are also in the fields of PE, or art and craft. In Booth's opinion, the work merits thinking about in helping children to make sense of many aspects of the world around them. It would have been interesting to see how primary science developed had the 'Oxford Project' had the massive resourcing of 'Nuffield'.

Science 5–13

'Science 5–13' was published by Macdonald Educational in 1972 as a series of 26 soft-covered books. This massive, loosely-structured project took four extensions of time limit and resourcing to reach completion. It spawned a number of smaller series, including four environmental titles and the 'Teaching Primary Science' books, both from Macdonald. The guide to the series was the book *With Objectives in Mind*, which related the project to the Piagetian stages of children's development. The book *Early Experiences* suggested work appropriate to the youngest primary children; the other books, in three stages, suggested work appropriate to children up to top of middle and lower secondary school. Topics ranged from 'Toys' and 'Change' to 'Minibeasts' and 'Ourselves'. All the books were designed for teacher use, forming a 'source', not a 'course'.

More particularly, the books provided the basis for some excellent in-service work for teachers; the project 'trained trainers', and used centres, from schools and colleges to the developing Teachers' Centres, to spread the message. The books were the most familiar of the Schools Council's projects to the ordinary classroom teacher, and as such were relatively successful. Like other projects before it, 'Science 5–13' has had a significant influence on other published projects. But this rich source of science work is a long way divorced from actual classroom practice, and good reasons can be identified for this disappointing state of affairs.

Firstly, there was no official index to the project until 1980, although a number of agencies had produced their own guides to the series, 'STEEL' (Science, Technology and Engineering Education in Lancashire), for example. For the first time, it was possible to take a topic, say 'colour' or 'food', and cut across the books to find the appropriate activities. The series then became accessible, although the contents still required adaptation for use in schools. Secondly, the project had little effect on the teaching of children at extreme ends of the age range. Despite *Early Experiences*, the project lacked ideas for younger infants and despite the 'Stage 3' books, the project has found little favour with the teachers of lower secondary schools. Thirdly, and most importantly, the series presumed a predilection towards science teaching that was not always demonstrated by teachers. Motivation was a prerequisite. The work was appropriate to children who routinely went out of school on visits and trips. It was suited to schools with good, or developing, practical resources. It demanded considerable preparation time on the part of the teachers. Where these preconditions were not present, the 26 units gathered dust. What was needed was a range of appropriate pupil materials. This was not to appear until 1982–3.

Progress in Learning Science – the 'Match and Mis-match' Materials

This unique work was published by Oliver and Boyd in 1977, as a result of the work of a Schools Council team matching appropriate science experience to children's development. The project capitalised on teachers' understanding of their own pupils, and their progress in the three key areas of attitudes, skills, and concepts. A wealth of items were listed – 'observing' or 'curiosity' for example – and three examples were given on distinct stages in the development of each of these items; thus observation ranges from 'limited' to 'wide-ranging', with the latter being selective of information 'relevant to a particular problem or enquiry'. Teachers could mark a child on a five-point scale according to how closely the child's observed behaviour related to the given statements. An individual record resulted, which was developmental in nature. Assessment in science is a difficult problem. *Progress in Learning Science* is an excellent example of how to tackle it.

Learning Through Science

This project represents the child materials for 'Science 5–13' produced in 1982–3 by some of the '5–13' team. It consists of work card packs, complete with teacher's notes, a 'Guide and Index' and some other publications already mentioned, including *Science for Children with Learning Difficulties*, and *Science Resources for Primary and Middle Schools*. The attractive, varnished cards are designed to lead children into investigations of their own, embracing what Roy Richards, the Project Director, describes as elbow room – i.e. space to develop original ideas. The index cross-references the cards and an appendix on 'the Structural Approach' illustrates the recording of children's progression.

As well as traditional areas – 'Ourselves', 'Electricity', 'Colour', and so on – there are packs on 'The Sky and Space', and on the 'Earth', written with the assistance of the appropriate professional organisations. Each pack contains two copies, each of 24 cards on the subject, together with the teacher notes, and a (very reasonable) list of appropriate apparatus.

The teacher is seen as the instigator of child activities, the regulator, recorder, and reference point. The whole series has been subject to very thorough trials. As a result, the reading demands are reasonable, the manual skills appropriate, and expectations realistic for children at the 'concrete' stage of development.

Science for Children with Learning Difficulties is a large-format book, with a selection of ideas appropriate to younger or less able children. They are chosen to be fairly self-centred – 'Me and My Friends', 'Me and My Reflection', or 'Me and My Shadow', for example. Some of the pages are copyright-free, and designed for photocopying. A little caution should be recommended in using the book; the chapter on 'Balls and Ball Games' for example, includes some measuring and mathematical work that would stretch the *able* child. Many people would be attracted to the book as a cut-price review of the 'Learning through Science' cards; but it must be emphasised that the book does not pretend to be a balanced scheme, or to give children all the experiences appropriate to primary science.

A lot of commercial schemes do, however claim this, and there is no space to consider each of them here. For a good, accurate factual account of nine current schemes (including 'Learning through Science'), see the ASE publication *Choosing Published Primary Science Materials for Use in the Classroom*. This covers a number of the commercial products, including some which have links with apparatus manufacturers and the 'My Body' Health Education project. Some significant schemes have come too late for inclusion; others, like Nelson's 'Sciencewise' books are simply not included. Most major publishers seem to have a scheme either marketed or in the pipeline and the criteria that the ASE set out in their book seem an excellent guide to objective assessment of them.

Under 'analysis' they consider the presentation, format and durability of the materials, together with what guidance is given for policy making and recording progress. Under 'Teacher Information' they look at practicalities to do with resources, safety, and adaptation to different teaching styles. What, for example, is the 'intended role of the teacher?' Lastly, the pupil materials are considered. Are they on-target for the intended group – encouraging individual ideas through the right level of language and realistic expectations of practical skills? Most important of all, what skills, abilities, and attitudes will be developed? A school which chose to select from the published schemes available would find the book enormously valuable, and the criteria are applicable to most published schemes.

Sources and resources

ASE, SNSS, SATRO, CLEAPSE – there is a wealth of initial letters related to primary science. Yet all these organisations – and many like them – can be major supports to a school, a teacher or a project. This guide offers a thumbnail sketch of the facilities offered by each.

The Association for Science Education – ASE
The Association for Science Education is based in a purpose-built headquarters in Hatfield. Its address is
> College Lane,
> Hatfield,
> Herts.
> AL10 9AA.

The primary subscriber membership had over 17,000 members in 1985. For a small annual fee, member schools could receive an excellent termly ideas sheet, 'Primary Science', liberally illustrated with examples of children's work, often on a particular theme. A termly *Primary Newsletter* keeps teachers in touch with recent developments; *Education in Science* periodically informs teachers across the age ranges, and discounts are offered on a range of published materials, including ASE's own series of study papers, drawn on when preparing this book. They will also advise on more local and regional activities. Experience has shown that primary membership of the ASE is excellent value, even if your school is unable to take part in locally-organised activities. All publications are the products of practitioners and bear the stamp of sound classroom experience. It is not surprising that the Department of Education and Science has chosen the ASE as the evaluating body for their Education Support Grant (ESG) projects in the Local Education Authorities.

Full membership of the ASE entitles you to receive the *School Science Review*, a periodical with both secondary and primary school contributors, and the most important publication for information on science education in the country, reflecting the ASE's position as the largest single-subject society. If you plan to take up full membership it would be as well to examine the *School Science Review* for its relevance to *primary* classrooms. Primary membership of the ASE is strongly advisable for teachers – especially post-holders – with science interests, or for whole schools. Similarly, schools might consider membership of the SNSS.

The School Natural Science Society – SNSS

Originally founded as the School Nature Study Union, the SNSS is concerned with all the aspects of natural science, including geology and astronomy. Its termly journal *Teaching Science* is free to members. Contributions are of interest to both specialists and non-specialists. The SNSS has a Teachers' Advisory Service to help with problems. It also publishes a wide range of pamphlets and booklets, available at a discount to members. These are very wide ranging, from practicalities of cage construction to biological indicators of stream pollution, but they are chiefly biological in nature. They are generally available for less than a pound. One regular contributor is Irene Finch, science writer and adviser to the old 'Science All Around' programmes on BBC television and now to 'Science Workshop'. Her work – especially her book *Nature Study and Science* – is unfailingly accurate and down to earth. Irene Finch is also the organiser of the group providing a comprehensive list of 'Primary School Science Skills' published by the SNSS and referred to in chapter 1. This, and other SNSS publications, is available from the ASE at their Hatfield address.

Consortium of Local Education Authorities for the Provision of Science Equipment – CLEAPSE (school science service)

Local Authority membership of CLEAPSE, based at

> Brunel University,
> Uxbridge,
> Middlesex.
> UB8 3PH

entitles contributory schools to a regular newsheet, *Science Equipment News*. This, as its name suggests, provides practice-based examples of work appropriate to primary children as well as news of newly-marketed science materials. Most important of all, it updates the CLEAPSE guides. These are enormously helpful booklets, providing a critical and confidential, *Which?*-style examination of the commercial equipment currently available for primary science teaching. If you are planning a large investment – a microscope or an environmental kit – the appropriate guide should be consulted. 'Best Buys' are listed, naturally, but sound criteria for equipment selection are provided, as well as a lot of practical advice on 'Working with Light' (Guide L156) for example, or 'Magnets' (Guide L161). These are available free to schools whose LEA contributes to CLEAPSE. An excellent example of the guides is L56, 'Small

Mammal Cages'. This reviews the types of cages currently available, and may introduce you to the clean, light, and hygienic polypropylene and stainless steel cages which are safer both for pets – the cages can be scrubbed with disinfectant and very hot water – and children – no sharp edges for cuts and infection. Teachers have to overcome a natural dislike of these laboratory-style cages. Our experience is that they made excellent, draught-free homes for classroom animals once you had got used to the clinical appearance. Pet shop cages compare poorly with recommended types.

CLEAPSE has bulk-buying and discounting arrangements with member Authorities; ask your Science Adviser.

The Surplus Buying Agency – SBA
The SBA is based in Sheffield at
 Woodbourn School,
 Woodbourn Road,
 Sheffield.
 S9 3LQ
 Tel: 0472 448647

and, as its name suggests, it buys up surplus stock which might have practical science applications. As a result, it is a relatively cheap source of many useful small items for science and craft, design and technology work; but understandably, it is not a comprehensive source, and it is not possible to equip from the SBA for the whole breadth of primary science work.

It *is* possible to buy as a personal caller to the SBA and for one or two larger items this is the only way of arranging delivery. Most often, though, the items are small – miniature bulbs, small switches, magnets, etc. – and are delivered by post.

In order to make use of the SBA's services, send them up to three stamped–addressed envelopes, addressed to your school, each year. You will receive a termly list, usually on a single sheet of A4 paper. You may need a specialist to help you decipher the descriptions – what are LEDs, for example? But once you have understood what is listed you will realise that the items – especially for low-voltage electrical work, and for simple craft, design and technology constructions – are much more reasonably priced than from an ordinary commercial supplier. Occasionally there are items with potential applications – electrical devices that strip down to give valuable spares. And once or twice there have been downright eccentric bargains – the authors could not resist toy doll mechanisms for 25 pence that (because they contained a tiny motor and 'record player') cried forlornly when connected to a battery!

The SBA is an excellent source of small, useful items. Send them an s.a.e. and find out what is on offer!

The British Association for the Advancement of Science – BAAS
The British Association has been running, for some years now, an Award Scheme for 'Young Investigators'. This is aimed at encouraging systematic investigation by young people between the ages of eight and twelve, and would most commonly be applied in a science club environment, rather than as the science curriculum. For a small registration fee, groups of more than five people receive a pack of materials (which do *not* contain the actual equipment involved) appropriate to one of the three levels of the scheme. All groups work for a Bronze award initially, and then (by way of further

5

Bronze awards if appropriate) they progress to a Silver, and finally a Gold award –
each award consisting of a certificate and badge. Bronze award tasks range from the
prescriptive (type A) to the open-ended (type B) and problem-solving (type C). They
can even be devised and agreed in co-ordination with a local awards co-ordinator.
Completion of each Bronze award will take a full school term. Silver awards are more
demanding, and would take two terms. Gold awards take a full year, marking a
significant achievement by a young person. Further details, and registration forms, are
available from
>BA Awards for Young Investigators
>The British Association for the Advancement of Science
>Fortress House
>23 Savile Row
>London
>W1X 1AB
>Tel: 01-734-6010.

Their BAYS group – British Association Young Scientists – is aimed at young people
of secondary age (11–18) and runs an annual BAYSDAY at an appropriate venue,
with displays, exhibitions and competitions. It is worthy of consideration by middle
school pupils.

SCIENCE EQUIPMENT – SOME SUGGESTIONS

The ideal school might contain all this in total; a great deal can be achieved using far
less, and a good start can be made using 'junk' materials at first, and adding specialist
equipment as the need arises. There are a number of specialist suppliers, and it is
always wise to shop around for discounts. In the experience of the authors, it is seldom
economic to buy prepared kits. They contain everything, of course, and when time is a
premium, this is an advantage, but you could end up paying heavily over the odds for
plastic bags and rubber bands. You will evolve sources as time goes on. A friendly
woodyard will offer offcuts, or a local pharmacist save sturdy airtight containers. A
good stock can be obtained from the Surplus Buying Agency, in Sheffield (address on
opposite page).

It is important to check with your LEA, if you are a local authority school, to see
whether they have preferential arrangements with suppliers through CLEAPSE for
the provision of science equipment. Schools rarely start from scratch, and you would
be well-advised to search the dimmer recesses of cupboards and stock-rooms. Often,
equipment lies unused because its true nature is not appreciated. Only after reviewing
what you already have should you start ordering what you need.

The following list presumes a central store for items of high value or needing special
care; note the comments in chapter 5, to post-holders, regarding the storage,
cataloguing and security of equipment. At 1986 prices, the materials listed could be
obtained for a total outlay of less than £1,500. It should be noted that a perfectly
effective science stock was built up in one school by an initial outlay of £300. Annual
costs thereafter were then between £50 and £100, with the majority of this money
going on expendables, and often being spent as petty cash in Woolworths. An
allowance was made for one 'large' item each year.

Stored centrally

(In no particular order of priority)

Binoculars   A good pair of binoculars is useful. It is important not to buy too high a magnification. In our experience, eight by thirty is about right. Anything higher than that is intensely frustrating. In adult hands, binoculars can be rapidly focussed. Children need practice in aiming the instrument along their line of sight towards the object. With binoculars of too high a magnification they have little hope of seeing a sitting bird, let alone one in flight. They will need advice about adjustment to suit their individual eyes before they start out, and it goes without saying that they need warning about the dangers of looking at the sun, or attempting to observe eclipses. Be content, initially, if junior children master the instrument; you may be disappointed if you fail to give them adequate practice before you ask them to observe something really important. By the time they have adjusted, aimed, and focussed the event you want them to observe will be over.

Microscopes   Well-meaning parent groups seem convinced that no science – as they remember it – can take place without a microscope. It is very easy to be carried away by their enthusiasm and to end up with an expensive instrument of limited use.

There are two types of microscope that may be of interest to you. They are the traditional monocular microscope beloved of forensic experts in television crime series, and the less traditional binocular. (There are also devices which resemble microscopes, but which are, in fact, photographic slide viewers. More of them later.)

Monocular microscopes demand a subject that is virtually still. The conveniently still object has to be sandwiched – in a bubble-free drop of water for preference – between two glass slides, one of which may be a 'coverslip', a fine sliver of glass no thicker than a razor blade. This is then placed on a stage beneath the barrel of the microscope, and a light source – natural or artificial – is reflected through it. Focussing is achieved by 'racking' the barrel up and down. All movements of the hand have to be reversed to succeed in bringing the object into the field of vision. Racking too far down (unless the machine is fitted with a stop) sends the barrel crashing through the glass. The object can be over-magnified so that only a small, and uninformative, part can actually be seen. Frequently, children see little more than their own eyelashes. You have no proof of this, since, except with exceptional microscopes beyond your need and pocket, you cannot see what the child is seeing. All this sounds rather damning, and in a way, it is meant to, since a rashly-bought monocular microscope can be an expensive and frustrating mistake. They do have their uses, however, and if you set out to buy one, avoid the 'toys' offering extremely high magnification (with correspondingly high levels of distortion), and go for a good, well-engineered device, capable of standing up to classroom life. Good examples are the Bausch and Lomb ESM10 and ESM40 models, and the Osmiroid 'Scientist' X20.

'Bioviewers' overcome the limitations of monocular microscopes, but are themselves limited in scope. Essentially viewers for prepared photographic slides, they ensure that the child achieves the best possible picture, but only, of course, from the range produced by the supplier (Appendix IV).

The most useful device for medium to high magnification in the experience of the authors is the binocular microscope, sometimes known as the stereomicroscope. These are sturdy and reliable. They do not offer the degree of enlargement that a monocular microscope does, but at primary level this is rarely necessary. They operate with a daylight or room light source, although you could provide a special light if you felt it necessary. Having two lenses, commonly adaptable for the varying distances between eyes, they give children a good chance of seeing the object of their interest. This object can be alive, and moving. Indeed, it can even be swimming in water, since a transparent container can be placed on the microscope stage, giving the creature both security and relative freedom. Either the lenses are racked down, or the stage can be racked up. The best binocular microscopes have a clutch device, which ensures that the lens cannot be racked into the object. With a little manouevering, it is possible for both teacher and pupil to have a lens each, so that you can actually see what the child sees. There are a number on the market; the sturdy cast zinc bodies of the Bausch and Lomb examples are virtually unbreakable, and two other good models are the Stereomaster 240 and the Zenith BM-51-2.

A microscope is useful when examining a whole range of materials.
(Reproduced with the permission of Osmiroid.)

Activities with light
The study of light can be a frustrating one since to experiment with light you must have dark. The result can be small groups crowded into stock-rooms and cupboards,

or working with with the blinds drawn. In the authors' experience, a good, reliable, low-voltage light source is worth a small investment; mains-operated projectors are dangerous, both electrically and because they become so hot, while torches and hand lanterns are not especially effective. Experiments with light being fairly critical anyway, it is important to get a good, sharp, light source. Most of the suppliers list ray boxes; Osmiroid's battery-powered one is worth looking at. Similarly, really effective pinhole cameras and periscopes are obtainable in pre-cut black card, and can save a lot of time and trouble. The angles in periscopes are critical for good results; pinhole cameras work best when used to 'photograph' a brightly-illuminated object.

Other materials that might be centrally stored are a cassette recorder and tapes; the various exciting construction sets, such as Technical Lego or Fischertechnik, that offer a wealth of experience with gears, levers, and pulleys; and the more expensive but infrequently-used devices such as electrical meters and a vacuum jar.

Specialist equipment available to areas, year groups, or classes

Simple magnifying aids are the 'nature viewers', like the SM475 model from Arnold, or the little Minispectors from Osmiroid. The latter are small, round, plastic boxes, with close-fitting lids – a point to remember if you do not want to suffocate small creatures. The lids are moulded into a magnifying lens (or 'magic-fying' as one child charmingly put it), and enlarge the object inside. The lids can even be stacked, producing a compound microscope effect; but the higher the magnification, the greater the distortion. Minispectors are a relatively cheap way of ensuring that a large number of children can experience magnification simultaneously.

Larger, more cup-sized, are the Midispectors from the same source. They incorporate a grid, ideal for measuring specimens. With their magnifying lids off, they are excellent for swimming creatures under the binocular microscope. More expensive, but worthy of consideration, are the beautiful mounted glass lenses, which offer greater sharpness and clarity. Some are like miniature coffee tables; others, like the Harris model, are mounted on flexible arms.

A useful device for the painless trapping of minibeasts is the 'pooter'. Essentially, this is a plastic beaker with two flexible tubes emerging. You put one over your prey, and suck through the other. A gauze prevents a mouthful of woodlouse! You can make these fairly easily, or they can be bought quite cheaply. Transfer of trapped creatures is best achieved with a soft paintbrush, but even here rough treatment must be avoided to prevent crushing.

For related environmental work, various nets are suitable; and for a deeper study of the surroundings, and a range of other uses, yet another Osmiroid product, the Thermostik, is invaluable. Essentially a thermometer that works on the bimetallic strip principle (i.e. without any liquids), the Thermostick can be put into liquids, pushed in the ground, suspended from a string, dipped in a pond, and all without the usual worries about thermometer breakage. The measured temperature can be read from a scale, and a moveable pointer can be set to read the base line. So, for example, it could be plunged into a can of ice, set with the starting temperature, and left to register the rise if the can is put in a warm room. The insulating properties of various materials could be measured by wrapping them round the can.

Of considerable use in environmental work is a selection of test papers. They are also helpful in food studies, and for learning the principle of colour-matching to a spectrum of possible results. The familiar Litmus paper in red and blue, Cobalt Chloride paper to test for water, and the various BDH universal papers can be supplemented with naturally-made indicators, such as red cabbage extract.

Effective filtering of soil samples, and separation of solids from liquids – e.g. sand from water – can be achieved with a filter funnel (plastic) and filter papers. You can cut your own, but the prepared circles of paper save time and are obtainable in various grades for various sizes of particle if you want that degree of sophistication. Incidentally, do not use filter paper for chromatography (colour separation) work, unless you have money to burn. Cheap blotting paper – even newsprint – can be as effective.

A selection of tubing – rubber and plastic, flexible and rigid – will be found useful, especially if it push-fits together.

Work with electricity can be exciting, whatever the level; but it is important to *preface and end every lesson with warnings about the dangers of current from the mains*, and to remind the children that the work in school is only done with low-voltage batteries. Bitter experience suggests that only children who are carefully supervised should be given screwdrivers; good connections can be made in a number of different ways without them. Children given screwdrivers will quickly dismantle apparatus into separate components! Select, then, from the following list. The Surplus Buying Agency and Woolworth should prove good sources; beware high street electrical stores where items are individually packaged, and expensive.

Multicore wire   it is essential to buy really flexible wire; single-core wire breaks very easily.

Fine insulated wire   for coils and electromagnets.

Resistance wire   which weakens current in proportion to its length, so that it can be used, coiled around card for convenience, to dim lamps or slow down motors.

Wire wool   with a current through it this burns away, effectively demonstrating the action of a fuse. Care must be taken to use only one strand at a time, over a tin plate.

Crocodile clips   wires can be screwed or soldered to these to make connections easy.

2.5 and 3.5 volt MES lamps   these are the small, screw-in lamps. They can be colour coded to save time when trying to identify the voltage.

Bulb-holders

Festoon lamps   a few of these add variety. They are shaped like a plug fuse, and can be fitted into:

Small coiled springs

Bicycle and bell batteries – not too strong, or they will 'blow' the bulbs. Their clip or spring terminals are ideal for crocodile clips, or you can buy

Torch batteries   and fit them into

Terry tool clips   these will hold the batteries, if screwed to a board; a screw at either end produces makeshift terminals.

A selection of *switches*, both commercial and home-made. For the latter, see the Nuffield science guides; for commercial switches, try to get a selection which might include

Toggle switches – miniature light switches. (These resemble mains switches, so emphasise the dangers.)

Knife switches   these enable two-way circuits to be made.

Bell pushes   children expect these to produce the buzz; show them that they are only special switches.

Micro-switches   these work by operating a tiny 'pip', and are present in many electrical appliances, where they carry a heavy load but are operated by a small movement; closing the door of the tumble drier, for example.

Rocker switches   these are the typical car switch. They, like others on this list, have *three* terminals; in finding out why, children will discover that some switches work in the ON position, some in the OFF.

Reed switches   these tiny, glass-tube switches work by magnetic induction. Either an electromagnet switches them on and off, or, in children's models, a permanent magnet comes close enough to trigger the switch. Easier to do than to explain.

Among other items that can come in handy are:

Electric buzzers   some printed-circuit type offer three levels of volume.

Electric bells   these take a higher voltage, or may need a couple of small batteries joined in series.

Electric motors   a variety can be obtained, relatively cheaply. Few have more than tiny solder tags as terminals, and it is worth looking for those that can be most easily connected-up.

Diodes   these are like 'one-way valves', and the children should experience them in a circuit.

Light-emitting diodes (LEDs)   these, as the name suggests, are diodes that light up. They are often used as tracers or reminder lights on appliances to tell you that you have left them on! Among the other hardware, we might list are:

A selection of metals and other materials.
Magnetic compasses
Soft iron rods
Wire-stripping pliers

If you plan to branch out into electrostatics, choose a dry day. Nothing destroys the magical effect of static electricity like damp in the air! Perhaps this is one field where a kit may be acceptable. Otherwise collect, individually, a selection of marked fabrics, a variety of rods – glass, ebonite, vulcanite – and pith balls or table tennis balls or balloons.

Returning to current electricity, there are a number of forms of specialised circuit boards available, with clip-in units ensuring perfect, even self-cleaning, connections. They enable reliable circuits to be made quickly and neatly, and may even have the circuit diagram of that item printed on them. They are a tremendous way of expanding the skills of older children after they have experienced a home-made set-up. Only the untidy mass of trailing wires can demonstrate that circuits do not have a special shape; provided we join things up in the right order, the wires can, and will, trail anywhere. This method teaches about poor connections, short-circuits, and fault-finding, the hard, and realistic way. A practical half-way house between the home-made and the more sophisticated circuit kits has become available from Osmiroid. The Science

Horizons Electricity Kit has push-fit connectors which, it is claimed 'even five-year-olds' can use. It certainly looks more successful than their previous kit, the clever, but fiddly and frustrating, Centric apparatus.

Work on mechanics can be enhanced by using a variety of simple pulleys, which are diffcult items to manufacture with any degree of success. Single, double, and triple sheave pulleys are expensive, and need some sort of simple but sturdy frame so that pulley systems can be set up, using strong cord, without the lines tangling horribly. An alternative is the kind of hoist manufactured to lift car engines; this is obtainable from accessory shops, but is neither variable nor cheap. 'S'-hooks, or butcher's hooks, are useful items; cover the points with insulating tape if you cannot file them off. Force meters of various strengths, G-clamps, and a variety of springs, levers and weights will all be useful. A lot of maths equipment is adaptable; the 'equaliser', for example, with its two arms and selection of washers or weights, is excellent to demonstrate the importance of lever length.

Work on light is possible with a variety of plastic mirrors, which are bendy and almost unbreakable. They are made in double-sided flat and concave/convex styles. You can buy special metal mirror clips to hold them upright, or use a blob of Blu-Tack. Similarly, plastic lenses in various configurations – bioconcave, bioconvex, planoconvex – are useful, and so is a ray box (already mentioned). Glass is the most satisfactory material for prisms, and Arnold (SW214) and ESA (7013/663) are among the suppliers. Colour filters are obtainable from theatrical suppliers, like Furse of Nottingham, or from apparatus manufacturers like Griffin Primary, with sets such as XGB 400–T. In principle, you can mix colours on Newton's famous wheel, and produce white – or at least a pale grey. In practice, only commercial wheels are effective, and a cheaper alternative is a Rainbow Top – Hestair Hope (K9051/075). It is a great help to any work with light if you can arrange to work at least in deep shade, if not in the dark.

Magnetism is a perennial favourite, and the traditional work can be greatly extended by the wide variety of magnets available, all with their own characteristics. Cheap bar magnets should be avoided; they are weak and quickly lose what magnetism they had. Size is no guide to magnet strength. As well as bar magnets, there are rods, horseshoes, buttons, and rings (which slide up and down a stick, illustrating beautifully how magnets attract and repel). They should always be stored neatly, with their keepers in place. They will have an effect on things stored with them, so keep them away from compasses and metal objects you wish to keep non-magnetic. There are also rubber magnets – more accurately, ferrite – which are available in sheet, strip, and string forms. A lodestone is a curio, and iron filings, steel needles, magnetic needles, and small magnetic, so-called 'field plotting' compasses are necessary for the more popular experiments. This selection of apparatus should enable you to branch out from the old favourites, to examine the characteristics of magnets, and to apply them in simple models and toys. Do not expect to achieve the impossible magnetic fields illustrated in so many books. Given half a chance, children will copy these and ignore the far more untidy products of real-life magnetism. A simple way of producing a record of the field shape is to sprinkle filings on to paper over the magnet, and then to sandwich them for a week with damp blotting paper. The resulting rust pattern is permanent. A useful accessory is a clean shoebrush; it removes filings in direct contact with magnets.

Equipment you can make yourself

It is beyond the scope of this book to present plans for the construction of home-made equipment, but plans can be found in any number of publications ranging from the early Nuffield Junior Science Guide on apparatus to the ingenious offerings of the Learning through Science book *Science Resources for Primary and Middle Schools*.

Simple caging for minibeasts can include insect cages from plastic lemonade bottles, a wood and glass (or better, plastic) sheet wormery, a 'snailery' and a home for an ants' nest – a formicarium. All these, even if available, are more cheaply made than bought, and there is a good deal of applied science in their construction. An equaliser can be constructed if none is available from the maths cupboard, and a safe 'hardness tester' can be made from a length of plastic drain pipe, a wood block and a nail. An adjustable ramp is useful for work with small cars, or can be manufactured from parcel tubes for rolling marbles. A length of guttering makes a good test tank for boats and plastic cups on wooden arms will produce a simple air speed indicator. An expensive item for weather studies – if you take them that far – is a Stevenson Screen.

If all this is beyond your time and resources, give careful thought to people who might have both the time and the enthusiasm to do the handwork. School caretakers, parents and the CDT departments of secondary schools might be approached. Indeed, some secondaries are so heavily involved as to produce simple kits, to teacher specification, for completion in primary classrooms. Discuss the idea with your science or CDT Adviser. Young people on the Manpower Services funded schemes might also become involved; again, they would welcome valuable, relevant, and genuinely-appreciated projects.

Materials from the maths store

A number of pieces of equipment appropriate for science work are common to the maths store, especially of course, those for weighing and measuring.

Waymaster make a number of suitable scales which you may find you can apply to a variety of scientific uses; the 400 model is a delicate letter scale, the 500, a kitchen scale. Salter make similar models, like the Waymix 0–2 kg kitchen scale. A bathroom scale like the Waymaster, or the Salter 400, is occasionally useful. Some scales are made to weigh in Newtons. Digital balances *can* be used; they have the same disadvantage as digital watches – can the children really understand them? Spring balances are valuable – weak ones, weighing to 1 kg by steps of 5 g, and stronger ones, weighing to 5 kg by 25 g steps, both have their uses. Masses, from 10 g to 5 kg, are essential. Specialist balances – the heavy duty bucket balance, suspended pan and see-saw scales– may be found useful.

Polypropylene is an excellent, sturdy, unbreakable material for measuring cylinders (100 and 1000 ml) and for beakers, if junk substitutes are not appropriate. (In the unlikely event that you need to heat liquids you will need glass containers of course. Pyrex beakers, of about 250 ml, and Pyrex test tubes, of about 125 × 16 mm, are suitable, but beware of 'bumping' – the sudden ejection of hot liquid from a test tube, usually countered by putting a small object (a dead match, for example) in the tube. There should be almost no need for this sort of technique, however, and you would be well advised to look for other ways of heating liquids.)

Sand timers are interesting – Osmiroid produce Transam timers in various sizes and hence times. Osmiroid also make little 'tocker timers' that rock to a standstill in a given time. Experiments some years ago with tocker timers suggested that they were wildly inaccurate – but they have been improved.

A *stopclock* is essential, and a number of companies produce sturdy models – but beware those with a 'reset' button on the top as it is almost impossible not to slam it down when stopping the timer, with the resultant loss of the measured time. A metronome can be interesting, and useful for setting a pace, or for hands-on tests against the clock.

For measurement of length, the standard 30 cm and metre ruler, tapes in 100 cm, 50 cm, 10 m, and 30 m, lengths are important, and so, too, is the click or trundle wheel. Callipers can be obtained, in both sliding (direct reading) and bow (reading from a ruler) forms. A height measure can be handy, as can a foot gauge.

A *micrometer screw gauge* is seldom used, but can be the only way of (say) grading card by thickness, or calculating the thickness of a single sheet of paper from a pile. Other specialist gauges include the depth gauge, feeler gauges for gaps, and a triangular-shaped internal diameter gauge. A map measure (like a miniature trundle wheel) is seldom used but has no junk substitute.

Plastic syringes (like those used for injections) are useful, but never use hospital cast-offs. With narrow gauge plastic tubing, they can endow working models with hydraulic power.

'Zoological' equipment

If you plan to do a lot of work with animals, then specific apparatus may be appropriate. Mammal cages, like those described in the section on keeping animals, will be found useful, together with feeding bottles and food hoppers. If you intend to keep an aquarium, then an electric aerator is valuable, and you may also need a water heater.

An incubator is an expensive item to buy outright. If you plan to incubate eggs, you would be well advised to discuss the whole project with your nearest college of agriculture or the authority's adviser for science or rural studies. Experience has shown that this can be an enormously successful and stimulating undertaking, or disappointing, and occasionally disastrous. It is not something to enter into lightly.

If you can borrow an appropriate incubator, begin by stabilising it, in the classroom, to the correct temperature range. A maximum-and-minimum thermometer is essential to see that the temperature is maintained, day and night, for several days. The incubator will need to be kept moist, too. Electricity and water are a dangerous mix, and so it is essential to use a safe, modern device. Prepare for the newly-hatched chicks, too. A large, deep box, with a temperature maintained by an infra-red bulb and correctly furnished with litter, water, and appropriate food, is essential. Chicks are no respecters of each other, and if the box becomes too cold, they will trample each other to come close to the source of heat. You will need a school key holder who is willing to help with the night-time egg turning (not essential throughout – check the textbooks according to the species of bird).

Only now (and given that you have a good home for the hatched chicks) can you acquire some fertile eggs. Ensure that their date of fertilisation fits your timescale – you will not want them to hatch in the middle of a holiday. Arrange for someone expert to 'candle' them to ensure that development is taking place. Then mark them to ensure that every egg is turned (traditionally with 'X' and 'O') and incubation can proceed. The authors have seen species ranging in size from quail to goose incubated in this way, but hens' eggs are the most common, and the most acceptable chicks to farms and colleges.

You are strongly advised against personalising the eggs or chicks. It is very easy for children to identify with a particular egg or chick, and thermostat failure, infertility or human error can easily prevent successful hatching. In one recent project, a power failure in the early hours sharply reduced the number of chicks hatched, with resultant disappointment to the children. Be prepared, too, for the very rapid rate of growth of the newly hatched chicks. Be ready to move them to their permanent home a few days after hatching – and certainly within a week.

Incubation has been described in some detail since it offers a once-in-a-lifetime experience, but is fraught with hazards. It is essential to take sound advice. Remember, too, that an incubator runs on mains electricity, and also that some children may show an allergy reaction to feathers.

Apparatus for weather recording and environmental work

Weather recording should not be seen as an end in itself. Even if the only application of recorded figures is to check them against the daily forecast in the newspaper or on the telephone, the recording will take on some significance. Better still to record them against natural events – the seasons, growth, life cycles, and change.

It is possible to spend an enormous amount of money on weather-recording instruments, but it is also possible to achieve satisfactory results from home-made equipment, and many science texts – notably Nuffield Junior Science and 'Science 5–13' – describe its construction. A Stephenson Screen (if required) can be made from louvred cupboard doors. A rain gauge (home-made), a wind-gauge (home-made, or the Osmiroid ventimeter), a humidity meter, and an aneroid barometer (from Metricaids) are probably all that are necessary, together with a thermometer, of which there are numerous types.

Most classrooms (indeed, probably all) will have the standard wall thermometer which has limited use since it is glass. The same is true of clinical thermometers, of course, and they have little value. If you want children to take their body temperatures, the Feverscan-type crystal thermometers are best. Dipping thermometers, which are meant to be hung on a cord in a pond or stream, are better protected than most glass thermometers. A useful device is the large-scale demonstration thermometer, which shows how the liquid expands to give the reading. This liquid expansion can also be seen with a home-made thermometer made with a plastic lemonade bottle into which a thin straw is fitted using plasticine or Blu-Tack. Coloured water will fountain amazingly if your warm hands are put round the bottle. Maximum and minimum thermometers have occasional value – especially for weather recording. A unique thermometer is Osmiroid's Thermostik, which works as an ordinary temperature measure but can also be used as a dipping thermometer and can be pushed into the ground or other soft materials to measure internal temperatures. This is a bimetallic strip thermometer – no glass or liquid is involved.

Apparatus for horticultural work

If you plan to grow plants and make studies of them on a large scale, then a number of tools will be found useful. Several suppliers offer small-scale garden tools that are appropriate for young children. Watering cans, trowels, and the like can be supplemented with a soil auger, which enables you to study the layers of the soil. Propagators, seed boxes and pots are all worth acquiring in reasonable quantities.

In buying all equipment look first for junk substitutes. Only buy kits as a last resort; the cost of packing them is understandably high.

ASSESSMENT AND RECORDING OF PUPIL PROGRESS

'The lesson went well; the children seemed to get a lot out of it.' We all think in phrases like these from the very beginning of teaching primary science. If we keep a record for the head, or for our own information, we may even jot down such a phrase. In so doing, we are *assessing* the activity, and the children's gains from it; if we use the information to improve the learning and teaching process later, we are *evaluating* it; and if we keep the note along with others about our primary science experiences, we are *recording* it. There is no magic about these three processes; teachers are performing them all the time. What is needed, to make the processes more valuable to teacher and to pupils, is a greater degree of objectivity.

Assessment

'What are the children gaining from this activity?' and 'Is that activity a good one for putting across what I am trying to teach?' are two sides of the same coin. In both cases, we are making professional judgements from evidence; and that evidence may be the children's degree of involvement, their application to the task, their reluctance to move to other activities, or simply how quiet it is in the classroom. A good teacher is making judgements like this all the time; but often they are subjective, and relative – 'I can't expect the work to go so well with the next group, they're comparatively immature.' Clear criteria are needed, alongside which children's learning can be objectively measured, or which accurately reflect the success or failure of a particular activity.

Let us look first at the assessment of children's progress in science. We can choose to assess this for a number of reasons, chief of which will be to place before the child or children relevant experiences in the future. This is the simple hierarchy of skills; it is no good expecting children to be able to eliminate variables, for example, until they have learnt a lot about experimental design. But there are other reasons for the assessment, e.g. pupil progress, among which are the identification of their difficulties, and the opportunity to give pupils themselves some sense of their own achievements. Other teachers and schools may expect, and act upon, our science records, and they are of value in any parent consultation, in that they contribute objective evidence of learning gains. It is important to recognise from the outset that assessment is not the same as testing; pencil-and-paper are seldom involved, and any modifications subsequent to the assessment are more likely to be in the mode of teaching groups – 'I must give them more experience of class observation' – rather than modifying the behaviour of individuals – 'must work harder'.

The Science 5–13 team were quite clear that science teaching was all about 'developing an inquiring mind and a scientific approach to problems.' The Assessment of Performance Unit are equally certain that science is a mode of thought or activity applicable to *other* subject areas. Any number of text books list the skills and subskills, the concepts, the knowledge, and the attitudes that may constitute a scientific way of thinking. What is necessary is the objective assessment of these criteria with a view to our presentation – and the children's understanding – of the complete picture.

In practice, the objective assessment of children's learning is a matter of clear criteria and applied teacher experience. As a first step, it is easy to record the activities that children have actually undertaken. A list of completed work cards does as much, and many of the commercial schemes provide such methods of recording. A slight refinement of this instrument is to record, separately, experience and understanding, though what is meant by understanding an activity may be a matter of degree.

Of far greater value is an objective assessment of the development of the skills underlying the work card assignments, and many of the techniques for this will be informal, even casual. You must work with a reasonable number; it is quite impossible to assess the understanding of a whole class, or of individuals in it, from the responses of two or three. Make it clear what you are about; or you may find that an engrossed group may try to fob you off with any answers simply to be rid of you and able to go back to the job in hand. Remember that it is *their answers*, not your questions, that count. *Let them talk*. You cannot expect them to respond in the precise way that your checklist demands. In the middle of an activity, they may be *predicting* what will happen next, when you want them *observing* what is happening now. Watch the skills that are demonstrated as they arise, not in the order of your prepared checklist. Above all, recognise that their progress is likely to be irregular; i.e. you cannot expect significant gains every week, or even every time you come to assess. And try to compare the performance of each individual not with some hypothetical norm but with their previous performance at that, or a similar, task.

The whole process takes a lot of time; more, of course, the greater the number of skills, attitudes, and concepts you set out to examine. Since lesson time is at a premium, it can help to make assessments from children's recordings of their work, where these are relevant. And, very occasionally, it can be appropriate to present the children with simple tests of their understanding, which can be practical or a written test of practical skills. The publications of the Assessment of Performance Unit, of course, provide a wealth of examples; the 'Look' project teachers' book *A Guide to Primary Science Policy* gives examples of simple tests tied closely to a commercial scheme.

By far the most elaborate and complete checklist of children's scientific development is from the classic study produced by the Progress in Learning Science project led by

Wynne Harlen; and commonly known as the 'Match and Mis-match' material. This examines skills like observing and pattern-seeking; concepts, like those of energy, change, and force; and attitudes, like curiosity, originality, and willingness to co-operate. Three statements are presented for each of these, describing behaviour at progressive stages of development. These behaviours are in terms of actions or responses which could be observed by a skilled teacher, not in a single, objective test, but in a variety of circumstances. Thus for 'finding patterns in observations', the three statements are made:

> Does not relate findings to the purpose of the enquiry or notice any patterns there are to be found without considerable help.

> Attempts to look for patterns in findings but rarely suggests possible explanations.

> Makes reasonable inferences which fit the evidence and makes some attempt to explain the patterns which he finds in his observation.

Five boxes provide a relative scale for recording both these and the intermediate stages; by dating or shading, it is possible to record an individual pupil profile. This record should develop with the individual.

Many attempts have been made to copy the 'Match and Mis-match' material; and other schemes have evolved in parallel. The Scottish 'Primary Science Development Project' material, for example, proposes a list of criteria from which an individual might be profiled:

> Very enthusiastic about science.
> Makes good use of her senses and is able to suggest explanations by applying previous experience.
> Usually needs some help to think beyond the first stage of an investigation.
> Contributes effectively to discussion.
> Written notes are clear and easy to follow.
> Requires help with recording in graph form.

One school produced a system using simplified statements on either side of a five-column recording grid. Thus children could be assessed on a scale ranging from 'observation, perfunctory and superficial' to 'observation accurate, with fine details identified'. By juggling the skills and attitudes up and down the scales from experience with the children the teacher who produced this simple checklist was able to produce a pattern of ticks which bore some relation to the children's scientific development. With experience, it was possible to see, from the curve of the record, the areas where the child might need wider experience and encouragement. This sort of use takes assessment into the field of planning, and evaluation.

Individual feedback on children can also be achieved by simple review activities, which might, for example, be set out on a table in one corner of the room. The activities could be practical, or pencil-and-paper. If, for example, you wanted to confirm that the children had understood the meanings of pitch in their sound activities you might provide numbers of bottles containing varying amounts of water; children could be asked to place the bottles in order of ascending pitch (using whatever words are appropriate to their age and ability level) and the bottles themselves would be a record, or they could write the numbers on the bottles in order, giving you a more permanent record.

Pencil-and-paper activities naturally demand a greater degree of abstraction;

pictures might show paired magnets with poles facing each other for children to draw on arrows saying which way they would expect the magnets to move when brought close together. Alternatively, the arrows could be provided and the children asked to write in the pole names. The practical tests are preferable; the paper-and-pencil work is very dependent upon degree of comprehension.

A number of schools are experimenting with children's recording of their own progress. They have found that older children are very aware of their own abilities and limitations. They can be very honest and accurate in their recording of their activities and experiences, although teacher supervision and checking is essential. If this seems appropriate to your situation, it would be as well to discuss it with a school already using the technique.

Evaluation

If you assess the science work that you are doing with the children with a view to improving it, you are evaluating. Evaluation can have far wider implications than individual assessment, in that it can lead to change in the science policy of an individual teacher, or of the whole school. It presumes a general understanding by the staff that a periodical questioning of what they are doing – and why – is a normal, healthy, and unthreatening activity. If an atmosphere of mutual confidence and professionalism is not apparent then the reasons for the evaluation may need to be carefully explained and justified. Thus one school gained greatly from a self-evaluation exercise once the staff clearly understood that the results would be of immediate benefit to their teaching, that individuals would not be identified, and that the outcome of the evaluation would always be confidential to the staff of the school. The process of self-evaluation showed that all the staff shared the same concerns about certain curriculum areas – notably moral and religious education, and the school's provision for special needs – while they felt generally happy and confident with the maths and language guidelines they had recently devised. When, two years later, the school was commended for its provision for children with special needs, the review and subsequent development were wholly vindicated. In the meantime, other areas of priority had been similarly identified.

What are the ways in which a school's current science teaching can be evaluated? *Self appraisal* by checklisting is formal but reliable. It can ensure (honestly answered!) that all the staff have read and understood the school policy (which they should have been previously involved in formulating) or the LEA policy (and their criticisms, if any, made known to the science adviser). A checklist can identify poor storage or poor access to equipment, or the lack of resources in all or some areas. It can identify general difficulties in the understanding of application of policies. Most importantly, it can enable staff to highlight, with a high degree of confidentiality, professional difficulties with, say, LEA officers or non-teaching staff.

Once established, such a self-appraisal checklist can form a vital part of an annual review of the school, or of its science work. Through such an annual review, *all* the staff, however vociferous their colleagues, can make their feelings known. Part of this annual review can be an *interview*, for each teacher, with the head teacher (or, in very large schools, a post-holder). Many schools do this voluntarily already. The interview highlights general areas of success and satisfaction in the last year, as well as bringing incidental difficulties forward. It enables head and teacher to set targets for the next year – particularly for post-holders. It is a valuable piece of professional development, properly-handled, that can present teachers with reasonable and achievable expectations to the benefit of the whole school. Such an interview could be of direct value in establishing and encouraging the development of science.

Staff discussion – between two or more teachers – can be a less formal, but equally valuable, channel of self-improvement. In particular, it can highlight opportunities for the initiation and development of science activities. It would seem to be true that if you have two or more teachers in a room together the conversation will eventually come around to schools. Quite why this should be – whether it is teachers' uncertainty, or their need for reassurance, or the performing nature of the job (rather as actors are immersed in their work), or whether it is simply a function of the fact that everyone in the room once had experience of schools – is not clear, but teachers will talk about teaching, and in that talking, they both teach and learn. When they compare their experience of primary science with that of others, they are informally evaluating, and probably planning improvement.

It is a small step from discussion to *mutual observation*, but a step that current staffing in schools seldom makes practicable. This is a pity, because such a lot is gained, both by observed and observer, when teachers can work and talk together; and while this is especially true when one of the pair is a science specialist, a simple briefing of any pair of teachers – 'notice how your colleague organises the class so that they are all occupied all the time' – can produce dividends.

Not as rewarding as mutual observation and discussion, because it is at second-hand, and in cold print, is the comparison and collation of *teachers' records*. While most schools keep records – and forecasts – of work, it may be only the head teacher who sees the whole picture, and there is a need to produce some feedback – not just to individuals, but generally – so that the whole school can move as one, along clearly-defined lines. Heads reading teachers' records are commonly looking at curriculum balance, and at progression. They may identify this for individual teachers, and pull the reins this way or that; but their universal view could enable them to point out that the school is neglecting physical science for natural history; or that the subskills necessary for successful CDT are not being taught in the lower juniors.

If this sounds like direction from the hierarchy, then the point should be made that a further way of steering the science policy of a school is by teacher reports to curriculum leaders and the head, thereby applying gentle pressure to those in authority to play their part. From formal accident reports – rare, but necessary – through records of pupil progress, to simple comments on the availability and suitability of resources, the practitioners influence the direction of the school's science policy. That progress can also be measured, in part, by the application of the kinds of assessment techniques described earlier, and the collation of their results to highlight areas of deficiency.

For many schools, the possession of a science policy would be a significant step forward. For those with such a policy, regular review should be seen as an essential feature of the school's development. It is not sufficient to establish the subject; without regular review, the science may become sterile and unimaginative, and individual members of staff may fail to recognise that they have a personal responsibility for the maintenance and development of the school's science policy.

REFERENCES

Archenhold, W. F., Jenkins, E. W., and Wood-Robinson, C. (1978) *School Science Laboratories*. London: Murray.

Association for Science Education (ASE) (1985) *Choosing Published Primary Science Materials for Use in the Classroom*. Hatfield: ASE.

Booth, N. (1980) An Approach to Primary Science. *Education 3–13* 8.1. pp. 23–27.

Centre for Life Studies (1984) *Guidelines for Keeping Animals and Plants*. London: ILEA.

Creedy, J. (1977) *A Laboratory Manual for Schools and Colleges*. London: Heinemann.

Department of Education and Science (1979) *Safety at School: General Advice*. London: HMSO.

Department of Education and Science (1981) *Safety in Practical Studies*. London: HMSO.

Gilbert, C., and Matthews, P. (1984) *The Look Project: A Guide to Primary Science Policy*. London: Addison-Wesley.

Nuffield Junior Science Project (1970) *Junior Science Source Book, Animals and Plants; Apparatus; Teachers Guide 1; Teachers Guide 2*. London: Collins.

Primary Science Development Project: Booklet 7: (1984) *Assessment, Evaluation and Record Keeping*. Edinburgh: Moray House College of Education.

Redman, S., Brereton, A., and Boyers, P. (1969) *An Approach to Primary Science*. London: Macmillan.

Schools Council (1972) *Science 5–13 Project Units for Teachers*. London: Macdonald.

Schools Council (1974) *Educational Use of Living Organisms Project*. London: English Universities Press.

Schools Council (1977) *Progress in Learning Science Project: Match and Mismatch*. Edinburgh: Oliver & Boyd.

Schools Council (1978) *Teaching Primary Science Project*. London: Macdonald.

Schools Council (1982) *Learning Through Science Project: Science Resources for Primary and Middle Schools*. London: Macdonald.

Schools Council (1983) *Learning Through Science Project: Science for Children with Learning Difficulties*. London: Macdonald.

Appendix I

EXAMPLES OF CONTENT GUIDELINES

(From Harlen, W. (1978) Does Content Matter in Primary Science? *The School Science Review*. 59.209 pp. 614–625)

By the age of nine or ten the ideas which children have should include the following:

About ourselves and other living things
– living things have the capability of reproducing themselves and this takes place in different ways in different plants and animals, but for each the pattern is the same in each generation;
– living things grow and develop, and this requires food;
– human beings must have certain kinds of food for growth, energy and to fight disease;
– human beings gain information about their surroundings through their senses; there are limits to the range and sensitivity of the sense organs, but these can be increased by using tools, or instruments.

About the physical surroundings
– patterns occur in weather conditions and cycles in the apparent movement of the sun and moon and in changes in plants in the immediate environment;
– the materials described as stone, wood, glass, plastic, metal, have certain sets of properties which help to identify them;
– there are definite differences in the way matter behaves when it is solid, liquid or gaseous;
– some substances dissolve in water very well, others only a little and some not at all;
– some substances float in water, others sink; substances which sink can be used to make things which float.

About forces, movement and energy
– to make anything move (or change the way it is moving) there has to be something pushing, pulling or twisting it;
– when a push or pull makes something move it requires energy which can come from various sources: food, fuel, electricity, a wound spring, etc.;

159

– all things are pulled down towards the earth; the amount of this pull is the weight of an object;
– the speed of an object means how far it moves in a certain time.

Basic concepts
– the length of an object remains the same when only its position is changed even though it may look different;
– the area is the amount of surface across the face of an object which is unaffected by moving or dividing up the surface;
– the capacity of a container is the amount of space within it which can be filled; the volume of an object is the amount of space it takes up;
– a quantity of water which exists at a certain time will still exist at a later time either in the same form or in different forms;
– objects or events can be classified in several ways according to their features or characteristics;
– certain actions always have the same consequences and this relationship can often be used to predict the effect of changes.

By the age of 11 or 12 the ideas which children have should include the above together with the following:

About ourselves and other living things
– the basic life processes are growth, feeding, respiration, excretion, reproduction, sensitivity to the surroundings, and some mechanism for movement and support;
– there is a great variety in the way in which these life processes are carried out by different living things;
– in the human body organs are grouped into systems, each concerned with one of the main processes;
– energy is needed by all living things to support life processes; animals take in food, plants use the sun's energy to produce food they can use and store;
– living things depend on each other for their survival and all animals depend ultimately on plants for their food;
– living things have changed very gradually through time by the process of adaptation to various external conditions; the most successful animals at any time are those best adapted to the present conditions.

About the physical surroundings
– air fills the space around us and contains oxygen, which living things need;
– air contains water vapour, some of which condenses out in various conditions to give rain, dew, mist, snow, hail, ice or water;
– soil is composed of small fragments from rocks, air, water and decayed remains from living material which provide substances needed by growing plants; these substances have to be replenished to keep soil fertile;
– all non-living things are made from substances found in the earth; their supply is not endless, so they must not be wasted;
– pollution of the air, water or land by waste, smoke, or noise can harm both living and non-living things;
– the earth is one of nine planets so far known to be circling the sun, which is our source of heat and light energy;
– the moon circles the earth, reflecting light from the sun;
– melting or evaporating requires energy in the form of heat;
– a complete circuit of conducting material is needed for electricity to flow.

About forces, movement and energy
- a force is needed to accelerate or decelerate a thing which is moving or to change the direction of its movement;
- when an object is not moving (or moving at a constant speed) the forces acting on it are equal and opposite;
- all things which are moving have energy and when they slow down some of their energy is changed into another form;
- friction is a force which commonly opposes motion;
- energy is changed from one form to another in a variety of processes; it is never lost, but what disappears in one form reappears in another.

Basic concepts
- the total volume of an object is not changed by dividing it up or changing its shape;
- the process of measurement is the repeated comparison of a quantity with an agreed unit of the quantity; all measurements, however careful or fine, are inexact to some degree;
- all changes in objects or substances are caused by interaction with other substances or by adding or taking away energy.

Appendix II

THE SCIENCE CONCEPTS WHICH MAY BE REQUIRED
IN CERTAIN SUB-CATEGORIES

(From Department of Education and Science (1981) *Assessment of Performance Unit: Science in Schools Age 11: Report No. 1*. London: HMSO. Reproduced with permission)

1. Living things depend on each other in various ways.
2. Some animals eat plants and some eat other animals, but animals ultimately depend on green plants.
3. Living things are usually well suited in form and function to their natural environment.
4. There is air around the earth.
5. Soil is a mixture of things coming from rocks and living things.
6. Substances taken from the soil by plants during growth must be replaced to maintain fertility.
7. Changes in the physical environment due to seasonal cycles are often matched by changes or events in the living world.
8. Air often contains water vapour.
9. There are many different plants and animals which between them show a variety of ways of carrying out life processes, such as growth, respiration, reproduction and movement.
10. Most living things need food, water and air for life processes.
11. Living things produce offspring of the same kind as themselves.
12. Living things of the same kind go through the same life cycles.
13. Living things are sensitive to their environment.
14. In humans the senses are sight, touch, hearing, taste and smell, which each provide different kinds of information about the environment.
15. The speed of an object depends on the distance it travels in a certain time.
16. The average speed of an object is found by dividing the distance moved by the time taken.
17. To make anything move (or change the way it moves) there has to be a force (push, pull or twist) acting on it.
18. To change the shape of an object there have to be forces acting on it.
19 The strength of an object or structure depends on its shape and on the material of which it is made.

20. The larger the area over which a force is spread the smaller the force on each part.
21. Water tends to flow until its surface reaches a common level.
22. Objects completely immersed in a liquid displace a volume of liquid equal to their own volume.
23. Whether an object floats or sinks depends both on the substance of which it is made and on its shape.
24. Magnets attract and repel other magnets and attract magnetic substances.
25. All things are pulled towards the earth; it is this force which makes them feel heavy.
26. The apparent movements of the sun, moon and stars follow a regular pattern.
27. There is a variety of sources of energy such as food, fuel, stretched springs and chemicals.
28. The faster an object is moving the more energy it has.
29. A complete circuit of conducting material is needed for a steady current to flow between the terminals of a battery.
30. Objects can be seen because of the light which they give out or reflect.
31. Light travels (in a uniform medium) in straight paths of rays.
32. Sound comes from vibrating objects.
33. In general a substance can be classified either as a solid or a liquid or a gas.
34. The processes of melting, freezing, evaporating and condensing do not change what a substance is made of.
35. Energy (often in the form of heat) is required for melting and for evaporation to take place.
36. Materials can be classified in many different ways into groups, such as metals, plastics and wood, according to their properties.
37. Some substances dissolve in water; others do not, but may dissolve in other liquids.

Appendix III

A SELECTION OF PRIMARY SCIENCE CURRICULUM MATERIALS, BOOKS AND SCHEMES

(*Note* the information given was accurate at the time of writing.)

Exploring Primary Science and Technology   Cambridge University Press

Christine Brown, Christopher Brown, Roy Edwards, Tony Roberts, Beverley Young.

7–11 years

Ourselves	0 521 32563 3	£ 8.95
Materials	0 521 32562 5	£17.90
Changes	0 521 32561 7	£15.50
Cycles	0 521 32560 9	£17.90
Energy	0 521 32559 5	£15.50
Habitats	0 521 32558 7	£ 8.95
Structures	0 521 32557 9	£ 8.95
Systems	0 521 32556 0	£13.50

The complete course consists of 4 units, one for each year from ages 7–11. There are 12 modules in each unit based on the eight major themes listed above.

Infant Science Masters and Primary Science Masters   Holmes McDougall

John Aitken, George Mills.

Infant Science Masters	5–7 years	0 7157 2217 4	£12.95
Primary Science Masters	Stage 1–8 years	0 7157 2006 6	£12.95
	Stage 2–9 years	0 7157 2007 4	£12.95
	Stage 3–10 years	0 7157 2008 2	£12.95
	Stage 4–11 years	0 7157 2009 0	£12.95

A structured programme on Pressure-fax Duplicating Masters, of teacher demonstrations and pupil activities.

Ladybird Science Series 621   Ladybird Books

	8 years +		£0.75 each
Magnets and Electricity		0 7214 0656 4	
Light (Filmstrip available)		0 7214 0657 2	
Air		0 7214 0658 0	
Simple Mechanics		0 7214 0659 9	
Simple Chemistry		0 7214 0660 2	
Botany		0 7214 0778 1	
Zoology		0 7214 0779 X	
Weather		0 7214 0825 7	

A basic introduction to Science and its practical applications, with simple experiments.

Learning Through Science   Macdonald Educational/
                                      Schools Council/Scottish Educational Council.

Roy Richards, Margaret Collis, Doug Kincaid.

	7–13 years	
Ourselves	0 356 07549 4	£11.95
Colour	0 356 07550 8	£11.95
Materials	0 356 07551 6	£11.95
Sky and Space	0 356 07552 4	£11.95
All Around	0 356 07553 2	£11.95
Out of Doors	0 356 07554 0	£11.95
On the Move	0 356 07555 9	£11.95
Moving Around	0 356 07556 7	£11.95
Earth	0 356 07557 5	£11.95
Electricity	0 356 07558 3	£11.95
Which and What?	0 356 07558 1	£11.95
Time, Growth and Change	0 356 07560 5	£11.95
Guide and Index	0 356 11258 6	£ 4.95
Formulating a School Policy,		
* with Index to Science 5–13*	0 356 06252 X	£ 4.95
Science for Children with		
* Learning Difficulties*	0 356 09364 6	£ 4.95
Science Resources for Primary		
* and Middle Schools*	0 356 07816 7	£ 3.95

Each pack contains a double set of 24 brightly coloured workcards plus a teacher's guide.

Look   Addison-Wesley Publishers Ltd.

Cyril Gilbert and Peter Matthews.

A First Look	4–8 years	201 15010 7	£31.50
Look! Pupils' Pack A	7–9 years	201 13740 2	£25.50
Look! Teacher's Guide A		201 13741 0	£ 6.95
Look! Pupils' Pack B	9–11 years	201 13742 9	£25.50
Look! Teacher's Guide B		201 13743 7	£ 7.50
A Guide to Primary Science Policy		201 18060 X	£ 1.95

A and B packs of science activity cards with accompanying Teachers Guides. A First Look consists of 71 topic-based activity cards for the teacher plus a background guide.

Looking at Science   Basil Blackwell

David Fielding.

8–12 years

Book 1: A First Look	0 631 91350 5	£ 2.65
Book 2: The Natural World	0 631 91360 2	£ 2.65
Book 3: Changes	0 631 91370 X	£ 2.65
Book 4: The Physical World	0 631 91380 7	£ 2.65
Book 5: A Closer Look	0 631 91390 4	£ 2.65

A series of Combined Science and Nature Study books interweaving information with enquiry.

My Body   Heinemann Educational Books

The Health Education Council.

10–12 years

Classroom Pack	0 435 04501 6	£14.95
Games Pack	0 435 04502 4	£ 5.75
Teacher's Notes	0 435 04500 8	£ 8.95

An integration of many curriculum areas into the common theme, to develop understanding and skills.

Primary Science   City of Sheffield Printing Services
Sheffield Education   Holly Resource Centre, Holly Street
Curriculum Development   Sheffield, S1 2GT

P. Elkington and teachers from Sheffield LEA Infant and First Schools.

Sound: using our ears
Air: using our nose
Wood
Life Cycles
Water
Hot and Cold – sense of touch
Magnets, Batteries and Bulbs
Light: using our eyes
Packaging

Metals
Ourselves
Minibeasts
Plants and Growing
Fabrics
Food
Changes
Eggs
Rocks and soil

£ 7.00 per
full set

A set of 4–8 page teachers' booklets.

Read and Do   Arnold-Wheaton

Doug Kincaid and Peter Coles.

6–8 years

Touch and Feel	0 08 026408 5	£1.65 each
Ears and Hearing	0 08 026409 3	
Taste and Smell	0 08 026410 7	
Eyes and Looking	0 08 026411 5	
Hot and Cold	0 08 030584 9	
Light and Dark	0 08 030586 5	
Quiet and Loud	0 08 030588 1	
Wet and Dry	0 08 030590 3	

An introduction to scientific observation through the five senses. Reading and Doing for children and a note for the teacher, listing the concepts covered, the vocabulary introduced and the materials used.

All About Me   Nelson
Schools Council Health Education Project.

Trefor Williams.

5–8 years

All About Me Teacher's Guide	0 17 423067 2	£ 7.75
All About Me Spirit Masters	0 17 423077 X	£ 8.95

Think Well

Trefor Williams, Ian McCafferty, Vaughan Johnson, Marilyn Stephens, Clyte Hampton.

9–13 years   0 17 423076 1   £34.50

A pack of eight units: Myself   Time to Spare
                          One of Many   Food for Thought
                          From Sickness to Health   Get Clean
                          Deadly Decisions   Skills and Spills

Think Well Spirit Masters for units 1, 2, 4   0 17 423078 8   £11.50
Think Well Resource Sheets for units 2, 4, 5, 6 0 17 423080 X   £16.95

Science Horizons   Macmillan Education
West Sussex Studies 5–14 Scheme

Co-ordinators – Jim Hudson and Derek Slack.

Level 1	5–8 years		£5.50 each
Observing Weather		0 333 28529 8	
Living with Electricity		0 333 28530 1	
Finding Out About Ourselves		0 333 28532 8	
Soil, Seeds and Trees		0 333 28533 6	
From Rain to Tap		0 333 31299 6	
Materials in the Home		0 333 31300 3	
Cooking and What We Eat		0 333 32156 1	
On the Move		0 333 32163 4	
Planet Earth		0 333 34906 7	
Healthy and Safe		0 333 34907 5	
Our Home		0 333 34908 3	
Watching Animals		0 333 34909 1	

Level 2a	7–11 years		£5.50 each
What is Air?		0 333 28534 4	
Looking at Animals		0 333 28535 2	
Floating and Sinking		0 333 28536 0	
Ourselves		0 333 28537 9	
Beneath our Feet		0 333 28538 7	
Light and Colour		0 333 28539 5	
Electricity		0 333 28540 9	
Water in the Home		0 333 32155 3	
Materials		0 333 32161 8	
Wheels		0 333 32162 6	
Keeping Our Home Warm		0 333 34910 5	
Safety at Home and School		0 333 34911 3	

Level 2b	10–12 years		£5.50 each
Flying Starts Here		0 333 28541 7	
Understanding the Weather		0 333 31301 1	

Shipshape	0 333 32153 7
Gardening Outdoors	0 333 32154 5
The Seashore	0 333 32158 8
Animals in the Air	0 333 32159 6

Teacher's Handbook for the		
West Sussex 5–14 Scheme	0 333 28571 9	£ 2.25

The units, which are held in a removable spine, include copyright-free pupil worksheets, together with teachers' notes.

Science in a Topic   Hulton Educational Publications Ltd.

Doug Kincaid and Peter Coles.

	8–12 years		£2.85 each
Ships		0 7175 0633 9	
Houses and Homes		0 7175 0669 X	
Clothes and Costume		0 7175 0713 0	
Communication		0 7175 0753 X	
Food		0 7175 0769 6	
Moving on Land		0 7175 0816 1	
Roads, Bridges and Tunnels		0 7175 0852 8	
In the Air		0 7175 0877 3	
Sports and Games		0 7175 0885 4	
Teacher's Guide	8–12 years	0 7175 1198 7	£ 3.50

The Science aspects of a variety of Topic areas, asking questions and suggesting ways in which children might find answers.

Science Skills   Collins Educational

George Mills.

Science Skills Box	0 003 17508 1	£29.50
Science Skills Spirit Masters	0 003 17509 X	£ 8.95
Science Skills Teacher's Guide	0 003 17510 3	£ 2.50
Early Science Skills, Ourselves	0 003 17511 1	£ 0.70
Early Science Skills, Living Things	0 003 17513 8	£ 0.70
Early Science Skills,		
Weather and Seasons	0 003 17512 X	£ 0.70
Early Science Skills, Materials	0 003 17514 6	£ 0.70

There are 112 work cards and 24 spirit masters.

Science Spirals   Hamish Hamilton

Julie Fitzpatrick.

                          7–9 years

In the Air	0 241 11205 2	£ 3.95
Magnets	0 241 11206 0	£ 3.95
Mirrors	0 241 11207 9	£ 3.95
On the Water	0 241 11208 7	£ 3.95
Balancing	0 241 11722 4	£ 4.50
Bounce, Stretch and Spring	0 241 11723 2	£ 4.50
Towers and Bridges	0 241 11724 0	£ 4.50
Wheels	0 241 11725 9	£ 4.50

A set of 32-page booklets consisting of short easy-to-read text, linked to carefully graded activities to encourage the development of science skills and an understanding of science facts.

Sciencewise   Nelson

Sheila Parker and Alan Ward.

                          7–8 years

Pupils Book 1	0 17 423011 7
Pupils Book 2	0 17 423013 3
Teachers Book 1	0 17 423033 8

                          8–9 years

Pupils Book 3	0 17 423015 X
Pupils Book 4	0 17 423017 6
Teachers Book 2	0 17 423034 6

                          9–10 years

Pupils Book 5	0 17 423017 2
Teachers Book 3	0 17 423027 3

                          10+ years

Pupils Book 6	0 17 423021 4
Teachers Book 4	0 17 423036 2

The books are arranged in four-page units around 3 basic concepts: Change, shape, size and structure. Teachers books provide extension material.

Science Workshop (TV Series)   Longman

Irene Finch.

	9–11 years	£2.95 each
Science Workshop		0 582 18348 0
Science Workshop 2		0 582 18350 2

Pupils' books designed to be used with the BBC TV programmes – or on their own.

Scienceworld   Longman

Ed. Brenda Prestt

Science Through Infant Topics A. Reception		0 582 18819 9	£35.00
Teachers Book A		0 582 18610 2	£ 9.50
Science Through Infant Topics B. Middle Infants		0 582 18820 2	£35.00
Teachers Book B		0 582 18821 0	£ 9.50
Science Through Infant Topics C. Top Infants		0 582 18823 7	£ 4.50
Teachers Book C		0 582 18822 0	£ 9.50
Junior Pupils Book 1	1st year Junior	0 582 18583 1	N.A.
Junior Pupils Book 2	2nd year Junior	0 582 18584 X	N.A.
Junior Pupils Book 3	3rd year Junior	0 582 18585 8	N.A.
Junior Pupils Book 4	4th year Junior	0 582 18586 6	N.A.
Junior Teachers Book 1 & 2		0 582 18627 7	N.A.
Junior Teachers Book 3 & 4		0 582 18639 0	N.A.

An emphasis on building up science skills and on teacher support through clear and humorous books.

Longman Scienceworld

Only the infant materials of Longman Scienceworld have been published in time for consideration. Early 'Evaluation Packs' contained *Teachers' Books, Starter Readers* (for use with older infants) and the *Starter Books* that introduce the Scienceworld characters and present discussion pictures.

The material is all bright and attractive, with full-colour illustrations. There are record sheets, too, which are easy to complete and help to keep track of skills development. The *Teachers' Books* contain practical ideas, well presented (although early criticisms of the books suggested that they spoon-fed teachers). There are some fairly complex appendices, however, which verge on the impenetrable – but this may not bother hard-pressed teachers, who will turn instead to the reassuring advice (and to the teachers' notes printed on the back of each *Starter Book* picture.)

The *Starter Books* serve as discussion tools. The purpose of the *Starter Readers* is less clear; they do not stand alone as story books, and there are obvious strains between the storyline and the contained science.

The junior materials are promised for 1987.

Ginn Science

The infant materials of the new 'Ginn Science' scheme will be published early in 1988, with the junior materials following shortly after. Ginn Science will offer a structured, flexible programme for children from 5–12 years of age, the extra year allowing for children in Scotland, and in some middle schools.

Over thirty carefully graded readers will be presented at infant level, with practical *Teacher Resource Books* to support appropriate practical activities. Five strands of practical science will be developed – 'Ourselves and Healthy Living', 'Other Animals and Plants', 'Materials', 'Energy and Forces', and 'Earth and Space' – in the infant and junior books, introduced through carefully planned activities following a skills and attitudes hierarchy. There will be assessment throughout the programme, and full exploration of the problem-solving and Craft, Design and Technology aspects.

The materials are being very thoroughly trialled in a large representative cross-section of primary schools. They will present yet another attractive alternative for schools implementing a science policy.

Appendix IV

SOME SOURCES OF REFERENCE AND USEFUL ADDRESSES
FOR PRIMARY SCIENCE RESOURCES

Museums and Galleries in Great Britain and Ireland	British Leisure Publications 1986
	0 948 05604 5 £2.50
See Britain at Work (Visits to craft workshops/factories)	Exley Publications 1981
Angela Lansbury	0 905 52154 4 £4.95
Voluntary Organisations	Bedford Square Press 1986
	0 719 91137 0 £5.95
Free Stuff for Kids	Exley Publications 1985
	1 850 15026 5 £2.95
Addresses for Science Teachers	From: Secretary, Centre for Studies in Science & Mathematics, Education Department, University of Leeds, Leeds. LS2 9JT 1983
W. F. Archenhold E. W. Jenkins C. Wood-Robinson	
	£1.00
Goldmine – Resources for Teachers	Epistemology 1985, 62 Newland Road, Worthing. BN11 1VX

ASE,
College Lane,
Hatfield,
Herts. AL10 9AA

Awards for Young Investigators,
British Association for the Advancement
    of Science,
Fortress House,
23 Savile Row,
London. W1X 1AB

BANTA Ltd. (Bioviewers, Biosets),
279 Church Road,
Upper Norwood,
London. SE19 2QQ

Ronald N. Baxter (Butterflies, Stick
    Insects, books),
Entomologists,
45 Chudleigh Crescent,
Ilford, Essex. 1G3 9AT

Beautiful Butterflies Ltd. (Eggs/larvae
    of Butterflies and Moths.),
High Street,
Bourton-on-the-Water,
Glos. GL54 2AN

Botanical Society of the British Isles,
c/o Department of Botany,
British Museum (Natural History),
Cromwell Road,
London. SW7 5BD

BP Educational Service,
PO Box 5,
Wetherby,
W. Yorks. LS23 7EH

BP Film Library,
15 Beaconsfield Road,
London. NW10 2LE

British Association for the Advancement
    of Science,
Fortress House,
23 Savile Row,
London. W1X 1AB

British Association for Young Scientists,
Fortress House,
23 Savile Row,
London. W1X 1AB

BBC (Publications),
School Orders Section,
144 Bermondsey Street,
London. SE1 3TH

British Computer Society,
13 Mansfield Street,
London. W1M 0BP

British Gas Education Service,
Room 707A,
British Gas,
326 High Holborn,
London. WC1V 7PT

British Museum (Natural History),
Publication Sales,
Cromwell Road,
London. SW7 5BD

British Red Cross Society,
9 Grosvenor Crescent,
London. SW1X 7EJ

British Sugar Bureau,
140 Park Lane,
London. W1Y 3AA

British Telecommunications plc,
Education Service,
81 Newgate Street,
London. EC1A 7AJ

British Trust for Conservation Volunteers,
36 St. Mary's Street,
Wallingford, Oxon. OX10 0UE

British Trust for Ornithology,
Beech Grove,
Tring,
Herts. HP23 5NR

British Wool Marketing Board,
Oak Mills,
Station Road,
Clayton,
Bradford,
Yorks. BD14 6JD

The Conservation Trust,
c/o George Palmer School,
Northumberland Avenue,
Reading,
Berks. RG2 7PW

CLEAPSE (Consortium of LEAs for
    Provision of Science Equipment),
School Science Service,
Brunel University,
Uxbridge,
Middx. UB8 3PH (Subscribers only)

Council for Environmental Conservation,
Zoological Gardens,
Regents Park,
London. NW1 4RY

Council for Environmental Education,
School of Education,
University of Reading,
London Road,
Reading. RG1 5AQ

Countryside Commission,
John Dover House,
Crescent Place,
Cheltenham,
Glos. GL50 3RA

Education Service of the Plastics and
    Rubber Institute,
Department of Creative Design,
Loughborough University,
Loughborough,
Leics. LE11 3TU

Equal Opportunities Commission,
Overseas House,
Quay Street,
Manchester. M3 3HN

Ever Ready Ltd.,
Technical Division,
Tanfield Lea,
Stanley,
Co. Durham. DH9 9QF

Freshwater Biological Association,
Windermere Laboratory,
The Ferry House,
Ambleside,
Cumbria. LA22 0LP

Friends of the Earth,
377 City Road,
London. EC1V 1NA

General Dental Council,
37 Wimpole Street,
London. W1M 8DQ

Geological Museum,
Exhibition Road,
South Kensington,
London. SW7 2DE

Philip Green (Science through Story
    Tapes)
KK Tape Services,
Ashurst Lodge,
14 Liverpool Gardens,
Worthing,
Sussex. BN11 1BR

Griffin & George,
285 Ealing Road,
Alperton,
Wembley,
Middx. HA0 1HS

Philip Harris Ltd.,
Lynn Lane,
Shenstone,
Staffs. WS14 0EE

Health Education Council,
78 New Oxford Street,
London. WC1A 1AH

Robert Lee (Bee Supplies) Ltd.,
Beehive Works,
High Street,
Cowley,
Uxbridge,
Middx. UB8 2BB

J. D. MacLennan (Craigie Kit),
Creative Learning Kits,
Overton House,
New Galloway,
Castle Douglas,
Kirkcudbright. DG7 3SD

Meterological Office,
London Road,
Bracknell,
Berks. RG12 2SZ

National Centre for Alternative
   Technology,
Llwyngwern Quarry,
Machynlleth,
Powys.

National Centre for School Technology,
Trent Polytechnic,
Burton Street,
Nottingham.

National Dairy Council,
National Dairy Centre,
John Princes Street,
London. W1M 0AP

Nature Conservancy Council,
19–20 Belgrave Square,
London. SW1X 5PY

Osmiroid Educational,
Osmiroid Works,
Gosport,
Hants. PO13 0AL

Reed Group Paper Division,
New Hythe House,
Aylesford,
Maidstone,
Kent. ME20 7PB

Royal Society for Nature Conservation,
The Green,
Nettleham,
Lincoln. LN2 2NR

RSPCA,
Manor House,
The Causeway,
Horsham,
Sussex. RH12 1HG

Royal Society for the Protection of Birds,
The Lodge,
Sandy,
Beds. SG19 2DL

The School Natural Science Society,
22 Chada Avenue,
Gillingham,
Kent.

The Science Museum,
Exhibition Road,
South Kensington,
London. SW7 2DD

Scottish Schools Science Equipment
    Research Centre,
103 Broughton Street,
Edinburgh. EH1 3RZ
(Scottish subscribers only)

Shell Education Service
Shell UK Limited,
Shell-Mex House,
Strand, London. WC22 0DZ

Town & Country Planning Association,
(Bulletin of Environmental Education)
Education Unit,
17 Carlton House Terrace,
London. SW17 5AS

The Tree Council,
35 Belgrave Square,
London. SW1X 8QN

Understanding Electricity Education
    Service,
Electricity Council,
30 Millbank,
London. SW1P 4RD

Unilever Education Section,
PO Box 68,
Unilever House,
London EC4P 4BQ

UFAW (Universities Federation for
    Animal Welfare),
8 Hamilton Close,
South Mimms,
Potters Bar,
Herts. EN6 3QD

WATCH (Junior Wing of the Nature
    Conservation Trust)
The Green,
Nettleham,
Lincoln, LN2 2NR

The Wildfowl Trust,
Slimbridge,
Glos. GL2 7BT

World Wildlife Fund,
Education Project,
Greenfield House,
Guiting Power,
Glos. GL54 5TZ

Index